LEARN C
THE HARD WAY

 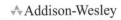

LEARN C THE HARD WAY

Practical Exercises on the
Computational Subjects You Keep
Avoiding (Like C)

Zed A. Shaw

✦Addison-Wesley

New York • Boston • Indianapolis • San Francisco
Toronto • Montreal • London • Munich • Paris • Madrid
Capetown • Sydney • Tokyo • Singapore • Mexico City

For information about buying this title in bulk quantities, or for special sales opportunities (which may include electronic versions; custom cover designs; and content particular to your business, training goals, marketing focus, or branding interests), please contact our corporate sales department at corpsales@pearsoned.com or (800) 382-3419.

For government sales inquiries, please contact governmentsales@pearsoned.com.

For questions about sales outside the U.S., please contact international@pearsoned.com.

Visit us on the Web: informit.com/aw

Library of Congress Cataloging-in-Publication Data

Shaw, Zed, author.
  Learn C the hard way : practical exercises on the computational subjects you keep avoiding (like C) / Zed A. Shaw.
     pages   cm
  Includes index.
  ISBN 978-0-321-88492-3 (pbk. : alk. paper)—ISBN 0-321-88492-2 (pbk. : alk. paper)
  1. C (Computer program language)—Problems, exercises, etc. I. Title.
  QA76.73.C15S473 2016
  005.13'3—dc23
                                                                          2015020858

ISBN-13: 978-0-321-88492-3
ISBN-10: 0-321-88492-2

Text printed in the United States on recycled paper at RR Donnelley in Crawfordsville, Indiana.
First printing, August 2015

Contents

Acknowledgments

I would like to thank three kinds of people who helped make this book what it is today: the haters, the helpers, and the painters.

The haters helped make this book stronger and more solid through their inflexibility of mind, irrational hero worship of old C gods, and complete lack of pedagogical expertise. Without their shining example of what not to be, I would have never worked so hard to make this book a complete introduction to becoming a better programmer.

The helpers are Debra Williams Cauley, Vicki Rowland, Elizabeth Ryan, the whole team at Addison-Wesley, and everyone online who sent in fixes and suggestions. Their work producing, fixing, editing, and improving this book has formed it into a more professional and better piece of writing.

The painters, Brian, Arthur, Vesta, and Sarah, helped me find a new way to express myself and to distract me from deadlines that Deb and Vicki clearly set for me but that I kept missing. Without painting and the gift of art these artists gave me, I would have a less meaningful and rich life.

Thank you to all of you for helping me write this book. It may not be perfect, because no book is perfect, but it's at least as good as I can possibly make it.

This Book Is Not Really about C

Please don't feel cheated, but this book is not about teaching you C programming. You'll learn to write programs in C, but the most important lesson you'll get from this book is *rigorous defensive programming*. Today, too many programmers simply assume that what they write works, but one day it will fail catastrophically. This is especially true if you're the kind of person who has learned mostly modern languages that solve many problems for you. By reading this book and following my exercises, you'll learn how to create software that defends itself from malicious activity and defects.

I'm using C for a very specific reason: C is broken. It is full of design choices that made sense in the 1970s but make zero sense now. Everything from its unrestricted, wild use of pointers to its severely broken NUL terminated strings are to blame for nearly all of the security defects that hit C. It's my belief that C is so broken that, while it's in wide use, it's the most difficult language to write securely. I would fathom that Assembly is actually easier to write securely than C. To be honest, and you'll find out that I'm very honest, I don't think that anybody should be writing new C code.

If that's the case, then why am I teaching you C? Because I want you to become a better, stronger programmer, and there are two reasons why C is an excellent language to learn if you want to get better. First, C's lack of nearly every modern safety feature means you have to be more vigilant and more aware of what's going on. If you can write secure, solid C code, you can write secure, solid code in any programming language. The techniques you learn will translate to every language you use from now on. Second, learning C gives you direct access to a mountain of legacy code, and teaches you the base syntax of a large number of descendant languages. Once you learn C, you can more easily learn C++, Java, Objective-C, and JavaScript, and even other languages become easier to learn.

I don't want to scare you away by telling you this, because I plan to make this book incredibly fun, easy, and devious. I'll make it fun to learn C by giving you projects that you might not have done in other programming languages. I'll make this book easy by using my proven pattern of exercises that has you *doing* C programming and building your skills slowly. I'll make it devious by teaching you how to break and then secure your code so you understand why these issues matter. You'll learn how to cause stack overflows, illegal memory access, and other common flaws that plague C programs so that you know what you're up against.

Getting through this book will be challenging, like all of my books, but when you're done you will be a far better and more confident programmer.

The Undefined Behaviorists

By the time you're done with this book, you'll be able to debug, read, and fix almost any C program you run into, and then write new, solid C code should you need to. However, I'm not really going to teach you official C. You'll learn the language, and you'll learn how to use it well, but official C isn't very secure. The vast majority of C programmers out there simply don't write solid code, and it's because of something called *Undefined Behavior* (UB). UB is a part of the American National Standards Institute (ANSI) C standard that lists all of the ways that a C compiler can disregard what you've written. There's actually a part of the standard that says if you write code like this, then all bets are off and the compiler doesn't have to do anything consistently. UB occurs when a C program reads off the end of a string, which is an incredibly common programming error in C. For a bit of background, C defines strings as blocks of memory that end in a NUL byte, or a 0 byte (to simplify the definition). Since many strings come from outside the program, it's common for a C program to receive a string without this NUL byte. When it does, the C program attempts to read past the end of this string and into the memory of the computer, causing your program to crash. Every other language developed after C attempts to prevent this, but not C. C does so little to prevent UB that every C programmer seems to think it means they don't have to deal with it. They write code full of potential NUL byte overruns, and when you point them out to these programmers, they say, "Well that's UB, and I don't have to prevent it." This reliance on C's large number of UBs is why most C code is so horribly insecure.

I write C code to try to avoid UB by either writing code that doesn't trigger it, or writing code that attempts to prevent it. This turns out to be an impossible task because there is *so much* UB that it becomes a Gordian knot of interconnected pitfalls in your C code. As you go through this book, I'll point out ways you can trigger UB, how to avoid it if you can, and how to trigger it in other people's code if possible. However, you should keep in mind that avoiding the nearly random nature of UB is almost impossible, and you'll just have to do your best.

WARNING! You'll find that hardcore C fans frequently will try to beat you up about UB. There's a class of C programmers who don't write very much C code but have memorized all of the UB just so they could beat up a beginner intellectually. If you run into one of these abusive programmers, please ignore them. Often, they aren't practicing C programmers, they are arrogant, abusive, and will only end up asking you endless questions in an attempt to prove their superiority rather than helping you with your code. Should you ever need help with your C code, simply email me at help@learncodethehardway.org, and I will gladly help you.

C Is a Pretty and Ugly Language

The presence of UB though is one more reason why learning C is a good move if you want to be a better programmer. If you can write good, solid C code in the way I teach you, then you can survive *any* language. On the positive side, C is a really elegant language in many ways. Its syntax is actually incredibly small given the power it has. There's a reason why so many other languages have copied its syntax over the last 45 or so years. C also gives you quite a lot using very little technology. When you're done learning C, you'll have an appreciation for a something that is very elegant and beautiful but also a little ugly at the same time. C is old, so like a beautiful monument, it will look fantastic from about 20 feet away, but when you step up close, you'll see all the cracks and flaws it has.

Because of this, I'm going to teach you the most recent version of C that I can make work with recent compilers. It's a practical, straightforward, simple, yet complete subset of C that works well, works everywhere, and avoids many pitfalls. This is the C that I use to get real work done, and not the encyclopedic version of C that hardcore fans try and fail to use.

I know the C that I use is solid because I spent two decades writing clean, solid C code that powered large operations without much failure at all. My C code has probably processed trillions of transactions because it powered the operations of companies like Twitter and airbnb. It rarely failed or had security attacks against it. In the many years that my code powered the Ruby on Rails Web world, it's run beautifully and even prevented security attacks, while other Web servers fell repeatedly to the simplest of attacks.

My style of writing C code is solid, but more importantly, my mind-set when writing C is one every programmer should have. I approach C, and any programming, with the idea of preventing errors as best I can and assuming that nothing will work right. Other programmers, even supposedly good C programmers, tend to write code and assume everything will work, but rely on UB or the operating system to save them, neither of which will work as a solution. Just remember that if people try to tell you that the code I teach in this book isn't "real C." If they don't have the same track record as me, maybe you can use what I teach you to show them why their code isn't very secure.

Does that mean my code is perfect? No, not at all. This is C code. Writing perfect C code is impossible, and in fact, writing perfect code in any language is impossible. That's half the fun and frustration of programming. I could take someone else's code and tear it apart, and someone could take my code and tear it apart. All code is flawed, but the difference is that I try to assume my code is always flawed and then prevent the flaws. My gift to you, should you complete this book, is to teach you the *defensive programming* mind-set that has served me well for two decades, and has helped me make high-quality, robust software.

What You Will Learn

The purpose of this book is to get you strong enough in C that you'll be able to write your own software with it or modify someone else's C code. After this book, you should read Brian Kernighan and Dennis Ritchie's *The C Programming Language*, Second Edition (Prentice Hall, 1988), a book by the creators of the C language, also called *K&R C*. What I'll teach you is

- The basics of C syntax and idioms

- Compilation, make files, linkers

- Finding bugs and preventing them

- Defensive coding practices

- Breaking C code

- Writing basic UNIX systems software

By the final exercise, you will have more than enough ammunition to tackle basic systems software, libraries, and other smaller projects.

How to Read This Book

This book is intended for programmers who have learned at least one other programming language. I refer you to my book *Learn Python the Hard Way* (Addison-Wesley, 2013) if you haven't learned a programming language yet. It's meant for beginners and works very well as a first book on programming. Once you've completed *Learn Python the Hard Way*, then you can come back and start this book.

For those who've already learned to code, this book may seem strange at first. It's not like other books where you read paragraph after paragraph of prose and then type in a bit of code here and there. Instead, there are videos of lectures for each exercise, you code right away, and then I explain what you just did. This works better because it's easier for me to explain something you've already done than to speak in an abstract sense about something you aren't familiar with at all.

Because of this structure, there are a few rules that you *must* follow in this book:

- Watch the lecture video first, unless the exercise says otherwise.

- Type in all of the code. Don't copy-paste!

- Type in the code exactly as it appears, even the comments.

- Get it to run and make sure it prints the same output.

- If there are bugs, fix them.

- Do the Extra Credit, but it's all right to skip anything you can't figure out.

- Always try to figure it out first before trying to get help.

If you follow these rules, do everything in the book, and still can't code C, then you at least tried. It's not for everyone, but just trying will make you a better programmer.

The Videos

Included in this course are videos for every exercise, and in many cases, more than one video for an exercise. These videos should be considered essential to get the full impact of the book's educational method. The reason for this is that *many* of the problems with writing C code are interactive issues with failure, debugging, and commands. C requires much more interaction to get the code running and to fix problems, unlike languages like Python and Ruby where code just runs. It's also much easier to show you a video lecture on a topic, such as pointers or memory management, where I can demonstrate how the machine is actually working.

I recommend that as you go through the course, you plan to watch the videos first, and then do the exercises unless directed to do otherwise. In some of the exercises, I use one video to present a problem and then another to demonstrate the solution. In most of the other exercises, I use a video to present a lecture, and then you do the exercise and complete it to learn the topic.

The Core Competencies

I'm going to guess that you have experience using a *lesser* language. One of those *usable* languages that lets you get away with sloppy thinking and half-baked hackery like Python or Ruby. Or, maybe you use a language like LISP that pretends the computer is some purely functional fantasy land with padded walls for little babies. Maybe you've learned Prolog, and you think the entire world should just be a database where you walk around in it looking for clues. Even worse, I'm betting you've been using an integrated development environment (IDE), so your brain is riddled with memory holes, and you can't even type an entire function's name without hitting CTRL-SPACE after every three characters.

No matter what your background is, you could probably use some improvement in these areas:

Reading and Writing

This is especially true if you use an IDE, but generally I find programmers do too much skimming and have problems reading for comprehension. They'll just skim code that they need to understand in detail without taking the time to understand it. Other languages provide tools that let programmers avoid actually writing any code, so when faced with a language like C, they break down. The simplest thing to do is just understand that *everyone* has this problem, and you can fix it by forcing yourself to slow down and be meticulous about your reading and writing. At first, it'll feel painful and annoying, but take frequent breaks, and then eventually it'll be easier to do.

Attention to Detail

Everyone is bad at this, and it's the biggest cause of bad software. Other languages let you get away with not paying attention, but C demands your full attention because it's right in the machine, and the machine is very picky. With C, there is no "kind of similar" or "close enough," so you need to pay attention. Double check your work. Assume everything you write is wrong until you prove it's right.

Spotting Differences

A key problem that people who are used to other languages have is that their brains have been trained to spot differences in *that* language, not in C. When you compare code you've written to my exercise code, your eyes will jump right over characters you think don't matter or that aren't familiar. I'll be giving you strategies that force you to see your mistakes, but keep in mind that if your code is not *exactly* like the code in this book, it's wrong.

Planning and Debugging

I love other, easier languages because I can just hang out. I can type the ideas I have into their interpreter and see results immediately. They're great for just hacking out ideas, but have you noticed that if you keep doing *hack until it works*, eventually nothing works? C is harder on you because it requires you to first plan out what you want to create. Sure, you can hack for a bit, but you have to get serious much earlier in C than in other languages. I'll be teaching you ways to plan out key parts of your program before you start coding, and this will likely make you a better programmer at the same time. Even just a little planning can smooth things out down the road.

Learning C makes you a better programmer because you are forced to deal with these issues earlier and more frequently. You can't be sloppy about what you write or nothing will work. The advantage of C is that it's a simple language that you can figure out on your own, which makes it a great language for learning about the machine and getting stronger in these core programming skills.

The Setup

The traditional first exercise, Excercise 0, is where you set up your computer for the rest of this book. In this exercise you'll install packages and software depending on the type of computer you have.

If you have problems following this exercise, then simply watch the Exercise 0 video for your computer and follow along with my setup instructions. That video should demonstrate how to do each step and help you solve any problems that might come up.

Linux

Linux is most likely the easiest system to configure for C development. For Debian systems you run this command from the command line:

```
$ sudo apt-get install build-essential
```

Here's how you would install the same setup on an RPM-based Linux like Fedora, RedHat, or CentOS 7:

```
$ sudo yum groupinstall development-tools
```

If you have a different variant of Linux, simply search for "c development tools" and your brand of Linux to find out what's required. Once you have that installed, you should be able to type:

```
$ cc --version
```

to see what compiler was installed. You will most likely have the GNU C Compiler (GCC) installed but don't worry if it's a different one from what I use in the book. You could also try installing the Clang C compiler using the *Clang's Getting Started* instructions for your version of Linux, or searching online if those don't work.

Mac OS X

On Mac OS X, the install is even easier. First, you'll need to either download the latest XCode from Apple, or find your install DVD and install it from there. The download will be massive and could take forever, so I recommend installing from the DVD. Also, search online for "installing xcode" for instructions on how to do it. You can also use the App Store to install it just as you would any other app, and if you do it that way you'll receive updates automatically.

To confirm that your C compiler is working, type this:

```
$ cc --version
```

You should see that you are using a version of the Clang C Compiler, but if your XCode is older you may have GCC installed. Either is fine.

Windows

For Microsoft Windows, I recommend you use the Cygwin system to acquire many of the standard UNIX software development tools. It should be easy to install and use, but watch the videos for this exercise to see how I do it. An alternative to Cygwin is the MinGW system; it is more minimalist but should also work. I will warn you that Microsoft seems to be phasing out C support in their development tools, so you may have problems using Microsoft's compilers to build the code in this book.

A slightly more advanced option is to use VirtualBox to install a Linux distribution and run a complete Linux system on your Windows computer. This has the added advantage that you can completely destroy this virtual machine without worrying about destroying your Windows configuration. It's also an opportunity to learn to use Linux, which is both fun and beneficial to your development as a programmer. Linux is currently deployed as the main operating system for many distributed computer and cloud infrastructure companies. Learning Linux will definitely improve your knowledge of the future of computing.

Text Editor

The choice of text editor for a programmer is a tough one. For beginners, I say just use Gedit since it's simple and it works for code. However, it doesn't work in certain international situations, and if you've been programming for a while, chances are you already have a favorite text editor.

With this in mind, I want you to try out a few of the standard programmer text editors for your platform and then stick with the one that you like best. If you've been using GEdit and like it, then stick with it. If you want to try something different, then try it out real quick and pick one.

The most important thing is *do not get stuck trying to pick the perfect editor*. Text editors all just kind of suck in odd ways. Just pick one, stick with it, and if you find something else you like, try it out. Don't spend days on end configuring it and making it perfect.

Some text editors to try out:

- GEdit on Linux and OS X.
- TextWrangler on OS X.

- Nano, which runs in Terminal and works nearly everywhere.

- Emacs and Emacs for OS X; be prepared to do some learning, though.

- Vim and MacVim.

There is probably a different editor for every person out there, but these are just a few of the free ones that I know work. Try out a few of these— and maybe some commercial ones—until you find one that you like.

Do Not Use an IDE

WARNING! Avoid using an integrated development environment (IDE) while you are learning a language. They are helpful when you need to get things done, but their help tends also to prevent you from really learning the language. In my experience, the stronger programmers don't use an IDE and also have no problem producing code at the same speed as IDE users. I also find that the code produced with an IDE is of lower quality. I have no idea why that is the case, but if you want deep, solid skills in a programming language, I highly recommend that you avoid IDEs while you're learning.

Knowing how to use a professional programmer's text editor is also a useful skill in your professional life. When you're dependent on an IDE, you have to wait for a new IDE before you can learn the newer programming languages. This adds a cost to your career: It prevents you from getting ahead of shifts in language popularity. With a generic text editor, you can code in any language, any time you like, without waiting for anyone to add it to an IDE. A generic text editor means freedom to explore on your own and manage your career as you see fit.

Dust Off That Compiler

After you have everything installed, you need to confirm that your compiler works. The easiest way to do that is to write a C program. Since you should already know at least one programming language, I believe you can start with a small but extensive example.

ex1.c

```
 1    #include <stdio.h>
 2
 3    /* This is a comment. */
 4    int main(int argc, char *argv[])
 5    {
 6        int distance = 100;
 7
 8        // this is also a comment
 9        printf("You are %d miles away.\n", distance);
10
11        return 0;
12    }
```

If you have problems getting the code up and running, watch the video for this exercise to see me do it first.

Breaking It Down

There are a few features of the C language in this code that you might or might not have figured out while you were typing it. I'll break this down, line by line, quickly, and then we can do exercises to understand each part better. Don't worry if you don't understand everything in this breakdown. I am simply giving you a quick dive into C and *promise* you will learn all of these concepts later in the book.

Here's a line-by-line description of the code:

ex1.c:1 An include, and it is the way to import the contents of one file into this source file. C has a convention of using .h extensions for *header* files, which contain lists of functions to use in your program.

ex1.c:3 This is a multiline comment, and you could put as many lines of text between the opening /* and closing */ characters as you want.

ex1.c:4 A more complex version of the main function you've been using so far. How C programs work is that the operating system loads your program, and then it runs the function named `main`. For the function to be totally complete it needs to return an `int` and take two parameters: an `int` for the argument count and an array of `char *` strings for the arguments. Did that just fly over your head? Don't worry, we'll cover this soon.

ex1.c:5   To start the body of any function, you write a `{` character that indicates the beginning of a *block*. In Python, you just did a `:` and indented. In other languages, you might have a `begin` or `do` word to start.

ex1.c:6   A variable declaration and assignment at the same time. This is how you create a variable, with the syntax `type  name = value;`. In C, statements (except for logic) end in a `;` (semicolon) character.

ex1.c:8   Another kind of comment. It works like in Python or Ruby, where the comment starts at the `//` and goes until the end of the line.

ex1.c:9   A call to your old friend `printf`. Like in many languages, function calls work with the syntax `name(arg1, arg2);` and can have no arguments or any number of them. The `printf` function is actually kind of weird in that it can take multiple arguments. You'll see that later.

ex1.c:11   A return from the main function that gives the operating system (OS) your exit value. You may not be familiar with how UNIX software uses return codes, so we'll cover that as well.

ex1.c:12   Finally, we end the main function with a closing brace `}` character, and that's the end of the program.

There's a lot of information in this breakdown, so study it line by line and make sure you at least have a grasp of what's going on. You won't know everything, but you can probably guess before we continue.

What You Should See

You can put this into an `ex1.c` and then run the commands shown here in this sample shell output. If you're not sure how this works, watch the video that goes with this exercise to see me do it.

Exercise 1 Session

```
$ make ex1
cc -Wall -g    ex1.c   -o ex1
$ ./ex1
You are 100 miles away.
$
```

The first command make is a tool that knows how to build C programs (and many others). When you run it and give it ex1 you are telling make to look for the ex1.c file, run the compiler to build it, and leave the results in a file named ex1. This ex1 file is an executable that you can run with ./ex1, which outputs your results.

How to Break It

In this book, I'm going to have a small section for each program teaching you how to break the program if it's possible. I'll have you do odd things to the programs, run them in weird ways, or change code so that you can see crashes and compiler errors.

For this program, simply try removing things at random and still get it to compile. Just make a guess at what you can remove, recompile it, and then see what you get for an error.

Extra Credit

- Open the ex1 file in your text editor and change or delete random parts. Try running it and see what happens.
- Print out five more lines of text or something more complex than "hello world."
- Run man 3 printf and read about this function and many others.
- For each line, write out the symbols you don't understand and see if you can guess what they mean. Write a little chart on paper with your guess so you can check it later to see if you got it right.

Using Makefiles to Build

We're going to use a program called make to simplify building your exercise code. The make program has been around for a very long time, and because of this it knows how to build quite a few types of software. In this exercise, I'll teach you just enough Makefile syntax to continue with the course, and then an exercise later will teach you more complete Makefile usage.

Using Make

How make works is you declare dependencies, and then describe how to build them or rely on the program's internal knowledge of how to build most common software. It has decades of knowledge about building a wide variety of files from other files. In the last exercise, you did this already using commands:

```
$ make ex1
# or this one too
$ CFLAGS="-Wall" make ex1
```

In the first command, you're telling make, "I want a file named ex1 to be created." The program then asks and does the following:

1. Does the file ex1 exist already?

2. No. Okay, is there another file that starts with ex1?

3. Yes, it's called ex1.c. Do I know how to build .c files?

4. Yes, I run this command cc ex1.c -o ex1 to build them.

5. I shall make you one ex1 by using cc to build it from ex1.c.

The second command in the listing above is a way to pass *modifiers* to the make command. If you're not familiar with how the UNIX shell works, you can create these *environment variables* that will get picked up by programs you run. Sometimes you do this with a command like export CFLAGS="-Wall" depending on the shell you use. You can, however, also just put them before the command you want to run, and that environment variable will be set only while that command runs.

In this example, I did CFLAGS="-Wall" make ex1 so that it would add the command line option -Wall to the cc command that make normally runs. That command line option tells the compiler cc to report all warnings (which, in a sick twist of fate, isn't actually all the warnings possible).

You can actually get pretty far with just using make in that way, but let's get into making a Makefile so you can understand make a little better. To start off, create a file with just the following in it.

ex2.1.mak

```
CFLAGS=-Wall -g

clean:
    rm -f ex1
```

Save this file as Makefile in your current directory. The program automatically assumes there's a file called Makefile and will just run it.

WARNING! Make sure you are only entering TAB characters, not mixtures of TAB and spaces.

This Makefile is showing you some new stuff with make. First, we set CFLAGS in the file so we never have to set it again, as well as adding the -g flag to get debugging. Then, we have a section named clean that tells make how to clean up our little project.

Make sure it's in the same directory as your ex1.c file, and then run these commands:

```
$ make clean
$ make ex1
```

What You Should See

If that worked, then you should see this:

Exercise 2 Session

```
$ make clean
rm -f ex1
$ make ex1
cc -Wall -g    ex1.c   -o ex1
ex1.c: In function 'main':
ex1.c:3: warning: implicit declaration of function 'puts'
$
```

Here you can see that I'm running make clean, which tells make to run our clean target. Go look at the Makefile again and you'll see that under this command, I indent and then put in the shell commands I want make to run for me. You could put as many commands as you wanted in there, so it's a great automation tool.

WARNING! If you fixed ex1.c to have #include <stdio.h>, then your output won't have the warning (which should really be an error) about puts. I have the error here because I didn't fix it.

Notice that even though we don't mention ex1 in the Makefile, make still knows how to build it *and* use our special settings.

How to Break It

That should be enough to get you started, but first let's break this Makefile in a particular way so you can see what happens. Take the line rm -f ex1 and remove the indent (move it all the way left) so you can see what happens. Rerun make clean, and you should get something like this:

```
$ make clean
Makefile:4: *** missing separator.  Stop.
```

Always remember to indent, and if you get weird errors like this, double check that you're consistently using tab characters because some make variants are very picky.

Extra Credit

- Create an all: ex1 target that will build ex1 with just the command make.
- Read man make to find out more information on how to run it.
- Read man cc to find out more information on what the flags -Wall and -g do.
- Research Makefiles online and see if you can improve this one.
- Find a Makefile in another C project and try to understand what it's doing.

Formatted Printing

Keep that Makefile around since it'll help you spot errors, and we'll be adding to it when we need to automate more things.

Many programming languages use the C way of formatting output, so let's try it:

ex3.c

```
1    #include <stdio.h>
2
3    int main()
4    {
5        int age = 10;
6        int height = 72;
7
8        printf("I am %d years old.\n", age);
9        printf("I am %d inches tall.\n", height);
10
11       return 0;
12   }
```

Once you've finished that, do the usual make ex3 to build and run it. Make sure you *fix all warnings*.

This exercise has a whole lot going on in a small amount of code, so let's break it down:

- First we're including another *header file* called stdio.h. This tells the compiler that you're going to use the standard Input/Output functions. One of those is printf.
- Then we're using a variable named age and setting it to 10.
- Next we're using a variable height and setting it to 72.
- Then we're adding the printf function to print the age and height of the tallest 10-year-old on the planet.
- In printf, you'll notice we're including a format string, as seen in many other languages.
- After this format string, we're putting in the variables that should be "replaced" into the format string by printf.

The result is giving printf some variables and it's constructing a new string and then printing it to the terminal.

What You Should See

When you do the whole build, you should see something like this:

```
$ make ex3
cc -Wall -g     ex3.c    -o ex3
$ ./ex3
I am 10 years old.
I am 72 inches tall.
$
```

Pretty soon I'm going to stop telling you to run make and what the build looks like, so please make sure you're getting this right and that it's working.

External Research

In the Extra Credit section of each exercise, you may have you go find information on your own and figure things out. This is an important part of being a self-sufficient programmer. If you're constantly running to ask someone a question before trying to figure things out yourself, then you'll never learn how to solve problems independently. You'll never build confidence in your skills and will always need someone else around to do your work.

The way to break this habit is to *force* yourself to try to answer your own question first, and then confirm that your answer is right. You do this by trying to break things, experimenting with your answer, and doing your own research.

For this exercise, I want you to go online and find out *all* of the printf escape codes and format sequences. Escape codes are \n or \t that let you print a newline or tab, respectively. Format sequences are the %s or %d that let you print a string or integer. Find them all, learn how to modify them, and see what kind of "precisions" and widths you can do.

From now on, these kinds of tasks will be in the Extra Credit sections, and you should do them.

How to Break It

Try a few of these ways to break this program, which may or may not cause it to crash on your computer:

- Take the age variable out of the first printf call, then recompile. You should get a couple of warnings.
- Run this new program and it will either crash or print out a really crazy age.

- Put the printf back the way it was, and then don't set age to an initial value by changing that line to int age;, and then rebuild it and run it again.

Exercise 3.bad Session

```
# edit ex3.c to break printf
$ make ex3
cc -Wall -g    ex3.c   -o ex3
ex3.c: In function 'main':
ex3.c:8: warning: too few arguments for format
ex3.c:5: warning: unused variable 'age'
$ ./ex3
I am -919092456 years old.
I am 72 inches tall.
# edit ex3.c again to fix printf, but don't init age
$ make ex3
cc -Wall -g    ex3.c   -o ex3
ex3.c: In function 'main':
ex3.c:8: warning: 'age' is used uninitialized in this function
$ ./ex3
I am 0 years old.
I am 72 inches tall.
$
```

Extra Credit

- Find as many other ways to break ex3.c as you can.

- Run man 3 printf and read about the other % format characters you can use. These should look familiar if you used them in other languages (they come from printf).

- Add ex3 to the all list in your Makefile. Use this to make clean all and build all of your exercises thus far.

- Add ex3 to the clean list in your Makefile as well. Use make clean to remove it when you need to.

Using a Debugger

This is a video-focused exercise where I show you how to use the debugger that comes with your computer to debug your programs, detect errors, and even debug processes that are currently running. Please watch the accompanying video to learn more about this topic.

GDB Tricks

Here's a list of simple tricks you can do with GNU Debugger (GDB):

gdb --args   Normally, gdb takes arguments you give it and assumes they are for itself. Using --args passes them to the program.

thread apply all bt   Dump a backtrace for *all* threads. It's very useful.

gdb --batch --ex r --ex bt --ex q --args   Run the program so that if it bombs, you get a backtrace.

GDB Quick Reference

The video is good for learning how to use a debugger, but you'll need to refer back to the commands as you work. Here is a quick reference to the GDB commands that I used in the video so you can use them later in the book:

run [args]   Start your program with [args].

break [file:]function   Set a break point at [file:]function. You can also use b.

backtrace   Dump a backtrace of the current calling stack. Shorthand is bt.

print expr   Print the value of expr. Shorthand is p.

continue   Continue running the program. Shorthand is c.

next   Next line, but step *over* function calls. Shorthand is n.

step   Next line, but step *into* function calls. Shorthand is s.

quit   Exit GDB.

help   List the types of commands. You can then get help on the class of command as well as the command.

cd, pwd, make   This is just like running these commands in your shell.

shell Quickly start a shell so you can do other things.

clear Clear a breakpoint.

info break, info watch Show information about breakpoints and watchpoints.

attach pid Attach to a running process so you can debug it.

detach Detach from the process.

list List out the next ten source lines. Add a - to list the previous ten lines.

LLDB Quick Reference

In OS X, you no longer have GDB and instead must use a similar program called LLDB Debugger (LLDB). The commands are almost the same, but here's a quick reference for LLDB:

run [args] Start your program with [args].

breakpoint set --name [file:]function Set a break point at [`file:`] `function`. You can also use b, which is way easier.

thread backtrace Dump a backtrace of the current calling stack. Shorthand is bt.

print expr Print the value of expr. Shorthand is p.

continue Continue running the program. Shorthand is c.

next Next line, but step *over* function calls. Shorthand is n.

step Next line, but step *into* function calls. Shorthand is s.

quit Exit LLDB.

help List the types of commands. You can then get help on the class of command as well as the command itself.

cd, pwd, make just like running these commands in your shell.

shell Quickly start a shell so you can do other things.

clear Clear a breakpoint.

info break, info watch Show information about breakpoints and watchpoints.

attach -p pid Attach to a running process so you can debug it.

detach Detach from the process.

list List out the next ten source lines. Add a - to list the previous ten sources.

You can also search online for quick reference cards and tutorials for both GDB and LLDB.

Memorizing C Operators

When you learned your first programming language, it most likely involved going through a book, typing in code you didn't quite understand, and then trying to figure out how it worked. That's how I wrote most of my other books, and that works very well for beginners. In the beginning, there are complex topics you need to understand before you can grasp what all the symbols and words mean, so it's an easy way to learn.

However, once you already know one programming language, this method of fumbling around learning the syntax by osmosis isn't the most efficient way to learn a language. It works, but there is a much faster way to build both your skills in a language and your confidence in using it. This method of learning a programming language might seem like magic, but you'll have to trust me that it works surprisingly well.

How I want you to learn C is to *first* memorize all the basic symbols and syntax, *then* apply them through a series of exercises. This method is very similar to how you might learn human languages by memorizing words and grammar, and then applying what you memorize in conversations. With just a simple amount of memorization effort in the beginning, you can gain foundational knowledge and have an easier time reading and writing C code.

WARNING! Some people are dead against memorization. Usually, they claim it makes you uncreative and boring. I'm proof that memorizing things doesn't make you uncreative and boring. I paint, play and build guitars, sing, code, write books, *and* I memorize lots of things. This belief is entirely unfounded and detrimental to efficient learning. Please ignore anyone telling you this.

How to Memorize

The best way to memorize something is a fairly simple process:

1. Create a set of flash cards that have a symbol on one side and the description on the other. You could also use a program called Anki to do this on your computer. I prefer creating my own because it helps me memorize them as I make them.

2. Randomize the flash cards and start going through them on one side. Try your best to remember the other side of the card without looking.

3. If you can't recall the other side of the card, then look at it and repeat the answer to yourself, then put that card into a separate pile.

4. Once you go through all the cards you'll have two piles: one pile of cards you recalled quickly, and another you failed to recall. *Pick up the fail pile and drill yourself on only those cards.*

5. At the very end of the session, which is usually 15–30 minutes, you'll have a set of cards you just can't recall. Take those cards with you wherever you go, and when you have free time, practice memorizing them.

There are many other tricks to memorizing things, but I've found that this is the best way to build instant recall on things you need to be able to use immediately. The symbols, keywords, and syntax of C are things you need instant recall on, so this method is the best one for this task.

Also remember that you need to do *both* sides of the cards. You should be able to read the description and know what symbol matches it, as well as knowing the description for a symbol.

Finally, *you don't have to stop* while you're memorizing these operators. The best approach is to combine this with exercises in this book so you can apply what you've memorized. See the next exercise for more on this.

The List of Operators

The first operators are the arithmetic operators, which are very similar to almost every other programming language. When you write the cards, the description side should say that it's an arithmetic operator, and what it does.

Arithmetic Operators	
Operator	**Description**
+	Add
–	Subtract
*	Multiply
/	Divide
%	Modulus
++	Increment
– –	Decrement

Relational operators test values for equality, and again, they are very common in programming languages.

Relational Operators	
Operator	**Description**
==	Equal
!=	Not equal
>	Greater than
<	Less than
>=	Greater than equal
<=	Less than equal

Logical operators perform logic tests, and you should already know what these do. The only odd one is the *logical ternary*, which you'll learn later in this book.

Logical Operators	
Operator	**Description**
&&	Logical and
||	Logical or
!	Logical not
? :	Logical ternary

Bitwise operators do something you likely won't experience often in modern code. They alter the bits that make up bytes and other data types in various ways. I won't cover this in my book, but they are very handy when working with certain types of lower-level systems.

Bitwise Operators	
Operator	**Description**
&	Bitwise and
|	Bitwise or
^	Bitwise xor
~	Bitwise one's complement
<<	Bitwise shift left
>>	Bitwise shift right

Assignment operators simply assign expressions to variables, but C combines a large number of other operators with assignment. So when I say and-equal, I mean the *bitwise* operators, not the logical operators.

Assignment Operators	
Operator	**Description**
=	Assign equal
+=	Assign plus-equal
-=	Assign minus-equal
*=	Assign multiply-equal
/=	Assign divide-equal
%=	Assign modulus-equal
<<=	Assign shift-left-equal
>>=	Assign shift-right-equal
&=	Assign and-equal
^=	Assign xor-equal
|=	Assign or-equal

I'm calling these *data operators* but they really deal with aspects of pointers, member access, and various elements of data structures in C.

Data Operators	
Operator	**Description**
sizeof()	Get the size of
[]	Array subscript
&	The address of
*	The value of
->	Structure dereference
.	Structure reference

Finally, there are a few miscellaneous symbols that are either frequently used for different roles (like ,), or don't fit into any of the previous categories for various reasons.

Miscellaneous Operators	
Operator	**Description**
,	Comma
( )	Parentheses
{ }	Braces
:	Colon

... continued on next page

Miscellaneous Operators	
Operator	**Description**
//	Single-line comment start
/*	Multi-line comment start
*/	Multi-line comment end

Study your flash cards while you continue with the book. If you spent 15–30 minutes a day before studying, and another 15–30 minutes before bed, you could most likely memorize all of these in a few weeks.

Memorizing C Syntax

After learning the operators, it's time to memorize the keywords and basic syntax structures you'll be using. Trust me when I tell you that the small amount of time spent memorizing these things will pay huge dividends later as you go through the book.

As I mentioned in Exercise 5, you don't have to stop reading the book while you memorize these things. You can and should do both. Use your flash cards as a warm up before coding that day. Take them out and drill on them for 15–30 minutes, then sit down and do some more exercises in the book. As you go through the book, try to use the code you're typing as more of a way to practice what you're memorizing. One trick is to build a pile of flash cards containing operators and keywords that you don't immediately recognize while you're coding. After you're done for the day, practice those flash cards for another 15–30 minutes.

Keep this up and you'll learn C much faster and more solidly than you would if you just stumbled around typing code until you memorized it secondhand.

The Keywords

The *keywords* of a language are words that augment the symbols so that the language reads well. There are some languages like APL that don't really have keywords. There are other languages like Forth and LISP that are almost nothing but keywords. In the middle are languages like C, Python, Ruby, and many more that mix sets of keywords with symbols to create the basis of the language.

WARNING!
The technical term for processing the symbols and keywords of a programming language is *lexical analysis*. The word for one of these symbols or keywords is a *lexeme*.

Keywords	
Operator	**Description**
auto	Give a local variable a local lifetime.
break	Exit out of a compound statement.
case	A branch in a switch-statement.
char	Character data type.
const	Make a variable unmodifiable.

Keywords	
Operator	**Description**
`continue`	Continue to the top of a loop.
`default`	Default branch in a `switch-statement`.
`do`	Start a do-while loop.
`double`	A double floating-point data type.
`else`	An else branch of an `if-statement`.
`enum`	Define a set of `int` constants.
`extern`	Declare an identifier is defined externally.
`float`	A floating-point data type.
`for`	Start a for-loop.
`goto`	Jump to a label.
`if`	Starts an `if-statement`.
`int`	An integer data type.
`long`	A long integer data type.
`register`	Declare a variable be stored in a CPU register.
`return`	Return from a function.
`short`	A short integer data type.
`signed`	A signed modifier for integer data types.
`sizeof`	Determine the size of data.
`static`	Preserve variable value after its scope exits.
`struct`	Combine variables into a single record.
`switch`	Start a `switch-statement`.
`typedef`	Create a new type.
`union`	Start a `union-statement`.
`unsigned`	An unsigned modifier for integer data types.
`void`	Declare a data type empty.
`volatile`	Declare a variable might be modified elsewhere.
`while`	Start a while-loop.

Syntax Structures

I suggest you memorize those keywords, as well as memorizing the syntax structures. A *syntax structure* is a pattern of symbols that make up a C program code form, such as the form of an `if-statement` or a `while-loop`. You should find most of these familiar, since you already know one language. The only trouble is then learning how C does it.

Here's how you read these:

1. Anything in ALLCAPS is meant as a replacement spot or hole.

2. Seeing [ALLCAPS] means that part is optional.

3. The best way to test your memory of syntax structures is to open a text editor, and where you see switch-statement, try to write the code form after saying what it does.

An if-statement is your basic logic branching control:

```
if(TEST) {
    CODE;
} else if(TEST) {
    CODE;
} else {
    CODE;
}
```

A switch-statement is like an if-statement but works on simple integer constants:

```
switch (OPERAND) {
    case CONSTANT:
        CODE;
        break;
    default:
        CODE;
}
```

A while-loop is your most basic loop:

```
while(TEST) {
    CODE;
}
```

You can also use continue to cause it to loop. Call this form while-continue-loop for now:

```
while(TEST) {
    if(OTHER_TEST) {
        continue;
    }
    CODE;
}
```

You can also use break to exit a loop. Call this form while-break-loop:

```
while(TEST) {
    if(OTHER_TEST) {
```

```
        break;
    }
    CODE;
}
```

The do-while-loop is an inverted version of a while-loop that runs the code *then* tests to see if it should run again:

```
do {
    CODE;
} while(TEST);
```

It can also have continue and break inside to control how it operates.

The for-loop does a controlled counted loop through a (hopefully) fixed number of iterations using a counter:

```
for(INIT; TEST; POST) {
    CODE;
}
```

An enum creates a set of integer constants:

```
enum { CONST1, CONST2, CONST3 } NAME;
```

A goto will jump to a label, and is only used in a few useful situations like error detection and exiting:

```
if(ERROR_TEST) {
    goto fail;
}

fail:
    CODE;
```

A function is defined this way:

```
TYPE NAME(ARG1, ARG2, ..) {
    CODE;
    return VALUE;
}
```

That may be hard to remember, so try this example to see what's meant by TYPE, NAME, ARG and VALUE:

```
int name(arg1, arg2) {
    CODE;
```

```
    return 0;
}
```

A `typedef` defines a new type:

```
typedef DEFINITION IDENTIFIER;
```

A more concrete form of this is:

```
typedef unsigned char byte;
```

Don't let the spaces fool you; the DEFINITION is `unsigned char` and the IDENTIFIER is byte in that example.

A `struct` is a packaging of many base data types into a single concept, which are used heavily in C:

```
struct NAME {
    ELEMENTS;
} [VARIABLE_NAME];
```

The [VARIABLE_NAME] is optional, and I prefer not to use it except in a few small cases. This is commonly combined with `typedef` like this:

```
typedef struct [STRUCT_NAME] {
    ELEMENTS;
} IDENTIFIER;
```

Finally, `union` creates something like a `struct`, but the elements will overlap in memory. This is strange to understand, so simply memorize the form for now:

```
union NAME {
    ELEMENTS;
} [VARIABLE_NAME];
```

A Word of Encouragement

Once you've created flash cards for each of these, drill on them in the usual way by starting with the name side, and then reading the description and form on the other side. In the video for this exercise, I show you how to use Anki to do this efficiently, but you can replicate the experience with simple index cards, too.

I've noticed some fear or discomfort in students who are asked to memorize something like this. I'm not exactly sure why, but I encourage you to do it anyway. Look at this as an opportunity to improve your memorization and learning skills. The more you do it, the better at it you get and the easier it gets.

It's normal to feel discomfort and frustration. Don't take it personally. You might spend 15 minutes and simply *hate* doing it and feel like a total failure. This is normal, and it doesn't mean you actually are a failure. Perseverance will get you past the initial frustration, and this little exercise will teach you two things:

1. You can use memorization as a self-evaluation of your competence. Nothing tells you how well you really know a subject like a memory test of its concepts.

2. The way to conquer difficulty is a little piece at a time. Programming is a great way to learn this because it's so easy to break down into small parts and focus on what's lacking. Take this as an opportunity to build your confidence in tackling large tasks in small pieces.

A Word of Warning

I'll add a final word of warning about memorization. Memorizing a large quantity of facts doesn't automatically make you good at applying those facts. You can memorize the entire ANSI C standards document and still be a terrible programmer. I've encountered many *supposed* C experts who know every square inch of standard C grammar but still write terrible, buggy, weird code, or don't code at all.

Never confuse an ability to regurgitate memorized facts with ability to actually do something well. To do that you need to apply these facts in different situations until you know how to use them. That's what the rest of this book will help you do.

Variables and Types

Y ou should be getting a grasp of how a simple C program is structured, so let's do the next simplest thing and make some variables of different types:

ex7.c

```
1    #include <stdio.h>
2
3    int main(intargc, char*argv[])
4    {
5        int distance = 100;
6        float power = 2.345f;
7        double super_power = 56789.4532;
8        char initial = 'A';
9        char first_name[] = "Zed";
10       char last_name[] = "Shaw";
11
12       printf("You are %d miles away.\n", distance);
13       printf("You have %f levels of power.\n", power);
14       printf("You have %f awesome super powers.\n", super_power);
15       printf("I have an initial %c.\n", initial);
16       printf("I have a first name %s.\n", first_name);
17       printf("I have a last name %s.\n", last_name);
18       printf("My whole name is %s %c. %s.\n",
19               first_name, initial, last_name);
20
21       int bugs = 100;
22       double bug_rate = 1.2;
23
24       printf("You have %d bugs at the imaginary rate of %f.\n",
25               bugs, bug_rate);
26
27       long universe_of_defects = 1L * 1024L * 1024L * 1024L;
28       printf("The entire universe has %ld bugs.\n", universe_of_defects);
29
30       double expected_bugs = bugs * bug_rate;
31       printf("You are expected to have %f bugs.\n", expected_bugs);
32
33       double part_of_universe = expected_bugs / universe_of_defects;
34       printf("That is only a %e portion of the universe.\n",
35               part_of_universe);
36
37       // this makes no sense, just a demo of something weird
38       char nul_byte = '\0';
```

```
39          int care_percentage = bugs * nul_byte;
40          printf("Which means you should care %d%%.\n", care_percentage);
41
42          return 0;
43      }
```

In this program, we're declaring variables of different types and then printing them using different printf format strings. I can break it down as follows:

ex7.c:1-4   The usual start of a C program.

ex7.c:5-6   Declare an int and double for some fake bug data.

ex7.c:8-9   Print out those two, so nothing new here.

ex7.c:11   Declare a huge number using a new type, long, for storing big numbers.

ex7.c:12-13   Print out that number using %ld that adds a modifier to the usual %d. Adding l (the letter) tells the program to print the number as a long decimal.

ex7.c:15-17   This is just more math and printing.

ex7.c:19-21   Craft a depiction of your bug rate compared to the bugs in the universe, which is a completely inaccurate calculation. It's so small that we have to use %e to print it in scientific notation.

ex7.c:24   Make a character, with a special syntax '\0' that creates a nul byte character. This is effectively the number 0.

ex7.c:25   Multiply bugs by this character, which produces 0, as in how much you should care. This demonstrates an ugly hack you might see sometimes.

ex7.c:26-27   Print that out, and notice we've used %% (two percent signs) so that we can print a % (percent) character.

ex7.c:28-30   The end of the main function.

This source file demonstrates how some math works with different types of variables. At the end of the program, it also demonstrates something you see in C but not in many other languages. To C, a *character* is just an integer. It's a really small integer, but that's all it is. This means you can do math on them, and a lot of software does just that—for good or bad.

This last bit is your first glance at how C gives you direct access to the machine. We'll be exploring that more in later exercises.

What You Should See

As usual, here's what you should see for the output:

```
$ make ex7
cc -Wall -g    ex7.c   -o ex7
$ ./ex7
You have 100 bugs at the imaginary rate of 1.200000.
The entire universe has 1073741824 bugs.
You are expected to have 120.000000 bugs.
That is only a 1.117587e-07 portion of the universe.
Which means you should care 0%.
$
```

How to Break It

Again, go through this and try to break the printf by passing in the wrong arguments. See what happens if you try to print out the nul_byte variable along with %s versus %c. When you break it, run it under the debugger to see what it says about what you did.

Extra Credit

- Make the number you assign to universe_of_defects various sizes until you get a warning from the compiler.

- What do these really huge numbers actually print out?

- Change long to unsigned long and try to find the number that makes it too big.

- Go search online to find out what unsigned does.

- Try to explain to yourself (before I do in the next exercise) why you can multiply a char and an int.

If, Else-If, Else

In C, there really isn't a *Boolean* type. Instead, any integer that's 0 is *false* or otherwise it's *true*. In the last exercise, the expression argc > 1 actually resulted in 1 or 0, not an explicit True or False like in Python. This is another example of C being closer to how a computer works, because to a computer, truth values are just integers.

However, C does have a typical if-statement that uses this numeric idea of true and false to do branching. It's fairly similar to what you would do in Python and Ruby, as you can see in this exercise:

ex8.c

```
1    #include <stdio.h>
2
3    int main(int argc, char *argv[])
4    {
5        int i = 0;
6
7        if (argc == 1) {
8            printf("You only have one argument. You suck.\n");
9        } else if (argc > 1 && argc < 4) {
10           printf("Here's your arguments:\n");
11
12           for (i = 0; i < argc; i++) {
13               printf("%s ", argv[i]);
14           }
15           printf("\n");
16       } else {
17           printf("You have too many arguments. You suck.\n");
18       }
19
20       return 0;
21   }
```

The format for the if-statement is this:

```
if(TEST) {
    CODE;
} else if(TEST) {
    CODE;
} else {
    CODE;
}
```

This is like most other languages except for some specific C differences:

- As mentioned before, the TEST parts are false if they evaluate to 0, or otherwise true.

- You have to put parentheses around the TEST elements, while some other languages let you skip that.

- You don't need the {} braces to enclose the code, but it is *very* bad form to not use them. The braces make it clear where one branch of code begins and ends. If you don't include them then obnoxious errors come up.

Other than that, the code works the way it does in most other languages. You don't need to have either else if or else parts.

What You Should See

This one is pretty simple to run and try out:

Exercise 8 Session

```
$ make ex8
cc -Wall -g     ex8.c    -o ex8
$ ./ex8
You only have one argument. You suck.
$ ./ex8 one
Here's your arguments:
./ex8 one
$ ./ex8 one two
Here's your arguments:
./ex8 one two
$ ./ex8 one two three
You have too many arguments. You suck.
$
```

How to Break It

This one isn't easy to break because it's so simple, but try messing up the tests in the if-statement:

- Remove the else at the end, and the program won't catch the edge case.

- Change the && to a || so you get an or instead of an and test and see how that works.

Extra Credit

- You were briefly introduced to &&, which does an and comparison, so go research online the different *Boolean operators*.

- Write a few more test cases for this program to see what you can come up with.

- Is the first test really saying the right thing? To you, the *first argument* isn't the same first argument a user entered. Fix it.

While-Loop and Boolean Expressions

The first looping construct I'll show you is the while-loop, and it's the simplest, useful loop you could possibly use in C. Here's this exercise's code for discussion:

ex9.c

```
1    #include <stdio.h>
2
3    int main(int argc, char *argv[])
4    {
5        int i = 0;
6        while (i < 25) {
7            printf("%d", i);
8            i++;
9        }
10
11       return 0;
12   }
```

From this code, and from your memorization of the basic syntax, you can see that a while-loop is simply this:

```
while(TEST) {
    CODE;
}
```

It simply runs the CODE as long as TEST is true (1). So to replicate how the for-loop works, we need to do our own initializing and incrementing of i. Remember that i++ increments i with the post-increment operator. Refer back to your list of tokens if you didn't recognize that.

What You Should See

The output is basically the same, so I just did it a little differently so that you can see it run another way.

Exercise 9 Session

```
$ make ex9
cc -Wall -g    ex9.c    -o ex9
$ ./ex9
arg 0: ./ex9
state 0: California
state 1: Oregon
```

```
state 2: Washington
state 3: Texas
$
$ ./ex9 test it
arg 0: ./ex9
arg 1: test
arg 2: it
state 0: California
state 1: Oregon
state 2: Washington
state 3: Texas
$
```

How to Break It

There are several ways to get a while-loop wrong, so I don't recommend you use it unless you must. Here are a few easy ways to break it:

- Forget to initialize the first int i;. Depending on what i starts with, the loop might not run at all, or run for an extremely long time.

- Forget to initialize the second loop's i so that it retains the value from the end of the first loop. Now your second loop might or might not run.

- Forget to do a i++ increment at the end of the loop and you'll get a *forever loop*, one of the dreaded problems common in the first decade or two of programming.

Extra Credit

- Make the loop count backward by using i-- to start at 25 and go to 0.

- Write a few more complex while-loops using what you know so far.

Switch Statements

In other languages, like Ruby, you have a switch-statement that can take any expression. Some languages, like Python, don't have a switch-statement because an if-statement with Boolean expressions is about the same thing. For these languages, switch-statements are more like alternatives to if-statements and work the same internally.

In C, the switch-statement is actually quite different and is really a *jump table*. Instead of random Boolean expressions, you can only put expressions that result in integers. These integers are used to calculate jumps from the top of the switch to the part that matches that value. Here's some code to help you understand this concept of jump tables:

ex10.c

```
1    #include <stdio.h>
2
3    int main(int argc, char *argv[])
4    {
5        int i = 0;
6
7        // go through each string in argv
8        // why am I skipping argv[0]?
9        for (i = 1; i < argc; i++) {
10           printf("arg %d: %s\n", i, argv[i]);
11       }
12
13       // let's make our own array of strings
14       char *states[] = {
15           "California", "Oregon",
16           "Washington", "Texas"
17       };
18
19       int num_states = 4;
20
21       for (i = 0; i < num_states; i++) {
22           printf("state %d: %s\n", i, states[i]);
23       }
24
25       return 0;
26   }
```

In this program, we take a single command line argument and print out all vowels in an incredibly tedious way to demonstrate a switch-statement. Here's how the switch-statement works:

- The compiler marks the place in the program where the switch-statement starts. Let's call this location Y.

- It then evaluates the expression in switch(letter) to come up with a number. In this case, the number will be the raw ASCII code of the letter in argv[1].

- The compiler also translates each of the case blocks like case 'A': into a location in the program that's that far away. So the code under case 'A' is at Y + A in the program.

- It then does the math to figure out where Y + letter is located in the switch-statement, and if it's too far, then it adjusts it to Y + default.

- Once it knows the location, the program *jumps* to that spot in the code, and then continues running. This is why you have break on some of the case blocks but not on others.

- If 'a' is entered, then it jumps to case 'a'. There's no break, so it "falls through" to the one right under it, case 'A', which has code and a break.

- Finally, it runs this code, hits the break, and then exits out of the switch-statement entirely.

This is a deep dive into how the switch-statement works, but in practice you just have to remember a few simple rules:

- Always include a default: branch so that you catch any missing inputs.

- Don't allow *fall through* unless you really want it. It's also a good idea to add a //fallthrough comment so people know it's on purpose.

- Always write the case and the break before you write the code that goes in it.

- Try to use if-statements instead if you can.

What You Should See

Here's an example of me playing with this, and also demonstrating various ways to pass in the argument:

Exercise 10 Session

```
$ make ex10
cc -Wall -gex10.c   -o ex10
$ ./ex10
ERROR: You need one argument.
$
$ ./ex10 Zed
0: Z is not a vowel
1: 'E'
2: d is not a vowel
$
$ ./ex10 Zed Shaw
ERROR: You need one argument.
$
$ ./ex10 "Zed Shaw"
```

```
0: Z is not a vowel
1: 'E'
2: d is not a vowel
3:   is not a vowel
4: S is not a vowel
5: h is not a vowel
6: 'A'
7: w is not a vowel
$
```

Remember that there's an if-statement at the top that exits with a return 1; when you don't provide enough arguments. A return that's not 0 indicates to the OS that the program had an error. You can test for any value that's greater than 0 in scripts and other programs to figure out what happened.

How to Break It

It's *incredibly* easy to break a switch-statement. Here are just a few ways you can mess one of these up:

- Forget a break, and it'll run two or more blocks of code you don't want it to run.
- Forget a default, and it'll silently ignore values you forgot.
- Accidentally put a variable into the switch that evaluates to something unexpected, like an int, which becomes weird values.
- Use uninitialized values in the switch.

You can also break this program in a few other ways. See if you can bust it yourself.

Extra Credit

- Write another program that uses math on the letter to convert it to lowercase, and then remove all of the extraneous uppercase letters in the switch.
- Use the ',' (comma) to initialize letter in the for-loop.
- Make it handle all of the arguments you pass it with yet another for-loop.
- Convert this switch-statement to an if-statement. Which do you like better?
- In the case for 'Y' I have the break outside of the if-statement. What's the impact of this, and what happens if you move it inside of the if-statement. Prove to yourself that you're right.

Arrays and Strings

This exercise shows you that C stores its strings simply as an array of bytes, terminated with the '\0' (nul) byte. You probably clued in to this in the last exercise since we did it manually. Here's how we do it in another way to make it even clearer by comparing it to an array of numbers:

ex11.c

```c
1    #include <stdio.h>
2
3    int main(int argc, char *argv[])
4    {
5        int numbers[4] = { 0 };
6        char name[4] = { 'a' };
7
8        // first, print them out raw
9        printf("numbers: %d %d %d %d\n",
10               numbers[0], numbers[1], numbers[2], numbers[3]);
11
12       printf("name each: %c %c %c %c\n",
13               name[0], name[1], name[2], name[3]);
14
15       printf("name: %s\n", name);
16
17       // set up the numbers
18       numbers[0] = 1;
19       numbers[1] = 2;
20       numbers[2] = 3;
21       numbers[3] = 4;
22
23       // set up the name
24       name[0] = 'Z';
25       name[1] = 'e';
26       name[2] = 'd';
27       name[3] = '\0';
28
29       // then print them out initialized
30       printf("numbers: %d %d %d %d\n",
31               numbers[0], numbers[1], numbers[2], numbers[3]);
32
33       printf("name each: %c %c %c %c\n",
34               name[0], name[1], name[2], name[3]);
35
36       // print the name like a string
37       printf("name: %s\n", name);
38
```

```
39          // another way to use name
40          char *another = "Zed";
41
42          printf("another: %s\n", another);
43
44          printf("another each: %c %c %c %c\n",
45                  another[0], another[1], another[2], another[3]);
46
47          return 0;
48      }
```

In this code, we set up some arrays the tedious way, by assigning a value to each element. In numbers, we are setting up numbers; but in name, we're actually building a string manually.

What You Should See

When you run this code, you should first see the arrays printed with their contents initialized to 0 (zero), then in its initialized form.

Exercise 11 Session

```
$ make ex11
cc -Wall -g    ex11.c    -o ex11
$ ./ex11
numbers: 0 0 0 0
name each: a
name: a
numbers: 1 2 3 4
name each: Z e d
name: Zed
another: Zed
another each: Z e d
$
```

You'll notice some interesting things about this program:

- I didn't have to give all four elements of the arrays to initialize them. This is a shortcut in C. If you set just one element, it'll fill in the rest with 0.

- When each element of numbers is printed, they all come out as 0.

- When each element of name is printed, only the first element 'a' shows up because the '\0' character is special and won't display.

- Then the first time we print name, it only prints the letter a. This is because the array will be filled with 0 after the first 'a' in the initializer, so the string is correctly terminated by a '\0' character.

- We then set up the arrays with a tedious, manual assignment to each thing and print them out again. Look at how they changed. Now the numbers are set, but do you see how the name string prints my name correctly?

- There are also two syntaxes for doing a string: `char name[4] = {'a'}` on line 6 versus `char *another = "name"` on line 44. The first one is less common and the second is what you should use for string literals like this.

Notice that I'm using the same syntax and style of code to interact with both an array of integers and an array of characters, but `printf` thinks that the name is just a string. Again, this is because the C language doesn't differentiate between a string and an array of characters.

Finally, when you make string literals you should typically use the `char *another = "Literal"` syntax. This works out to be the same thing, but it's more idiomatic and easier to write.

How to Break It

The source of almost all bugs in C come from forgetting to have enough space, or forgetting to put a `'\0'` at the end of a string. In fact, it's so common and hard to get right that the majority of good C code just doesn't use C-style strings. In later exercises, we'll actually learn how to avoid C strings completely.

In this program, the key to breaking it is to forget to put the `'\0'` character at the end of the strings. There are a few ways to do this:

- Get rid of the initializers that set up name.
- Accidentally set `name[3] = 'A';` so that there's no terminator.
- Set the initializer to `{'a','a','a','a'}` so that there are too many `'a'` characters and no space for the `'\0'` terminator.

Try to come up with some other ways to break this, and run all of these under the debugger so you can see exactly what's going on and what the errors are called. Sometimes you'll make these mistakes and even a debugger can't find them. Try moving where you declare the variables to see if you get an error. This is part of the voodoo of C: Sometimes just where the variable is located changes the bug.

Extra Credit

- Assign the characters into `numbers`, and then use `printf` to print them one character at a time. What kind of compiler warnings do you get?
- Do the inverse for name, trying to treat it like an array of `int` and print it out one `int` at a time. What does the debugger think of that?

- In how many other ways can you print this out?

- If an array of characters is 4 bytes long, and an integer is 4 bytes long, then can you treat the whole name array like it's just an integer? How might you accomplish this crazy hack?

- Take out a piece of paper and draw each of these arrays as a row of boxes. Then do the operations you just did on paper to see if you get them right.

- Convert name to be in the style of another and see if the code keeps working.

Sizes and Arrays

In the last exercise, you did math but with, a '\0' (nul) character. This may seem odd if you're coming from other languages, since they try to treat *strings* and *byte arrays* as different beasts. C treats strings as just arrays of bytes, and it's only the different printing functions that recognize a difference.

Before I can really explain the significance of this, I have to introduce a couple more concepts: sizeof and arrays. Here's the code we'll be talking about:

ex12.c

```
1    #include <stdio.h>
2
3    int main(int argc, char *argv[])
4    {
5        int areas[] = { 10, 12, 13, 14, 20 };
6        char name[] = "Zed";
7        char full_name[] = {
8            'Z', 'e', 'd',
9            ' ', 'A', '.', ' ',
10           'S', 'h', 'a', 'w', '\0'
11       };
12
13       // WARNING: On some systems you may have to change the
14       // %ld in this code to a %u since it will use unsigned ints
15       printf("The size of an int: %ld\n", sizeof(int));
16       printf("The size of areas (int[]): %ld\n", sizeof(areas));
17       printf("The number of ints in areas: %ld\n",
18               sizeof(areas) / sizeof(int));
19       printf("The first area is %d, the 2nd %d.\n", areas[0], areas[1]);
20
21       printf("The size of a char: %ld\n", sizeof(char));
22       printf("The size of name (char[]): %ld\n", sizeof(name));
23       printf("The number of chars: %ld\n", sizeof(name) / sizeof(char));
24
25       printf("The size of full_name (char[]): %ld\n", sizeof(full_name));
26       printf("The number of chars: %ld\n",
27               sizeof(full_name) / sizeof(char));
28
29       printf("name=\"%s\" and full_name=\"%s\"\n", name, full_name);
30
31       return 0;
32   }
```

In this code, we create a few arrays with different data types in them. Because arrays of data are so central to how C works, there are a huge number of ways to create them. For now, just use the syntax `type name[] = {initializer}`; and we'll explore more later. What this syntax means is, "I want an array of type that is initialized to {..}." When C sees this, it knows to:

- Look at the type, and in this first case, it's `int`.

- Look at the `[]` and see that there's no length given.

- Look at the initializer `{10, 12, 13, 14, 20}` and figure out that you want those five integers in your array.

- Create a piece of memory in the computer that can hold 5 integers one after another.

- Take the name you want, `areas`, and assign it this location.

In the case of `areas`, it's creating an array of five integers that contain those numbers. When it gets to `char name[] = "Zed";` it's doing the same thing, except it's creating an array of three characters and assigning that to name. The final array we make is `full_name`, but we use the annoying syntax of spelling it out one character at a time. To C, name and `full_name` are identical methods of creating a char array.

In the rest of the file, we're using a keyword called `sizeof` to ask C how big things are in *bytes*. C is all about the size and location of pieces of memory, and what you do with them. To help you keep this straight, it gives you `sizeof` so that you can ask how big something is before you work with it.

This is where stuff gets tricky, so let's run this code first and then explain it later.

What You Should See

```
$ make ex12
cc -Wall -g    ex12.c    -o ex12
$ ./ex12
The size of an int: 4
The size of areas (int[]): 20
The number of ints in areas: 5
The first area is 10, the 2nd 12.
The size of a char: 1
The size of name (char[]): 4
The number of chars: 4
The size of full_name (char[]): 12
The number of chars: 12
name="Zed" and full_name="Zed A. Shaw"
$
```

Now you see the output of these different `printf` calls and start to get a glimpse of what C is doing. Your output could actually be totally different from mine, since your computer might have different size integers. I'll go through my output:

5   My computer thinks an `int` is 4 bytes in size. Your computer might use a different size if it's a 32-bit versus 64-bit CPU.

6   The `areas` array has five integers in it, so it makes sense that my computer requires 20 bytes to store it.

7   If we divide the size of `areas` by the size of an `int`, then we get five elements. Looking at the code, this matches what we put in the initializer.

8   We then did an array access to get `areas[0]` and `areas[1]`, which means C is *zero indexed* like Python and Ruby.

9-11   We repeat this for the name array, but do you notice something odd about the size of the array? It says it's *4* bytes long, but we only typed "Zed" for three characters. Where's the fourth one coming from?

12-13   We do the same thing with `full_name`, and now notice it gets this correct.

13   Finally, we just print out the name and `full_name` to prove that they actually are "strings" according to `printf`.

Make sure you can go through and see how these output lines match what was created. We'll be building on this, and exploring more about arrays and storage next.

How to Break It

Breaking this program is fairly easy. Try some of these:

- Get rid of the `'\0'` at the end of `full_name` and rerun it. Run it under the debugger too. Now, move the definition of `full_name` to the top of `main` before `areas`. Try running it under the debugger a few times and see if you get some new errors. In some cases, you might still get lucky and not catch any errors.

- Change it so that instead of `areas[0]` you try to print `areas[10]`. See what the debugger thinks of that.

- Try other ways to break it like this, doing it to name and `full_name`, too.

Extra Credit

- Try assigning to elements in the areas array with areas[0] = 100; and similar.
- Try assigning to elements of name and full_name.
- Try setting one element of areas to a character from name.
- Search online for the different sizes used for integers on different CPUs.

For-Loops and Arrays of Strings

You can make an array of various types with the idea that a string and an array of bytes are the same thing. The next step is to do an array that has strings in it. We'll also introduce your first looping construct, the for-loop, to help print out this new data structure.

The fun part of this is that there's been an array of strings hiding in your programs for a while now: the char *argv[] in the main function arguments. Here's code that will print out any command line arguments you pass it:

ex13.c

```c
#include <stdio.h>

int main(int argc, char *argv[])
{
    if (argc != 2) {
        printf("ERROR: You need one argument.\n");
        // this is how you abort a program
        return 1;
    }

    int i = 0;
    for (i = 0; argv[1][i] != '\0'; i++) {
        char letter = argv[1][i];

        switch (letter) {
            case 'a':
            case 'A':
                printf("%d: 'A'\n", i);
                break;

            case 'e':
            case 'E':
                printf("%d: 'E'\n", i);
                break;

            case 'i':
            case 'I':
                printf("%d: 'I'\n", i);
                break;

            case 'o':
            case 'O':
                printf("%d: 'O'\n", i);
                break;
```

```
35
36                  case 'u':
37                  case 'U':
38                      printf("%d: 'U'\n", i);
39                      break;
40
41                  case 'y':
42                  case 'Y':
43                      if (i > 2) {
44                          // it's only sometimes Y
45                          printf("%d: 'Y'\n", i);
46                      }
47                      break;
48
49                  default:
50                      printf("%d: %c is not a vowel\n", i, letter);
51              }
52          }
53
54          return 0;
55      }
```

The format of a for-loop is this:

```
for(INITIALIZER; TEST; INCREMENTER) {
    CODE;
}
```

Here's how the for-loop works:

- The INITIALIZER is code that's run to set up the loop, which in this case is $i = 0$.

- Next, the TEST Boolean expression is checked. If it's false (0), then CODE is skipped, doing nothing.

- The CODE runs and does whatever it does.

- After the CODE runs, the INCREMENTER part is run, usually incrementing something, such as in i++.

- And it continues again with step 2 until the TEST is false (0).

This for-loop is going through the command line arguments using argc and argv like this:

- The OS passes each command line argument as a string in the argv array. The program's name (./ex10) is at 0, with the rest coming after it.

- The OS also sets argc to the number of arguments in the argv array, so you can process them without going past the end. Remember that if you give one argument, the program's name is the first, so argc is 2.

- The for-loop sets up with i = 1 in the initializer.

- It then tests that i is less than argc with the test i < argc. Since $1 < 2$, it'll pass.

- It then runs the code that just prints out the i and uses i to index into argv.

- The incrementer is then run using the i++ syntax, which is a handy way of writing i = i + 1.

- This then repeats until i < argc is finally false (0), the loop exits, and the program continues on.

What You Should See

To play with this program, then, you have to run it two ways. The first way is to pass in some command line arguments so that argc and argv get set. The second is to run it with no arguments so you can see that the first for-loop doesn't run if i < argc is false.

Exercise 13 Session

```
$ make ex13
cc -Wall -g      ex13.c    -o ex13
$ ./ex13 i am a bunch of arguments
arg 1: i
arg 2: am
arg 3: a
arg 4: bunch
arg 5: of
arg 6: arguments
state 0: California
state 1: Oregon
state 2: Washington
state 3: Texas
$
$ ./ex13
state 0: California
state 1: Oregon
state 2: Washington
state 3: Texas
$
```

Understanding Arrays of Strings

In C you make an *array of strings* by combining the char *str = "blah" syntax with the char str[] = {'b','l','a','h'} syntax to construct a two-dimensional array. The syntax char *states[] = {...} on line 14 is this two-dimensional combination, each string being one element, and each character in the string being another.

Confusing? The concept of multiple dimensions is something most people never think about, so what you should do is build this array of strings on paper:

- Make a grid with the index of each *string* on the left.

- Then put the index of each *character* on the top.

- Then fill in the squares in the middle with what single character goes in each square.

- Once you have the grid, trace through the code using this grid of paper.

Another way to figure this is out is to build the same structure in a programming language you are more familiar with, like Python or Ruby.

How to Break It

- Take your favorite other language and use it to run this program, but include as many command line arguments as possible. See if you can bust it by giving it way too many arguments.

- Initialize i to 0 and see what that does. Do you have to adjust argc as well, or does it just work? Why does 0-based indexing work here?

- Set num_states wrong so that it's a higher value and see what it does.

Extra Credit

- Figure out what kind of code you can put into the parts of a for-loop.

- Look up how to use the comma character (,) to separate multiple statements in the parts of the for-loop, but between the semicolon characters (;).

- Read about what a NULL is and try to use it in one of the elements from the states array to see what it'll print.

- See if you can assign an element from the states array to the argv array before printing both. Try the inverse.

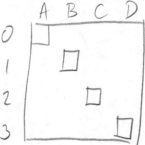

Writing and Using Functions

Up until now, we've just used functions that are part of the stdio.h header file. In this exercise, you'll write some functions and use some other functions.

ex14.c

```
1    #include <stdio.h>
2    #include <ctype.h>
3
4    // forward declarations
5    int can_print_it(char ch);
6    void print_letters(char arg[]);
7
8    void print_arguments(int argc, char *argv[])
9    {
10       int i = 0;
11
12       for (i = 0; i < argc; i++) {
13           print_letters(argv[i]);
14       }
15   }
16
17   void print_letters(char arg[])
18   {
19       int i = 0;
20
21       for (i = 0; arg[i] != '\0'; i++) {
22           char ch = arg[i];
23
24           if (can_print_it(ch)) {
25               printf("'%c' == %d ", ch, ch);
26           }
27       }
28
29       printf("\n");
30   }
31
32   int can_print_it(char ch)
33   {
34       return isalpha(ch) || isblank(ch);
35   }
36
37   int main(int argc, char *argv[])
38   {
39       print_arguments(argc, argv);
40       return 0;
41   }
```

In this example we're creating functions to print out the characters and ASCII codes for any that are *alpha* or *blanks*. Here's the breakdown:

ex14.c:2   Include a new header file, so we can gain access to isalpha and isblank.

ex14.c:5-6   Tell C that you'll be using some functions later in your program without actually having to define them. This is a *forward declaration* and it solves the chicken-and-egg problem of needing to use a function before you've defined it.

ex14.c:8-15   Define the print_arguments function, which knows how to print the same array of strings that main typically gets.

ex14.c:17-30   Define the next function, print_letters, which is called by print_arguments and knows how to print each of the characters and their codes.

ex14.c:32-35   Define can_print_it, which simply returns the truth value (0 or 1) of isalpha(ch) || isblank(ch) back to its caller, print_letters.

ex14.c:38-42   Finally, main simply calls print_arguments to make the whole chain of functions go.

I shouldn't have to describe what's in each function, because they're all things you've run into before. What you should be able to see, though, is that I've simply defined functions the same way you've been defining main. The only difference is you have to help C out by telling it ahead of time if you're going to use functions it hasn't encountered yet in the file. That's what the forward declarations do.

What You Should See

To play with this program, you just feed it different command line arguments, which get passed through your functions. Here's me playing with it to demonstrate:

Exercise 14 Session

```
$ make ex14
cc -Wall -g     ex14.c     -o ex14

$ ./ex14
'e' == 101 'x' == 120

$ ./ex14 hi this is cool
'e' == 101 'x' == 120
'h' == 104 'i' == 105
't' == 116 'h' == 104 'i' == 105 's' == 115
'i' == 105 's' == 115
'c' == 99 'o' == 111 'o' == 111 'l' == 108
```

```
$ ./ex14 "I go 3 spaces"
'e' == 101 'x' == 120
'I' == 73 ' ' == 32 'g' == 103 'o' == 111 ' ' == 32 ' ' == 32\
        's' == 115 'p' == 112 'a' == 97 'c' == 99 'e' == 101 's' == 115
$
```

The isalpha and isblank do all the work of figuring out if the given character is a letter or a blank. When I do the last run, it prints everything but the 3 character since that's a digit.

How to Break It

There are two different kinds of breaking in this program:

- Remove the forward declarations to confuse the compiler and cause it to complain about can_print_it and print_letters.

- When you call print_arguments inside main, try adding 1 to argc so that it goes past the end of the argv array.

Extra Credit

- Rework these functions so that you have fewer functions. For example, do you really need can_print_it?

- Have print_arguments figure out how long each argument string is by using the strlen function, and then pass that length to print_letters. Then, rewrite print_letters so it only processes this fixed length and doesn't rely on the '\0' terminator. You'll need the #include <string.h> for this.

- Use man to look up information on isalpha and isblank. Use other similar functions to print out only digits or other characters.

- Go read about how other people like to format their functions. Never use the K&R syntax (it's antiquated and confusing) but understand what it's doing in case you run into someone who likes it.

Pointers, Dreaded Pointers

Pointers are famous mystical creatures in C. I'll attempt to demystify them by teaching you the vocabulary to deal with them. They actually aren't that complex, but they're frequently abused in weird ways that make them hard to use. If you avoid the stupid ways to use pointers, then they're fairly easy.

To demonstrate pointers in a way that we can talk about them, I've written a frivolous program that prints a group of people's ages in three different ways.

ex15.c

```
1    #include <stdio.h>
2
3    int main(int argc, char *argv[])
4    {
5        // create two arrays we care about
6        int ages[] = { 23, 43, 12, 89, 2 };
7        char *names[] = {
8            "Alan", "Frank",
9            "Mary", "John", "Lisa"
10       };
11
12       // safely get the size of ages
13       int count = sizeof(ages) / sizeof(int);
14       int i = 0;
15
16       // first way using indexing
17       for (i = 0; i < count; i++) {
18           printf("%s has %d years alive.\n", names[i], ages[i]);
19       }
20
21       printf("---\n");
22
23       // set up the pointers to the start of the arrays
24       int *cur_age = ages;
25       char **cur_name = names;
26
27       // second way using pointers
28       for (i = 0; i < count; i++) {
29           printf("%s is %d years old.\n",
30                   *(cur_name + i), *(cur_age + i));
31       }
32
33       printf("---\n");
34
35       // third way, pointers are just arrays
36       for (i = 0; i < count; i++) {
```

```
37                    printf("%s is %d years old again.\n", cur_name[i], cur_age[i]);
38            }
39
40            printf("---\n");
41
42            // fourth way with pointers in a stupid complex way
43            for (cur_name = names, cur_age = ages;
44                    (cur_age - ages) < count; cur_name++, cur_age++) {
45                printf("%s lived %d years so far.\n", *cur_name, *cur_age);
46            }
47
48            return 0;
49      }
```

Before explaining how pointers work, let's break this program down line by line so you get an idea of what's going on. As you go through this detailed description, try to answer the questions for yourself on a piece of paper, then see if what you guessed matches my description of pointers later.

ex15.c:6-10 Create two arrays: ages storing some int data, and names storing an array of strings.

ex15.c:12-13 These are some variables for our for-loops later.

ex15.c:16-19 This is just looping through the two arrays and printing how old each person is. This is using i to index into the array.

ex15.c:24 Create a pointer that points at ages. Notice the use of int * to create a pointer to integer type of pointer. That's similar to char *, which is a pointer to char, and a string is an array of chars. Seeing the similarity yet?

ex15.c:25 Create a pointer that points at names. A char * is already a pointer to char, so that's just a string. However, you need two levels since names is two-dimensional, which then means you need char ** for a pointer to (a pointer to char) type. Study that and try to explain it to yourself, too.

ex15.c:28-31 Loop through ages and names but use the pointers *plus an offset of i* instead. Writing *(cur_name+i) is the same as writing name[i], and you read it as "the value of (pointer cur_name plus i)."

ex15.c:35-39 This shows how the syntax to access an element of an array is the same for a pointer and an array.

ex15.c:44-50 This is another admittedly insane loop that does the same thing as the other two, but instead it uses various pointer arithmetic methods:

  ex15.c:44 Initialize our for-loop by setting cur_name and cur_age to the beginning of the names and ages arrays.

ex15.c:45 The test portion of the for-loop then compares the *distance* of the pointer cur_age from the start of ages. Why does that work?

ex15.c:46 The increment part of the for-loop then increments both cur_name and cur_age so that they point at the *next* element of the name and age arrays.

ex15.c:48-49 The pointers cur_name and cur_age are now pointing at one element of the arrays that they work on, and we can print them out using just *cur_name and *cur_age, which means "the value of wherever cur_name is pointing."

This seemingly simple program has a large amount of information, and my goal is to get you to attempt to figure pointers out for yourself before I explain them. *Don't continue until you've written down what you think a pointer does.*

What You Should See

After you run this program, try to trace back each line printed out to the line in the code that produced it. If you have to, alter the printf calls to make sure you've got the right line number.

Exercise 15 Session

```
$ make ex15
cc -Wall -g     ex15.c   -o ex15
$ ./ex15
Alan has 23 years alive.
Frank has 43 years alive.
Mary has 12 years alive.
John has 89 years alive.
Lisa has 2 years alive.
---
Alan is 23 years old.
Frank is 43 years old.
Mary is 12 years old.
John is 89 years old.
Lisa is 2 years old.
---
Alan is 23 years old again.
Frank is 43 years old again.
Mary is 12 years old again.
John is 89 years old again.
Lisa is 2 years old again.
---
Alan lived 23 years so far.
Frank lived 43 years so far.
Mary lived 12 years so far.
John lived 89 years so far.
Lisa lived 2 years so far.
$
```

A pointer is another name for a variable.

It points back at the place in memory where a given variable starts.

Explaining Pointers

When you type something like ages[i], you're *indexing* into the array ages, and you're using the number that's held in i to do it. If i is set to zero then it's the same as typing ages[0]. We've been calling this number i an *index* since it's a location inside ages that we want. It could also be called an address, which is a way of saying "I want the integer in ages that's at address i."

If i is an index, then what's ages? To C, ages is a location in the computer's memory where all of these integers start. It's *also* an address, and the C compiler will replace ages anywhere you type it with the address of the very first integer in ages. Another way to think of ages is that it's the "address of the first integer in ages." But here's the trick: ages is an address inside the *entire computer*. It's not like i that's just an address inside ages. The ages array name is actually an address in the computer.

That leads to a certain realization: C thinks your whole computer is one massive array of bytes. Obviously, this isn't very useful, but then what C does is layer on top of this massive array of bytes the concept of *types* and *sizes* of those types. You already saw how this worked in previous exercises, but now you start to get an idea of how C is doing the following with your arrays:

- Creating a block of memory inside your computer
- *Pointing* the name ages at the beginning of that block
- *Indexing* into the block by taking the base address of ages and getting the element that's i away from there
- Converting that address at ages+i into a valid int of the right size, such that the index works to return what you want: the int at index i

If you can take a base address, like ages, and add to it with another address like i to produce a new address, then can you just make something that points right at this location all the time? Yes, and that thing is called a *pointer*. This is what the pointers cur_age and cur_name are doing: They are variables pointing at the location where ages and names live in your computer's memory. The example program is then moving them around or doing math on them to get values out of the memory. In one instance, they just add i to cur_age, which is the same as what the program does with array[i]. In the last for-loop, though, these two pointers are being moved on their own, without i to help out. In that loop, the pointers are treated like a combination of array and integer offset rolled into one.

A pointer is simply an address pointing somewhere inside the computer's memory with a type specifier so that you get the right size of data with it. It's kind of like a combination of ages and i rolled into one data type. C knows where pointers are pointing, knows the data type they point at, the size of those types, and how to get the data for you. Just like with i, you can increment, decrement, subtract, or add to them. But, just like ages, you can also get values out, put new values in, and use all of the array operations.

The purpose of a pointer is to let you manually index data into blocks or memory when an array won't do it right. In almost all other cases, you actually want to use an array. But, there are times when you *have to* work with a raw block of memory and that's where a pointer comes in. A pointer gives you raw, direct access to a block of memory so you can work with it.

The final thing to grasp at this stage is that you can use either syntax for most array or pointer operations. You can take a pointer to something, but use the array syntax to access it. You can take an array and do pointer arithmetic with it.

Practical Pointer Usage

There are primarily four useful things you can do with pointers in C code:

- Ask the OS for a chunk of memory and use a pointer to work with it. This includes strings and something you haven't seen yet, `structs`.
- Pass large blocks of memory (like large structs) to functions with a pointer, so you don't have to pass the whole thing to them.
- Take the address of a function, so you can use it as a dynamic callback.
- Scan complex chunks of memory, converting bytes off of a network socket into data structures or parsing files.

For nearly everything else, you might see people use pointers when they should be using arrays. In the early days of C programming, people used pointers to speed up their programs, because the compilers were really bad at optimizing array usage. These days, the syntax to access an array versus a pointer are translated into the same machine code and optimized in the same way, so it's not as necessary. Instead, you should go with arrays whenever you can, and then only use pointers as a performance optimization if you absolutely have to.

The Pointer Lexicon

I'm now going to give you a little lexicon to use for reading and writing pointers. Whenever you run into a complex pointer statement, just refer to this and break it down bit by bit (or just don't use it since it's probably not good code.)

type *ptr   A pointer of type named ptr

***ptr**   The value of whatever ptr is pointed at

***(ptr + i)**   The value of (whatever ptr is pointed at plus i)

&thing   The address of thing

type *ptr = &thing   A pointer of type named ptr set to the address of thing

ptr++   Increment where ptr points

We'll be using this simple lexicon to break down all of the pointers we use from now on in the book.

Pointers Aren't Arrays

No matter what, you should never think that pointers and arrays are the same thing. They aren't the same thing, even though C lets you work with them in many of the same ways. For example, if you do sizeof(cur_age) in the code above, you would get the size of the *pointer*, not the size of what it points at. If you want the size of the full array, you have to use the array's name, age, as I did on line 12.

To do: Expand on this some more with what doesn't work the same on pointers and arrays.

How to Break It

You can break this program by simply pointing the pointers at the wrong things:

- Try to make cur_age point at names. You'll need to use a C cast to force it, so go look that up and try to figure it out.
- In the final for-loop, try getting the math wrong in weird ways.
- Try rewriting the loops so that they start at the end of the arrays and go to the beginning. This is harder than it looks.

Extra Credit

- Rewrite all of the arrays in this program as pointers.
- Rewrite all of the pointers as arrays.
- Go back to some of the other programs that use arrays and try to use pointers instead.
- Process command line arguments using just pointers, similar to how you did names in this one.
- Play with combinations of getting the value of and the address of things.
- Add another for-loop at the end that prints out the addresses that these pointers are using. You'll need the %p format for printf.
- Rewrite this program to use a function for each of the ways you're printing out things. Try to pass pointers to these functions so that they work on the data. Remember you can declare a function to accept a pointer, but just use it like an array.
- Change the for-loops to while-loops and see what works better for which kind of pointer usage.

Structs And Pointers to Them

In this exercise, you'll learn how to make a struct, point a pointer at it, and use it to make sense of internal memory structures. We'll also apply the knowledge of pointers from the last exercise, and then get you constructing these structures from raw memory using malloc.

As usual, here's the program we'll talk about, so type it in and make it work.

ex16.c

```
1    #include <stdio.h>
2    #include <assert.h>
3    #include <stdlib.h>
4    #include <string.h>
5
6    struct Person {
7        char *name;
8        int age;
9        int height;
10       int weight;
11   };
12
13   struct Person *Person_create(char *name, int age, int height,
14           int weight)
15   {
16       struct Person *who = malloc(sizeof(struct Person));
17       assert(who != NULL);
18
19       who->name = strdup(name);
20       who->age = age;
21       who->height = height;
22       who->weight = weight;
23
24       return who;
25   }
26
27   void Person_destroy(struct Person *who)
28   {
29       assert(who != NULL);
30
31       free(who->name);
32       free(who);
33   }
34
35   void Person_print(struct Person *who)
36   {
```

```
37          printf("Name: %s\n", who->name);
38          printf("\tAge: %d\n", who->age);
39          printf("\tHeight: %d\n", who->height);
40          printf("\tWeight: %d\n", who->weight);
41      }
42
43      int main(int argc, char *argv[])
44      {
45          // make two people structures
46          struct Person *joe = Person_create("Joe Alex", 32, 64, 140);
47
48          struct Person *frank = Person_create("Frank Blank", 20, 72, 180);
49
50          // print them out and where they are in memory
51          printf("Joe is at memory location %p:\n", joe);
52          Person_print(joe);
53
54          printf("Frank is at memory location %p:\n", frank);
55          Person_print(frank);
56
57          // make everyone age 20 years and print them again
58          joe->age += 20;
59          joe->height -= 2;
60          joe->weight += 40;
61          Person_print(joe);
62
63          frank->age += 20;
64          frank->weight += 20;
65          Person_print(frank);
66
67          // destroy them both so we clean up
68          Person_destroy(joe);
69          Person_destroy(frank);
70
71          return 0;
72      }
```

To describe this program, I'm going to use a different approach than before. I'm not going to give you a line-by-line breakdown of the program, I'm going to make *you* write it. I'm giving you a guide of the program based on the parts it contains, and your job is write out what each line does.

includes   I include some new header files here to gain access to some new functions. What does each give you?

struct Person   This is where I'm creating a structure that has four elements to describe a person. The final result is a new compound type that lets me reference these elements all as one or each piece by name. It's similar to a row of a database table or a class in an object-oriented programming (OOP) language.

function Person_create I need a way to create these structures, so I've made a function to do that. Here are the important things:

- I use malloc for memory allocate to ask the OS to give me a piece of raw memory.

- I pass to malloc the sizeof(struct Person), which calculates the total size of the structure, given all of the fields inside it.

- I use assert to make sure that I have a valid piece of memory back from malloc. There's a special constant called NULL that you use to mean "unset or invalid pointer." This assert is basically checking that malloc didn't return a NULL invalid pointer.

- I initialize each field of struct Person using the x->y syntax, to say what part of the structure I want to set.

- I use the strdup function to duplicate the string for the name, just to make sure that this structure actually owns it. The strdup actually is like malloc, and it also copies the original string into the memory it creates.

function Person_destroy If I have a create function, then I always need a destroy function, and this is what destroys Person structures. I again use assert to make sure I'm not getting bad input. Then I use the function free to return the memory I got with malloc and strdup. If you don't do this, you get a *memory leak*.

function Person_print I then need a way to print out people, which is all this function does. It uses the same x->y syntax to get the field from the structure to print it.

function main In the main function, I use all of the previous functions and the struct Person to do the following:

- Create two people, joe and frank.

- Print them out, but notice I'm using the %p format so you can see *where* the program has actually put your structure in memory.

- Age both of them by 20 years with changes to their bodies, too.

- Print each one after aging them.

- Finally, destroy the structures so we can clean up correctly.

Go through this description carefully, and do the following:

- Look up every function and header file you don't know. Remember that you can usually do man 2 function or man 3 function, and it'll tell you about it. You can also search online for the information.

- Write a *comment* above each and every single line that says what the line does in English.

- Trace through each function call and variable so you know where it comes from in the program.

- Look up any symbols you don't understand.

What You Should See

After you augment the program with your description comments, make sure it really runs and produces this output:

```
$ make ex16
cc -Wall -g    ex16.c   -o ex16

$ ./ex16
Joe is at memory location 0xeba010:
Name: Joe Alex
  Age: 32
  Height: 64
  Weight: 140
Frank is at memory location 0xeba050:
Name: Frank Blank
  Age: 20
  Height: 72
  Weight: 180
Name: Joe Alex
  Age: 52
  Height: 62
  Weight: 180
Name: Frank Blank
  Age: 40
  Height: 72
  Weight: 200
```

Explaining Structures

If you've done the work, then structures should be making sense, but let me explain them explicitly just to make sure you've understood it.

A structure in C is a collection of other data types (variables) that are stored in one block of memory where you can access each variable independently by name. They are similar to a record in a database table, or a very simplistic class in an OOP language. We can break one down this way:

- In the above code, we make a struct that has fields for a person: name, age, weight, and height.

- Each of those fields has a type, like int.

- C then packs those together so that they can all be contained in one single struct.

- The struct Person is now a *compound data type*, which means you can refer to struct Person using the same kinds of expressions you would for other data types.

- This lets you pass the whole cohesive grouping to other functions, as you did with Person_print.

- You can then access the individual parts of a struct by their names using x->y if you're dealing with a pointer.

- There's also a way to make a struct that doesn't need a pointer, and you use the x.y (period) syntax to work with it. We'll do this in the Extra Credit section.

If you didn't have struct, you'd need to figure out the size, packing, and location of pieces of memory with contents like this. In fact, in most early Assembler code (and even some now), this is what you would do. In C, you can let it handle the memory structuring of these compound data types and then focus on what you do with them.

How to Break It

The ways in which to break this program involve how you use the pointers and the malloc system:

- Try passing NULL to Person_destroy see what it does. If it doesn't abort, then you must not have the -g option in your Makefile's CFLAGS.

- Forget to call Person_destroy at the end, and then run it under the debugger to see it report that you forgot to free the memory. Figure out the options you need to pass to the debugger to get it to print how you leaked this memory.

- Forget to free who->name in Person_destroy and compare the output. Again, use the right options to see how the debugger tells you exactly where you messed up.

- This time, pass NULL to Person_print and see what the debugger thinks of that. You'll figure out that NULL is a quick way to crash your program.

Extra Credit

In this part of the exercise, I want you to attempt something difficult for the extra credit: Convert this program to *not* use pointers and malloc. This will be hard, so you'll want to research the following:

- How to create a struct on the *stack*, just like you're making any other variable.

- How to initialize it using the x.y (period) character instead of the x->y syntax.

- How to pass a structure to other functions without using a pointer.

Heap and Stack Memory Allocation

In this exercise, you're going to make a big leap in difficulty and create an entire small program to manage a database. This database isn't very efficient and doesn't store very much, but it does demonstrate most of what you've learned so far. It also introduces memory allocation more formally, and gets you started working with files. We use some file I/O functions, but I won't be explaining them too well so that you can try to figure them out first.

As usual, type this whole program in and get it working, then we'll discuss it.

ex17.c

```c
1    #include <stdio.h>
2    #include <assert.h>
3    #include <stdlib.h>
4    #include <errno.h>
5    #include <string.h>
6
7    #define MAX_DATA 512
8    #define MAX_ROWS 100
9
10   struct Address {
11       int id;
12       int set;
13       char name[MAX_DATA];
14       char email[MAX_DATA];
15   };
16
17   struct Database {
18       struct Address rows[MAX_ROWS];
19   };
20
21   struct Connection {
22       FILE *file;
23       struct Database *db;
24   };
25
26   void die(const char *message)
27   {
28       if (errno) {
29           perror(message);
30       } else {
31           printf("ERROR: %s\n", message);
32       }
33
34       exit(1);
```

```
35      }
36
37      void Address_print(struct Address *addr)
38      {
39          printf("%d %s %s\n", addr->id, addr->name, addr->email);
40      }
41
42      void Database_load(struct Connection *conn)
43      {
44          int rc = fread(conn->db, sizeof(struct Database), 1, conn->file);
45          if (rc != 1)
46              die("Failed to load database.");
47      }
48
49      struct Connection *Database_open(const char *filename, char mode)
50      {
51          struct Connection *conn = malloc(sizeof(struct Connection));
52          if (!conn)
53              die("Memory error");
54
55          conn->db = malloc(sizeof(struct Database));
56          if (!conn->db)
57              die("Memory error");
58
59          if (mode == 'c') {
60              conn->file = fopen(filename, "w");
61          } else {
62              conn->file = fopen(filename, "r+");
63
64              if (conn->file) {
65                  Database_load(conn);
66              }
67          }
68
69          if (!conn->file)
70              die("Failed to open the file");
71
72          return conn;
73      }
74
75      void Database_close(struct Connection *conn)
76      {
77          if (conn) {
78              if (conn->file)
79                  fclose(conn->file);
80              if (conn->db)
81                  free(conn->db);
82              free(conn);
83          }
84      }
```

```
85
86     void Database_write(struct Connection *conn)
87     {
88         rewind(conn->file);
89
90         int rc = fwrite(conn->db, sizeof(struct Database), 1, conn->file);
91         if (rc != 1)
92             die("Failed to write database.");
93
94         rc = fflush(conn->file);
95         if (rc == -1)
96             die("Cannot flush database.");
97     }
98
99     void Database_create(struct Connection *conn)
100    {
101        int i = 0;
102
103        for (i = 0; i < MAX_ROWS; i++) {
104            // make a prototype to initialize it
105            struct Address addr = {.id = i,.set = 0 };
106            // then just assign it
107            conn->db->rows[i] = addr;
108        }
109    }
110
111    void Database_set(struct Connection *conn, int id, const char *name,
112            const char *email)
113    {
114        struct Address *addr = &conn->db->rows[id];
115        if (addr->set)
116            die("Already set, delete it first");
117
118        addr->set = 1;
119        // WARNING: bug, read the "How To Break It" and fix this
120        char *res = strncpy(addr->name, name, MAX_DATA);
121        // demonstrate the strncpy bug
122        if (!res)
123            die("Name copy failed");
124
125        res = strncpy(addr->email, email, MAX_DATA);
126        if (!res)
127            die("Email copy failed");
128    }
129
130    void Database_get(struct Connection *conn, int id)
131    {
132        struct Address *addr = &conn->db->rows[id];
133
134        if (addr->set) {
```

```
135                 Address_print(addr);
136             } else {
137                 die("ID is not set");
138             }
139     }
140
141     void Database_delete(struct Connection *conn, int id)
142     {
143         struct Address addr = {.id = id,.set = 0 };
144         conn->db->rows[id] = addr;
145     }
146
147     void Database_list(struct Connection *conn)
148     {
149         int i = 0;
150         struct Database *db = conn->db;
151
152         for (i = 0; i < MAX_ROWS; i++) {
153             struct Address *cur = &db->rows[i];
154
155             if (cur->set) {
156                 Address_print(cur);
157             }
158         }
159     }
160
161     int main(int argc, char *argv[])
162     {
163         if (argc < 3)
164             die("USAGE: ex17 <dbfile> <action> [action params]");
165
166         char *filename = argv[1];
167         char action = argv[2][0];
168         struct Connection *conn = Database_open(filename, action);
169         int id = 0;
170
171         if (argc > 3) id = atoi(argv[3]);
172         if (id >= MAX_ROWS) die("There's not that many records.");
173
174         switch (action) {
175             case 'c':
176                 Database_create(conn);
177                 Database_write(conn);
178                 break;
179
180             case 'g':
181                 if (argc != 4)
182                     die("Need an id to get");
183
184                 Database_get(conn, id);
```

```
185                    break;
186
187            case 's':
188                if (argc != 6)
189                    die("Need id, name, email to set");
190
191                Database_set(conn, id, argv[4], argv[5]);
192                Database_write(conn);
193                break;
194
195            case 'd':
196                if (argc != 4)
197                    die("Need id to delete");
198
199                Database_delete(conn, id);
200                Database_write(conn);
201                break;
202
203            case 'l':
204                Database_list(conn);
205                break;
206            default:
207                die("Invalid action: c=create, g=get, s=set, d=del, l=list");
208        }
209
210        Database_close(conn);
211
212        return 0;
213    }
```

In this program, we're using a set of structures, or structs, to create a simple database for an address book. There are some things you've never seen, so you should go through it line by line, explain what each line does, and look up any functions that you don't recognize. There are a few key things that you should pay attention to, as well:

#define for constants   We use another part of the C preprocessor (CPP) to create constant settings of MAX_DATA and MAX_ROWS. I'll cover more of what the CPP does later, but this is a way to create a constant that will work reliably. There are other ways, but they don't apply in certain situations.

Fixed sized structs   The Address struct then uses these constants to create a piece of data that is fixed in size, making it less efficient but easier to store and read. The Database struct is then also a fixed size because it's a fixed length array of Address structs. That lets you write the whole thing to disk in one move later.

die function to abort with an error   In a small program like this, you can make a single function that kills the program with an error if there's anything wrong. I call this die, and it's used to exit the program with an error after any failed function calls or bad inputs.

errno and perror() for error reporting   When you have an error return from a function, it will usually set an external variable called `errno` to say exactly what happened. These are just numbers, so you can use `perror` to print the error message.

FILE functions   I'm using all new functions like `fopen`, `fread`, `fclose`, and `rewind` to work with files. Each of these functions works on a `FILE` struct that's just like your other structs, but it's defined by the C standard library.

nested struct pointers   There's a use for nested structures and getting the address of array elements that you should study. Specifically, code like `&conn->db->rows[i]` that reads "get the i element of rows, which is in db, which is in conn, then get the address of (&) it."

copying struct prototypes   Best shown in `Database_delete`, you can see I'm using a temporary local `Address`, initializing its `id` and `set` fields, and then simply copying it into the `rows` array by assigning it to the element I want. This trick makes sure that all fields except `set` and `id` are initialized to zeros and it's actually easier to write. Incidentally, you shouldn't be using `memcpy` to do these kinds of struct copying operations. Modern C allows you to simply assign one struct to another and it'll handle the copying for you.

processing complex arguments   I'm doing some more complex argument parsing, but this isn't really the best way to do it. We'll get into a better option for parsing later in the book.

converting strings to ints   I use the `atoi` function to take the string for the id on the command line and convert it to the `int id` variable. Read up on this and similar functions.

allocating large data on the heap   The whole point of this program is that I'm using `malloc` to ask the OS for a large amount of memory when I create the `Database`. We'll cover this in more detail later.

NULL is 0, so Boolean works   In many of the checks, I'm testing that a pointer is not NULL by simply doing `if(!ptr) die("fail!")`, because NULL will evaluate to false. You could be explicit and say `if(ptr == NULL) die("fail!")`, as well. In some rare systems, NULL will be stored in the computer (represented) as something not 0, but the C standard says you should still be able to write code as if it has a 0 value. From now on when I say "NULL is 0," I mean its value for anyone who is overly pedantic.

What You Should See

You should spend as much time as you can testing that it works, and running it with a debugger to confirm that you've got all of the memory usage right. Here's a session of me testing it normally, and then using the debugger to check the operations:

```
$ make ex17
cc -Wall -g    ex17.c    -o ex17
$ ./ex17 db.dat c
$ ./ex17 db.dat s 1 zed zed@zedshaw.com
$ ./ex17 db.dat s 2 frank frank@zedshaw.com
$ ./ex17 db.dat s 3 joe joe@zedshaw.com
$
$ ./ex17 db.dat l
1 zed zed@zedshaw.com
2 frank frank@zedshaw.com
3 joe joe@zedshaw.com
$ ./ex17 db.dat d 3
$ ./ex17 db.dat l
1 zed zed@zedshaw.com
2 frank frank@zedshaw.com
$ ./ex17 db.dat g 2
2 frank frank@zedshaw.com
```

Heap versus Stack Allocation

You kids have it great these days. You play with your Ruby or Python and just make objects and variables without any care for where they live. You don't care if it's on the *stack,* and what about on the *heap*? Fuggedaboutit. You don't even know, and you know what, chances are your language of choice doesn't even put the variables on stack at all. It's all heap, and you don't even *know* if it is.

C is different because it's using the real CPU's actual machinery to do its work, and that involves a chunk of RAM called the stack and another called the heap. What's the difference? It all depends on where you get the storage.

The heap is easier to explain since it's just all the remaining memory in your computer, and you access it with the function malloc to get more. Each time you call malloc, the OS uses internal functions to register that piece of memory to you, and then returns a pointer to it. When you're done with it, you use free to return it to the OS so that it can be used by other programs. Failing to do this will cause your program to *leak* memory, but Valgrind will help you track these leaks down.

The stack is a special region of memory that stores temporary variables, which each function creates as locals to that function. How it works is that each argument to a function is *pushed* onto the stack and then used inside the function. It's really a stack data structure, so the last thing in is the first thing out. This also happens with all local variables like char action and int id in main. The advantage of using a stack for this is simply that when the function exits, the C compiler pops these variables off of the stack to clean up. This is simple and prevents memory leaks if the variable is on the stack.

The easiest way to keep this straight is with this mantra: If you didn't get it from `malloc`, or a function that got it from `malloc`, then it's on the stack.

There are three primary problems with stacks and heaps to watch out for:

- If you get a block of memory from `malloc`, and have that pointer on the stack, then when the function exits the pointer will get popped off and lost.

- If you put too much data on the stack (like large structs and arrays), then you can cause a *stack overflow* and the program will abort. In this case, use the heap with `malloc`.

- If you take a pointer to something on the stack, and then pass or return it from your function, then the function receiving it will *segmentation fault* (segfault), because the actual data will get popped off and disappear. You'll be pointing at dead space.

This is why I created a `Database_open` that allocates memory or dies, and then a `Database_close` that frees everything. If you create a create function that makes the whole thing or nothing, and then a destroy function that safely cleans up everything, then it's easier to keep it all straight.

Finally, when a program exits, the OS will clean up all of the resources for you, but sometimes not immediately. A common idiom (and one I use in this exercise) is to just abort and let the OS clean up on error.

How to Break It

This program has a lot of places where you can break it, so try some of these but also come up with your own:

- The classic way is to remove some of the safety checks so that you can pass in arbitrary data. For example, remove the check on line 160 that prevents you from passing in any record number.

- You can also try corrupting the data file. Open it in any editor and change random bytes, and then close it.

- You could also find ways to pass bad arguments to the program when it's run. For example, getting the file and action backward will make it create a file named after the action, and then do an action based on the first character.

- There's a bug in this program because `strncpy` is poorly designed. Go read about `strncpy` and try to find out what happens when the name or address you give is *greater* than 512 bytes. Fix this by simply forcing the last character to `'\0'` so that it's always set no matter what (which is what `strncpy` should do).

- In the Extra Credit section, I have you augment the program to create arbitrary size databases. Try to see what the biggest database is before you cause the program to die due to lack of memory from malloc.

Extra Credit

- The die function needs to be augmented to let you pass the conn variable, so it can close it and clean up.

- Change the code to accept parameters for MAX_DATA and MAX_ROWS, store them in the Database struct, and write that to the file, thus creating a database that can be arbitrarily sized.

- Add more operations you can do with the database, like find.

- Read about how C does it's struct packing, and then try to see why your file is the size it is. See if you can calculate a new size after adding more fields.

- Add some more fields to Address and make them searchable.

- Write a shell script that will do your testing automatically for you by running commands in the right order. Hint: Use set -e at the top of a bash to make it abort the whole script if any command has an error.

- Try reworking the program to use a single global for the database connection. How does this new version of the program compare to the other one?

- Go research stack data structure and write one in your favorite language, then try to do it in C.

Pointers to Functions

Functions in C are actually just pointers to a spot in the program where some code exists. Just like you've been creating pointers to structs, strings, and arrays, you can point a pointer at a function, too. The main use for this is to pass callbacks to other functions, or to simulate classes and objects. In this exercise, we'll do some callbacks, and in the next exercise, we'll make a simple object system.

The format of a function pointer looks like this:

```
int (*POINTER_NAME)(int a, int b)
```

A way to remember how to write one is to do this:

- Write a normal function declaration: `int callme(int a, int b)`
- Wrap the function name with the pointer syntax: `int (*callme)(int a, int b)`
- Change the name to the pointer name: `int (*compare_cb)(int a, int b)`

The key thing to remember is that when you're done with this, the *variable* name for the pointer is called *compare_cb* and you use it just like it's a function. This is similar to how pointers to arrays can be used just like the arrays they point to. Pointers to functions can be used like the functions they point to but with a different name.

```
int (*tester)(int a, int b) = sorted_order;
printf("TEST: %d is same as %d\n", tester(2, 3), sorted_order(2, 3));
```

This will work even if the function pointer returns a pointer to something:

- Write it: `char *make_coolness(int awesome_levels)`
- Wrap it: `char *(*make_coolness)(int awesome_levels)`
- Rename it: `char *(*coolness_cb)(int awesome_levels)`

The next problem to solve with using function pointers is that it's hard to give them as parameters to a function, such as when you want to pass the function callback to another function. The solution is to use `typedef`, which is a C keyword for making new names for other, more complex types.

The only thing you need to do is put typedef before the same function pointer syntax, and then after that you can use the name like it's a type. I demonstrate this in the following exercise code:

```c
1    #include <stdio.h>
2    #include <stdlib.h>
3    #include <errno.h>
4    #include <string.h>
5
6    /** Our old friend die from ex17. */
7    void die(const char *message)
8    {
9        if (errno) {
10            perror(message);
11        } else {
12            printf("ERROR: %s\n", message);
13        }
14
15        exit(1);
16   }
17
18   // a typedef creates a fake type, in this
19   // case for a function pointer
20   typedef int (*compare_cb) (int a, int b);
21
22   /**
23    * A classic bubble sort function that uses the
24    * compare_cb to do the sorting.
25    */
26   int *bubble_sort(int *numbers, int count, compare_cb cmp)
27   {
28        int temp = 0;
29        int i = 0;
30        int j = 0;
31        int *target = malloc(count * sizeof(int));
32
33        if (!target)
34            die("Memory error.");
35
36        memcpy(target, numbers, count * sizeof(int));
37
38        for (i = 0; i < count; i++) {
39            for (j = 0; j < count - 1; j++) {
40                if (cmp(target[j], target[j + 1]) > 0) {
41                    temp = target[j + 1];
42                    target[j + 1] = target[j];
43                    target[j] = temp;
44                }
45            }
46        }
```

```
47
48          return target;
49     }
50
51     int sorted_order(int a, int b)
52     {
53          return a - b;
54     }
55
56     int reverse_order(int a, int b)
57     {
58          return b - a;
59     }
60
61     int strange_order(int a, int b)
62     {
63          if (a == 0 || b == 0) {
64              return 0;
65          } else {
66              return a % b;
67          }
68     }
69
70     /**
71      * Used to test that we are sorting things correctly
72      * by doing the sort and printing it out.
73      */
74     void test_sorting(int *numbers, int count, compare_cb cmp)
75     {
76          int i = 0;
77          int *sorted = bubble_sort(numbers, count, cmp);
78
79          if (!sorted)
80              die("Failed to sort as requested.");
81
82          for (i = 0; i < count; i++) {
83              printf("%d ", sorted[i]);
84          }
85          printf("\n");
86
87          free(sorted);
88     }
89
90     int main(int argc, char *argv[])
91     {
92          if (argc < 2) die("USAGE: ex18 4 3 1 5 6");
93
94          int count = argc - 1;
95          int i = 0;
96          char **inputs = argv + 1;
```

```
97
98          int *numbers = malloc(count * sizeof(int));
99          if (!numbers) die("Memory error.");
100
101         for (i = 0; i < count; i++) {
102             numbers[i] = atoi(inputs[i]);
103         }
104
105         test_sorting(numbers, count, sorted_order);
106         test_sorting(numbers, count, reverse_order);
107         test_sorting(numbers, count, strange_order);
108
109         free(numbers);
110
111         return 0;
112     }
```

In this program, you're creating a dynamic sorting algorithm that can sort an array of integers using a comparison callback. Here's the breakdown of this program, so you can clearly understand it:

ex18.c:1-6   The usual includes that are needed for all of the functions that we call.

ex18.c:7-17   This is the die function from the previous exercise that I'll use to do error checking.

ex18.c:21   This is where the typedef is used, and later I use compare_cb like it's a type similar to int or char in bubble_sort and test_sorting.

ex18.c:27-49   A bubble sort implementation, which is a very inefficient way to sort some integers. Here's a breakdown:

> **ex18.c:27** I use the typedef for compare_cb as the last parameter cmp. This is now a function that will return a comparison between two integers for sorting.

> **ex18.c:29-34** The usual creation of variables on the stack, followed by a new array of integers on the heap using malloc. Make sure you understand what count * sizeof(int) is doing.

> **ex18.c:38** The outer loop of the bubble sort.

> **ex18.c:39** The inner loop of the bubble sort.

> **ex18.c:40** Now I call the cmp callback just like it's a normal function, but instead of being the name of something that we defined, it's just a pointer to it. This lets the caller pass in anything it wants as long as it matches the signature of the compare_cb typedef.

> **ex18.c:41-43** The actual swapping operation where a bubble sort needs to do what it does.

> **ex18.c:48** Finally, this returns the newly created and sorted result array target.

ex18.c:51-68   Three different versions of the `compare_cb` function type, which needs to have the same definition as the `typedef` that we created. The C compiler will complain to you if you get this wrong and say the types don't match.

ex18.c:74-87   This is a tester for the `bubble_sort` function. You can see now how I'm also using `compare_cb` to pass to `bubble_sort`, demonstrating how these can be passed around like any other pointers.

ex18.c:90-103   A simple main function that sets up an array based on integers to pass on the command line, and then it calls the `test_sorting` function.

ex18.c:105-107   Finally, you get to see how the `compare_cb` function pointer typedef is used. I simply call `test_sorting` but give it the name of `sorted_order`, `reverse_order`, and `strange_order` as the function to use. The C compiler then finds the address of those functions, and makes it a pointer for `test_sorting` to use. If you look at `test_sorting`, you'll see that it then passes each of these to `bubble_sort`, but it actually has no idea what they do. The compiler only knows that they match the `compare_cb` prototype and should work.

ex18.c:109   Last thing we do is free up the array of numbers that we made.

What You Should See

Running this program is simple, but you should try different combinations of numbers, or even other characters, to see what it does.

Exercise 18 Session

```
$ make ex18
cc -Wall -g    ex18.c    -o ex18
$ ./ex18 4 1 7 3 2 0 8
0 1 2 3 4 7 8
8 7 4 3 2 1 0
3 4 2 7 1 0 8
$
```

How to Break It

I'm going to have you do something kind of weird to break this. These function pointers are like every other pointer, so they point at blocks of memory. C has this ability to take one pointer and convert it to another so you can process the data in different ways. It's usually not necessary, but to show you how to hack your computer, I want you to add this at the end of `test_sorting`:

```
unsigned char *data = (unsigned char *)cmp;

for(i = 0; i < 25; i++) {
```

```
        printf("%02x:", data[i]);
    }

    printf("\n");
```

This loop is sort of like converting your function to a string, and then printing out its contents. This won't break your program unless the CPU and OS you're on has a problem with you doing this. What you'll see after it prints the sorted array is a string of hexadecimal numbers, like this:

```
    55:48:89:e5:89:7d:fc:89:75:f8:8b:55:fc:8b:45:
```

That should be the raw assembler byte code of the function itself, and you should see that they start the same but then have different endings. It's also possible that this loop isn't getting all of the function, or it's getting too much and stomping on another piece of the program. Without more analysis you won't know.

Extra Credit

- Get a hex editor and open up ex18, and then find the sequence of hex digits that start a function to see if you can find the function in the raw program.

- Find other random things in your hex editor and change them. Rerun your program and see what happens. Strings you find are the easiest things to change.

- Pass in the wrong function for the compare_cb and see what the C compiler complains about.

- Pass in NULL and watch your program seriously bite it. Then, run the debugger and see what that reports.

- Write another sorting algorithm, then change test_sorting so that it takes *both* an arbitrary sort function and the sort function's callback comparison. Use it to test both of your algorithms.

Zed's Awesome Debug Macros

There's a reoccurring problem in C that we've been dancing around, but I'm going to solve it in this exercise using a set of macros I developed. You can thank me later when you realize how insanely awesome these macros are. Right now, you don't know how awesome they are, so you'll just have to use them, and then you can walk up to me one day and say, "Zed, those debug macros were the bomb. I owe you my firstborn child because you saved me a decade of heartache and prevented me from killing myself more than once. Thank you, good sir, here's a million dollars and the original Snakehead Telecaster prototype signed by Leo Fender."

Yes, they are that awesome.

The C Error-Handling Problem

Handling errors is a difficult activity in almost every programming language. There are entire programming languages that try as hard as they can to avoid even the concept of an error. Other languages invent complex control structures like exceptions to pass error conditions around. The problem exists mostly because programmers assume errors don't happen, and this optimism infects the types of languages they use and create.

C tackles the problem by returning error codes and setting a global errno value that you check. This makes for complex code that simply exists to check if something you did had an error. As you write more and more C code, you'll write code with this pattern:

- Call a function.
- Check if the return value is an error (and it must look that up each time, too).
- Then, clean up all the resources created so far.
- Lastly, print out an error message that hopefully helps.

This means for every function call (and yes, *every* function), you are potentially writing three or four more lines just to make sure it worked. That doesn't include the problem of cleaning up all of the junk you've built to that point. If you have ten different structures, three files, and a database connection, you'd have 14 more lines when you get an error.

In the past, this wasn't a problem because C programs did what you've been doing when there was an error: die. No point in bothering with cleanup when the OS will do it for you. Today, though, many C programs need to run for weeks, months, or years, and handle errors from many different sources gracefully. You can't just have your Web server die at the slightest touch, and you definitely can't have a library that you've written nuke the program it's used in. That's just rude.

Other languages solve this problem with exceptions, but those have problems in C (and in other languages, too). In C, you only have one return value, but exceptions make up an entire stack-based return system with arbitrary values. Trying to marshal exceptions up the stack in C is difficult, and no other libraries will understand it.

The Debug Macros

The solution I've been using for years is a small set of debug macros that implements a basic debugging and error-handling system for C. This system is easy to understand, works with every library, and makes C code more solid and clearer.

It does this by adopting the convention that whenever there's an error, your function will jump to an error: part of the function that knows how to clean up everything and return an error code. You can use a macro called check to check return codes, print an error message, and then jump to the cleanup section. You can combine that with a set of logging functions for printing out useful debug messages.

I'll now show you the entire contents of the most awesome set of brilliance you've ever seen.

dbg.h

```
#ifndef __dbg_h__
#define __dbg_h__

#include <stdio.h>
#include <errno.h>
#include <string.h>

#ifdef NDEBUG
#define debug(M, ...)
#else
#define debug(M, ...) fprintf(stderr, "DEBUG %s:%d: " M "\n",\
        __FILE__, __LINE__, ##__VA_ARGS__)
#endif

#define clean_errno() (errno == 0 ? "None" : strerror(errno))

#define log_err(M, ...) fprintf(stderr,\
        "[ERROR] (%s:%d: errno: %s) " M "\n", __FILE__, __LINE__,\
        clean_errno(), ##__VA_ARGS__)

#define log_warn(M, ...) fprintf(stderr,\
        "[WARN] (%s:%d: errno: %s) " M "\n",\
        __FILE__, __LINE__, clean_errno(), ##__VA_ARGS__)

#define log_info(M, ...) fprintf(stderr, "[INFO] (%s:%d) " M "\n",\
        __FILE__, __LINE__, ##__VA_ARGS__)

#define check(A, M, ...) if(!(A)) {\
    log_err(M, ##__VA_ARGS__); errno=0; goto error; }
```

```
#define sentinel(M, ...)  { log_err(M, ##__VA_ARGS__);\
    errno=0; goto error; }

#define check_mem(A) check((A), "Out of memory.")

#define check_debug(A, M, ...) if(!(A)) { debug(M, ##__VA_ARGS__);\
    errno=0; goto error; }

#endif
```

Yes, that's it, and here's a breakdown of every line:

dbg.h:1-2 The usual defense against accidentally including the file twice, which you saw in the last exercise.

dbg.h:4-6 Includes for the functions that these macros need.

dbg.h:8 The start of a #ifdef that lets you recompile your program so that all of the debug log messages are removed.

dbg.h:9 If you compile with NDEBUG defined, then "no debug" messages will remain. You can see in this case the #define debug() is just replaced with nothing (the right side is empty).

dbg.h:10 The matching #else for the above #ifdef.

dbg.h:11 The alternative #define debug that translates any use of debug("format", arg1, arg2) into an fprintf call to stderr. Many C programmers don't know this, but you can create macros that actually work like printf and take variable arguments. Some C compilers (actually CPP) don't support this, but the ones that matter do. The magic here is the use of ##__VA_ARGS__ that says "put whatever they had for extra arguments (...) here." Also notice the use of __FILE__ and __LINE__ to get the current file:line for the debug message. *Very* helpful.

dbg.h:12 The end of the #ifdef.

dbg.h:14 The clean_errno macro that's used in the others to get a safe, readable version of errno. That strange syntax in the middle is a ternary operator and you'll learn what it does later.

dbg.h:16-20 The log_err, log_warn, and log_info, macros for logging messages that are meant for the end user. They work like debug but can't be compiled out.

dbg.h:22 The best macro ever, check, will make sure the condition A is true, and if not, it logs the error M (with variable arguments for log_err), and then jumps to the function's error: for cleanup.

dbg.h:24 The second best macro ever, sentinel, is placed in any part of a function that shouldn't run, and if it does, it prints an error message and then jumps to the error:

label. You put this in if-statements and switch-statements to catch conditions that shouldn't happen, like the default:.

dbg.h:26 A shorthand macro called check_mem that makes sure a pointer is valid, and if it isn't, it reports it as an error with "Out of memory."

dbg.h:28 An alternative macro, check_debug, which still checks and handles an error, but if the error is common, then it doesn't bother reporting it. In this one, it will use debug instead of log_err to report the message. So when you define NDEBUG, the check still happens, and the error jump goes off, but the message isn't printed.

Using dbg.h

Here's an example of using all of dbg.h in a small program. This doesn't actually do anything but demonstrate how to use each macro. However, we'll be using these macros in all of the programs we write from now on, so be sure to understand how to use them.

ex19.c

```
1    #include "dbg.h"
2    #include <stdlib.h>
3    #include <stdio.h>
4
5    void test_debug()
6    {
7        // notice you don't need the \n
8        debug("I have Brown Hair.");
9
10       // passing in arguments like printf
11       debug("I am %d years old.", 37);
12   }
13
14   void test_log_err()
15   {
16       log_err("I believe everything is broken.");
17       log_err("There are %d problems in %s.", 0, "space");
18   }
19
20   void test_log_warn()
21   {
22       log_warn("You can safely ignore this.");
23       log_warn("Maybe consider looking at: %s.", "/etc/passwd");
24   }
25
26   void test_log_info()
27   {
28       log_info("Well I did something mundane.");
29       log_info("It happened %f times today.", 1.3f);
30   }
```

```
31
32   int test_check(char *file_name)
33   {
34       FILE *input = NULL;
35       char *block = NULL;
36
37       block = malloc(100);
38       check_mem(block);                    // should work
39
40       input = fopen(file_name, "r");
41       check(input, "Failed to open %s.", file_name);
42
43       free(block);
44       fclose(input);
45       return 0;
46
47   error:
48       if (block) free(block);
49       if (input) fclose(input);
50       return -1;
51   }
52
53   int test_sentinel(int code)
54   {
55       char *temp = malloc(100);
56       check_mem(temp);
57
58       switch (code) {
59           case 1:
60               log_info("It worked.");
61               break;
62           default:
63               sentinel("I shouldn't run.");
64       }
65
66       free(temp);
67       return 0;
68
69   error:
70       if (temp)
71           free(temp);
72       return -1;
73   }
74
75   int test_check_mem()
76   {
77       char *test = NULL;
78       check_mem(test);
79
80       free(test);
```

```
81          return 1;
82
83    error:
84          return -1;
85    }
86
87    int test_check_debug()
88    {
89          int i = 0;
90          check_debug(i != 0, "Oops, I was 0.");
91
92          return 0;
93    error:
94          return -1;
95    }
96
97    int main(int argc, char *argv[])
98    {
99          check(argc == 2, "Need an argument.");
100
101         test_debug();
102         test_log_err();
103         test_log_warn();
104         test_log_info();
105
106         check(test_check("ex19.c") == 0, "failed with ex19.c");
107         check(test_check(argv[1]) == -1, "failed with argv");
108         check(test_sentinel(1) == 0, "test_sentinel failed.");
109         check(test_sentinel(100) == -1, "test_sentinel failed.");
110         check(test_check_mem() == -1, "test_check_mem failed.");
111         check(test_check_debug() == -1, "test_check_debug failed.");
112
113         return 0;
114
115    error:
116         return 1;
117    }
```

Pay attention to how check is used, and when it's false, it jumps to the error: label to do a cleanup. The way to read those lines is, "check that A is true, and if not, say M and jump out."

What You Should See

When you run this, give it some bogus first parameter to see this:

```
$ make ex19
cc -Wall -g -DNDEBUG    ex19.c   -o ex19
$ ./ex19 test
```

```
[ERROR] (ex19.c:16: errno: None) I believe everything is broken.
[ERROR] (ex19.c:17: errno: None) There are 0 problems in space.
[WARN] (ex19.c:22: errno: None) You can safely ignore this.
[WARN] (ex19.c:23: errno: None) Maybe consider looking at: /etc/passwd.
[INFO] (ex19.c:28) Well I did something mundane.
[INFO] (ex19.c:29) It happened 1.300000 times today.
[ERROR] (ex19.c:38: errno: No such file or directory) Failed to open test.
[INFO] (ex19.c:57) It worked.
[ERROR] (ex19.c:60: errno: None) I shouldn't run.
[ERROR] (ex19.c:74: errno: None) Out of memory.
```

See how it reports the exact line number where the check failed? That's going to save you hours of debugging later. Also, see how it prints the error message for you when errno is set? Again, that will save you hours of debugging.

How the CPP Expands Macros

It's now time for you to get a short introduction to the CPP so that you know how these macros actually work. To do this, I'm going to break down the most complex macro from dbg.h, and have you run cpp so you can see what it's actually doing.

Imagine that I have a function called dosomething() that returns the typical 0 for success and -1 for an error. Every time I call dosomething, I have to check for this error code, so I'd write code like this:

```
int rc = dosomething();

if(rc != 0) {
    fprintf(stderr, "There was an error: %s\n", strerror());
    goto error;
}
```

What I want to use the CPP for is to encapsulate this if-statement into a more readable and memorable line of code. I want what you've been doing in dbg.h with the check macro:

```
int rc = dosomething();
check(rc == 0, "There was an error.");
```

This is *much* clearer and explains exactly what's going on: Check that the function worked, and if not, report an error. To do this, we need some special CPP tricks that make the CPP useful as a code generation tool. Take a look at the check and log_err macros again:

```
#define log_err(M, ...) fprintf(stderr,\
    "[ERROR] (%s:%d: errno: %s) " M "\n", __FILE__, __LINE__,\
    clean_errno(), ##__VA_ARGS__)
#define check(A, M, ...) if(!(A)) {\
    log_err(M, ##__VA_ARGS__); errno=0; goto error; }
```

The first macro, log_err, is simpler. It simply replaces itself with a call to fprintf to stderr. The only tricky part of this macro is the use of ... in the definition log_err(M, ...). What this does is let you pass variable arguments to the macro, so you can pass in the arguments that should go to fprintf. How do they get injected into the fprintf call? Look at the end for the ##__VA_ARGS__, which is telling the CPP to take the args entered where the ... is, and inject them at that part of the fprintf call. You can then do things like this:

```
log_err("Age: %d, name: %s", age, name);
```

The arguments age, name are the ... part of the definition, and those get injected into the fprintf output:

```
fprintf(stderr, "[ERROR] (%s:%d: errno: %s) Age %d: name %d\n",
    __FILE__, __LINE__, clean_errno(), age, name);
```

See the age, name at the end? That's how ... and ##__VA_ARGS__ work together, which will work in macros that call other variable argument macros. Look at the check macro now and see that it calls log_err, but check is *also* using the ... and ##__VA_ARGS__ to do the call. That's how you can pass full printf style format strings to check, which go to log_err, and then make both work like printf.

The next thing to study is how check crafts the if-statement for the error checking. If we strip out the log_err usage, we see this:

```
if(!(A)) { errno=0; goto error; }
```

Which means: If A is false, then clear errno and goto the error label. The check macro is being replaced with the if-statement, so if we manually expand out the macro check(rc == 0, "There was an error."), we get this:

```
if(!(rc == 0)) {
    log_err("There was an error.");
    errno=0;
    goto error;
}
```

What you should be getting from this trip through these two macros is that the CPP replaces macros with the expanded version of their definition, and it will do this *recursively*, expanding all of the macros in macros. The CPP, then, is just a recursive templating system, as I mentioned before. Its power comes from its ability to generate whole blocks of parameterized code, thus becoming a handy code generation tool.

That leaves one question: Why not just use a function like die? The reason is that you want file:line numbers and the goto operation for an error handling exit. If you did this inside a function, you wouldn't get a line number where the error actually happened, and the goto would be much more complicated.

Another reason is that you still have to write the raw if-statement, which looks like all of the other if-statements in your code, so it's not as clear that this one is an error check. By wrapping the if-statement in a macro called check, you make it clear that this is just error checking, and not part of the main flow.

Finally, CPP has the ability to *conditionally compile* portions of code, so you can have code that's only present when you build a developer or debug version of the program. You can see this already in the dbg.h file where the debug macro only has a body if the compiler asks for it. Without this ability, you'd need a wasted if-statement that checks for debug mode, and then wastes CPU capacity doing that check for no value.

Extra Credit

- Put #define NDEBUG at the top of the file and check that all of the debug messages go away.
- Undo that line, and add -DNDEBUG to CFLAGS at the top of the Makefile, and then recompile to see the same thing.
- Modify the logging so that it includes the function name, as well as the file:line.

Advanced Debugging Techniques

I've already taught you about my awesome debug macros, and you've been using them. When I debug code I use the debug() macro almost exclusively to analyze what's going on and track down the problem. In this exercise, I'm going to teach you the basics of using GDB to inspect a simple program that runs and doesn't exit. You'll learn how to use GDB to attach to a running process, stop it, and see what's happening. After that, I'll give you some little tips and tricks that you can use with GDB.

This is another video-focused exercise where I show you advanced debugging tricks with my technique. The discussion below reinforces the video, so watch the video first. Debugging will be much easier to learn by watching me do it first.

Debug Printing versus GDB

I approach debugging primarily with a "scientific method" style: I come up with possible causes and then rule them out or prove that they cause the defect. The problem many programmers have with this approach is that they feel like it will slow them down. They panic and rush to solve the bug, but in their rush they fail to notice that they're really just flailing around and gathering no useful information. I find that logging (debug printing) forces me to solve a bug scientifically, and it's also just easier to gather information in most situations.

In addition, I have these reasons for using debug printing as my primary debugging tool:

- You see an entire tracing of a program's execution with debug printing of variables, which lets you track how things are going wrong. With GDB, you have to place watch and debug statements all over the place for everything you want, and it's difficult to get a solid trace of the execution.

- The debug prints can stay in the code, and when you need them, you can recompile and they come back. With GDB, you have to configure the same information uniquely for every defect you have to hunt down.

- It's easier to turn on debug logging on a server that's not working right, and then inspect the logs while it runs to see what's going on. System administrators know how to handle logging, but they don't know how to use GDB.

- Printing things is just easier. Debuggers are always obtuse and weird with their own quirky interfaces and inconsistencies. There's nothing complicated about debug("Yo, dis right? %d", my_stuff);.

- When you write debug prints to find a defect, you're forced to actually analyze the code and use the scientific method. You can think of debug usage as, "I hypothesize that the code is broken here." Then when you run it, you get your hypothesis tested, and if it's not broken, then you can move to another part where it could be. This may seem like it takes longer, but it's actually faster because you go through a process of differential diagnosis and rule out possible causes until you find the real one.

- Debug printing works better with unit testing. You can actually just compile the debugs while you work, and when a unit test explodes, just go look at the logs at any time. With GDB, you'd have to rerun the unit test under GDB and then trace through it to see what's going on.

Despite all of these reasons that I rely on debug over GDB, I still use GDB in a few situations, and I think you should have any tool that helps you get your work done. Sometimes, you just have to connect to a broken program and poke around. Or, maybe you've got a server that's crashing and you can only get at core files to see why. In these and a few other cases, GDB is the way to go, and it's always good to have as many tools as possible to help solve problems.

Here's a breakdown of when I use GDB versus Valgrind versus debug printing:

- I use Valgrind to catch all memory errors. I use GDB if Valgrind is having problems or if using Valgrind would slow the program down too much.

- I use print with debug to diagnose and fix defects related to logic or usage. This amounts to about 90% of the defects after you start using Valgrind.

- I use GDB for the remaining mysteriously weird stuff or emergency situations to gather information. If Valgrind isn't turning anything up, and I can't even print out the information that I need, then I bust out GDB and start poking around. My use of GDB in this case is entirely to gather information. Once I have an idea of what's going on, I'll go back to writing a unit test to cause the defect, and then do print statements to find out why.

A Debugging Strategy

This process will actually work with any debugging technique you're using. I'm going to describe it in terms of using GDB since it seems people skip this process the most when using debuggers. Use this for every bug until you only need it on the very difficult ones.

- Start a little text file called `notes.txt` and use it as a kind of lab notes for ideas, bugs, problems, and so on.

- Before you use GDB, write out the bug you're going to fix and what could be causing it.

- For each cause, write out the files and functions where you think the cause is coming from, or just write that you don't know.

- Now start GDB and pick the first possible cause with good file and function variables and set breakpoints there.

- Use GDB to then run the program and confirm whether that is the cause. The best way is to see if you can use the `set` command to either fix the program easily or cause the error immediately.

- If this isn't the cause, then mark in the `notes.txt` that it wasn't, and why. Move on to the next possible cause that's easiest to debug, and keep adding information.

In case you haven't noticed, this is basically the scientific method. You write down a set of hypotheses, then you use debugging to prove or disprove them. This gives you insight into more possible causes and eventually you find it. This process helps you avoid going over the same possible causes repeatedly after you've found that they aren't possible.

You can also do this with debug printing, the only difference is that you actually write out your hypotheses in the source code instead of in the `notes.txt`. In a way, debug printing forces you to tackle bugs scientifically because you have to write out hypotheses as print statements.

Extra Credit

- Find a graphical debugger and compare using it to raw GDB. These are useful when the program you're looking at is local, but they are pointless if you have to debug a program on a server.

- You can enable core dumps on your OS, and when a program crashes, you'll get a core file. This core file is like a postmortem of the program that you can load up to see what happened right at the crash and what caused it. Change `ex18.c` so that it crashes after a few iterations, then try to get a core dump and analyze it.

Advanced Data Types and Flow Control

This exercise will be a complete compendium of the available C data types and flow control structures you can use. It will work as a reference to complete your knowledge, and won't have any code for you to enter. I'll have you memorize some of the information by creating flash cards so you can get the important concepts solid in your mind.

For this exercise to be useful, you should spend at least a week hammering in the content and filling out all of the elements that are missing here. You'll be writing out what each one means, and then writing a program to confirm what you've researched.

Available Data Types

Type	Description
int	Stores a regular integer, defaulting to 32 bits in size.
double	Holds a large floating-point number.
float	Holds a smaller floating-point number.
char	Holds a single 1-byte character.
void	Indicates "no type" and is used to say that a function returns nothing, or a pointer has no type, as in void *thing.
enum	Enumerated types, which work as and convert to integers, but give you symbolic names for sets. Some compilers will warn you when you don't cover all elements of an enum in switch-statements.

Type Modifiers

Modifier	Description
unsigned	Changes the type so that it doesn't have negative numbers, giving you a larger upper bound but nothing lower than 0.
signed	Gives you negative and positive numbers, but halves your upper bound in exchange for the same lower bound negative.
long	Uses a larger storage for the type so that it can hold bigger numbers, usually doubling the current size.
short	Uses smaller storage for the type so it stores less, but takes half the space.

Type Qualifiers

Qualifier	Description
`const`	Indicates that the variable won't change after being initialized.
`volatile`	Indicates that all bets are off, and the compiler should leave this alone and try not to do any fancy optimizations to it. You usually only need this if you're doing really weird stuff to your variables.
`register`	Forces the compiler to keep this variable in a register, and the compiler can just ignore you. These days compilers are better at figuring out where to put variables, so only use this if you can actually measure an improvement in speed.

Type Conversion

C uses a sort of stepped type promotion mechanism, where it looks at two operands on either side of an expression, and promotes the smaller side to match the larger side before doing the operation. If one side of an expression is on this list, then the other side is converted to that type before the operation is done. It goes in this order:

1. `long double`
2. `double`
3. `float`
4. `int` (but only char and short `int`);
5. `long`

Always promote up, not down

If you find yourself trying to figure out how your conversions are working in an expression, then don't leave it to the compiler. Use explicit casting operations to make it exactly what you want. For example, if you have

`long + char - int * double`

Rather than trying to figure out if it will be converted to double correctly, just use casts:

`(double)long - (double)char - (double)int * double`

Putting the type you want in parentheses before the variable name is how you force it into the type you really need. The important thing, though, is *always promote up, not down*. Don't cast `long` into `char` unless you know what you're doing.

Type Sizes

The stdint.h defines both a set of typdefs for exact-sized integer types, as well as a set of macros for the sizes of all the types. This is easier to work with than the older limits.h since it is consistent. Here are the types defined:

Type	Definition
int8_t	8-bit signed integer
uint8_t	8-bit unsigned integer
int16_t	16-bit signed integer
uint16_t	16-bit unsigned integer
int32_t	32-bit signed integer
uint32_t	32-bit unsigned integer
int64_t	64-bit signed integer
uint64_t	64-bit unsigned integer

The pattern here is in the form (u)int(*BITS*)_t where a *u* is put in front to indicate "unsigned," and *BITS* is a number for the number of bits. This pattern is then repeated for macros that return the maximum values of these types:

INT(N)_MAX   Maximum positive number of the signed integer of bits *(N)*, such as INT16_MAX.

INT(N)_MIN   Minimum negative number of signed integer of bits *(N)*.

UINT(N)_MAX   Maximum positive number of unsigned integer of bits *(N)*. Since it's unsigned, the minimum is 0 and it can't have a negative value.

WARNING! Pay attention! Don't go looking for a literal INT(N)_MAX definition in any header file. I'm using the (N) as a placeholder for any number of bits your platform currently supports. This (N) could be any number—8, 16, 32, 64, maybe even 128. I use this notation in this exercise so that I don't have to literally write out every possible combination.

There are also macros in `stdint.h` for sizes of the `size_t` type, integers large enough to hold pointers, and other handy size defining macros. Compilers have to at least have these, and then they can allow other, larger types.

Here is a full list that should be in `stdint.h`:

Type	Definition
`int_least(N)_t`	Holds at least *(N)* bits
`uint_least(N)_t`	Holds at least *(N)* bits unsigned
`INT_LEAST(N)_MAX`	Maximum value of the matching least *(N)* type
`INT_LEAST(N)_MIN`	Minimum value of the matching least *(N)* type
`UINT_LEAST(N)_MAX`	Unsigned maximum of the matching *(N)* type
`int_fast(N)_t`	Similar to `int_least*N*_t` but asking for the "fastest" with at least that precision
`uint_fast(N)_t`	Unsigned fastest least integer
`INT_FAST(N)_MAX`	Maximum value of the matching fastest *(N)* type
`INT_FAST(N)_MIN`	Minimum value of the matching fastest *(N)* type
`UINT_FAST(N)_MAX`	Unsigned maximum value of the matching fastest *(N)* type
`intptr_t`	*Signed* integer large enough to hold a pointer
`uintptr_t`	*Unsigned* integer large enough to hold a pointer
`INTPTR_MAX`	Maximum value of a `intptr_t`
`INTPTR_MIN`	Minimum value of a `intptr_t`
`UINTPTR_MAX`	Unsigned maximum value of a `uintptr_t`
`intmax_t`	Biggest number possible on that system
`uintmax_t`	Biggest unsigned number possible
`INTMAX_MAX`	Largest value for the biggest signed number
`INTMAX_MIN`	Smallest value for the biggest signed number
`UINTMAX_MAX`	Largest value for the biggest unsigned number
`PTRDIFF_MIN`	Minimum value of `ptrdiff_t`
`PTRDIFF_MAX`	Maximum value of `ptrdiff_t`
`SIZE_MAX`	Maximum of a `size_t`

Available Operators

This is a comprehensive list of all the operators in the C language. In this list, I'm indicating the following:

Operator	Definition
(binary)	The operator has a left and right: X + Y.
(unary)	The operator is on its own: -X.
(prefix)	The operator comes before the variable: ++X.
(postfix)	This is usually the same as the (prefix) version, but placing it after gives it a different meaning: X++.
(ternary)	There's only one of these, so it's actually called the ternary, but it means "three operands": X ? Y : Z.

Math Operators

These perform your basic math operations, plus I include () since it calls a function and is close to a math operation.

Operator	Definition
()	Function call
* (binary)	Multiply
/	Divide
+ (binary)	Add
+ (unary)	Positive number
++ (postfix)	Read, then increment
++ (prefix)	Increment, then read
-- (postfix)	Read, then decrement
-- (prefix)	Decrement, then read
- (binary)	Subtract
- (unary)	Negative number

Data Operators

These are used to access data in different ways and forms.

Operator	Definition
->	Struct pointer access
.	Struct value access
[]	Array index
sizeof	Size of a type or variable
& (unary)	Address of
* (unary)	Value of

Logic Operators

These handle testing equality and inequality of variables.

Operator	Definition
!=	Does not equal
<	Less than
<=	Less than or equal
==	Equal (not assignment)
>	Greater than
>=	Greater than or equal

Bit Operators

These are more advanced and are for shifting and modifying the raw bits in integers.

& (binary)	Bitwise and
<<	Shift left
>>	Shift right
^	Bitwise xor (exclusive or)
		Bitwise or
~	Complement (flips all the bits)

Boolean Operators

These are used in truth testing. Study the ternary operator carefully. It's very handy.

Operator	Definition
!	Not
&&	And
||	Or
?:	Ternary truth test, read X ? Y : Z as "if X then Y else Z"

Assignment Operators

Here are compound assignment operators that assign a value, and/or perform an operation at the same time. Most of the above operations can also be combined into a compound assignment operator.

Operator	Definition
=	Assign
%=	Modulus assign
&=	Bitwise and assign
*=	Multiply assign
+=	Plus assign
-=	Minus assign
/=	Divide assign
<<=	Shift left, assign
>>=	Shift right, assign
^=	Bitwise xor, assign
|=	Bitwise or, assign

Available Control Structures

There are a few control structures that you haven't encountered yet.

do-while   do { ... } while(X); First does the code in the block, then tests the X expression before exiting.

break   Puts a break in a loop, ending it early.

continue   Stops the body of a loop and jumps to the test so it can continue.

goto   Jumps to a spot in the code where you've placed a `label:`, and you've been using this in the `dbg.h` macros to go to the `error:` label.

Extra Credit

- Read `stdint.h` or a description of it, and write out all the available size identifiers.

- Go through each item here and write out what it does in code. Research it online so you know you got it right.

- Get this information memorized by making flash cards and spending 15 minutes a day practicing it.

- Create a program that prints out examples of each type, and confirm that your research is right.

The Stack, Scope, and Globals

The concept of scope seems to confuse quite a few people when they first start programming. It originally came from the use of the system stack (which we lightly covered earlier), and how it was used to store temporary variables. In this exercise, we'll learn about scope by learning how a stack data structure works, and then feeding that concept back in to how modern C does scoping.

The real purpose of this exercise, though, is to learn where the hell things live in C. When someone doesn't grasp the concept of scope, it's almost always a failure in understanding where variables are created, exist, and die. Once you know where things are, the concept of scope becomes easier.

This exercise will require three files:

ex22.h   A header file that sets up some external variables and some functions.

ex22.c   This isn't your main like normal, but instead a source file that will become the object file ex22.o, which will have some functions and variables in it defined from ex22.h.

ex22_main.c   The actual main that will include the other two, and demonstrate what they contain, as well as other scope concepts.

ex22.h and ex22.c

Your first step is to create your own header file named ex22.h that defines the functions and extern variables:

ex22.h

```
#ifndef _ex22_h
#define _ex22_h

// makes THE_SIZE in ex22.c available to other .c files
extern int THE_SIZE;

// gets and sets an internal static variable in ex22.c
int get_age();
void set_age(int age);

// updates a static variable that's inside update_ratio
double update_ratio(double ratio);
```

```
void print_size();

#endif
```

The important thing to see here is the use of extern int THE_SIZE, which I'll explain after you create this matching ex22.c:

```
1    #include <stdio.h>
2    #include "ex22.h"
3    #include "dbg.h"
4
5    int THE_SIZE = 1000;
6
7    static int THE_AGE = 37;
8
9    int get_age()
10   {
11       return THE_AGE;
12   }
13
14   void set_age(int age)
15   {
16       THE_AGE = age;
17   }
18
19   double update_ratio(double new_ratio)
20   {
21       static double ratio = 1.0;
22
23       double old_ratio = ratio;
24       ratio = new_ratio;
25
26       return old_ratio;
27   }
28
29   void print_size()
```

```
30    {
31        log_info("I think size is: %d", THE_SIZE);
32    }
```

These two files introduce some new kinds of storage for variables:

> **extern**   This keyword is a way to tell the compiler "the variable exists, but it's in another 'external' location." Typically this means that one .c file is going to use a variable that's been defined in another .c file. In this case, we're saying ex22.c has a variable THE_SIZE that will be accessed from ex22_main.c.

> **static (file)**   This keyword is kind of the inverse of extern, and says that the variable is only used in this .c file and should not be available to other parts of the program. Keep in mind that static at the file level (as with THE_AGE here) is different than in other places.

> **static (function)**   If you declare a variable in a function static, then that variable acts like a static defined in the file, but it's only accessible from that function. It's a way of creating constant state for a function, but in reality it's *rarely* used in modern C programming because they are hard to use with threads.

In these two files, you should understand the following variables and functions:

> **THE_SIZE**   This is the variable you declared extern that you'll play with from ex22_main.c.

> **get_age and set_age**   These are taking the static variable THE_AGE, but exposing it to other parts of the program through functions. You can't access THE_AGE directly, but these functions can.

> **update_ratio**   This takes a new ratio value, and returns the old one. It uses a function level static variable ratio to keep track of what the ratio currently is.

> **print_size**   This prints out what ex22.c thinks THE_SIZE is currently.

ex22_main.c

Once you have that file written, you can then make the main function, which uses all of these and demonstrates some more scope conventions.

ex22_main.c

```
1    #include "ex22.h"
2    #include "dbg.h"
3
```

```
4    const char *MY_NAME = "Zed A. Shaw";
5
6    void scope_demo(int count)
7    {
8        log_info("count is: %d", count);
9
10       if (count > 10) {
11           int count = 100;      // BAD! BUGS!
12
13           log_info("count in this scope is %d", count);
14       }
15
16       log_info("count is at exit: %d", count);
17
18       count = 3000;
19
20       log_info("count after assign: %d", count);
21   }
22
23   int main(int argc, char *argv[])
24   {
25       // test out THE_AGE accessors
26       log_info("My name: %s, age: %d", MY_NAME, get_age());
27
28       set_age(100);
29
30       log_info("My age is now: %d", get_age());
31
32       // test out THE_SIZE extern
33       log_info("THE_SIZE is: %d", THE_SIZE);
34       print_size();
35
36       THE_SIZE = 9;
37
38       log_info("THE SIZE is now: %d", THE_SIZE);
39       print_size();
40
41       // test the ratio function static
42       log_info("Ratio at first: %f", update_ratio(2.0));
```

```
43        log_info("Ratio again: %f", update_ratio(10.0));
44        log_info("Ratio once more: %f", update_ratio(300.0));
45
46        // test the scope demo
47        int count = 4;
48        scope_demo(count);
49        scope_demo(count * 20);
50
51        log_info("count after calling scope_demo: %d", count);
52
53        return 0;
54    }
```

I'll break this file down line by line, but as I do, you should find each variable and where it lives.

ex22_main.c:4   A const, which stands for constant, and is an alternative to using a define to create a constant variable.

ex22_main.c:6   A simple function that demonstrates more scope issues in a function.

ex22_main.c:8   This prints out the value of count as it is at the top of the function.

ex22_main.c:10   An if-statement that starts a new *scope block*, and then has another count variable in it. This version of count is actually a whole new variable. It's kind of like the if-statement started a new mini function.

ex22_main.c:11   The count that is local to this block is actually different from the one in the function's parameter list.

ex22_main.c:13   This prints it out so you can see it's actually 100 here, not what was passed to scope_demo.

ex22_main.c:16   Now for the freaky part. You have count in two places: the parameters to this function, and in the if-statement. The if-statement created a new block, so the count on line 11 *does not impact the parameter with the same name*. This line prints it out, and you'll see that it prints the value of the parameter, not 100.

ex22_main.c:18-20   Then, I set the parameter count to 3000 and print that out, which will demonstrate that you can change function parameters and they don't impact the caller's version of the variable.

Make sure that you trace through this function, but don't think that you understand scope quite yet. Just start to realize that if you make a variable inside a block (as in if-statements or while-loops), then those variables are *new* variables that exist only in that block. This is crucial to understand, and is also a *source of many bugs*. We'll address why you shouldn't make a variable inside a block shortly.

The rest of the ex22_main.c then demonstrates all of these by manipulating and printing them out:

ex22_main.c:26   This prints out the current values of MY_NAME, and gets THE_AGE from ex22.c by using the accessor function get_age.

ex22_main.c:27-30   This uses set_age in ex22.c to change THE_AGE and then print it out.

ex22_main.c:33-39   Then I do the same thing to THE_SIZE from ex22.c, but this time I'm accessing it directly. I'm also demonstrating that it's actually changing in that file by printing it here and with print_size.

ex22_main.c:42-44   Here, I show how the static variable ratio inside update_ratio is maintained between function calls.

ex22_main.c:46-51   Finally, I'm running scope_demo a few times so you can see the scope in action. The big thing to notice is that the local count variable remains unchanged. You *must* understand that passing in a variable like this won't let you change it in the function. To do that, you need our old friend the pointer. If you were to pass a pointer to this count, then the called function would have the address of it and could change it.

That explains what's going on, but you should trace through these files and make sure you know where everything is as you study it.

What You Should See

This time, instead of using your Makefile, I want you to build these two files manually so you can see how the compiler actually puts them together. Here's what you should do and see for output:

Exercise 22 Session

```
$ cc -Wall -g -DNDEBUG   -c -o ex22.o ex22.c
$ cc -Wall -g -DNDEBUG    ex22_main.c ex22.o   -o ex22_main
$ ./ex22_main
[INFO] (ex22_main.c:26) My name: Zed A. Shaw, age: 37
[INFO] (ex22_main.c:30) My age is now: 100
[INFO] (ex22_main.c:33) THE_SIZE is: 1000
[INFO] (ex22.c:32) I think size is: 1000
[INFO] (ex22_main.c:38) THE SIZE is now: 9
[INFO] (ex22.c:32) I think size is: 9
```

```
[INFO] (ex22_main.c:42) Ratio at first: 1.000000
[INFO] (ex22_main.c:43) Ratio again: 2.000000
[INFO] (ex22_main.c:44) Ratio once more: 10.000000
[INFO] (ex22_main.c:8) count is: 4
[INFO] (ex22_main.c:16) count is at exit: 4
[INFO] (ex22_main.c:20) count after assign: 3000
[INFO] (ex22_main.c:8) count is: 80
[INFO] (ex22_main.c:13) count in this scope is 100
[INFO] (ex22_main.c:16) count is at exit: 80
[INFO] (ex22_main.c:20) count after assign: 3000
[INFO] (ex22_main.c:51) count after calling scope_demo: 4
```

Make sure you trace how each variable is changing and match it to the line that gets output. I'm using log_info from the dbg.h macros so you can get the exact line number where each variable is printed, and find it in the files for tracing.

Scope, Stack, and Bugs

If you've done this right, you should now see many of the different ways you can place variables in your C code. You can use extern or access functions like get_age to create globals. You can make new variables inside any blocks, and they'll retain their own values until that block exits, leaving the outer variables alone. You also can pass a value to a function, and change the parameter but without changing the caller's version of it.

The most important thing to realize is that all of this causes bugs. C's ability to place things in many places in your machine, and then let you access it in those places, means that you can get easily confused about where something lives. If you don't know where it lives, then there's a chance you won't manage it properly.

With that in mind, here are some rules to follow when writing C code so you can avoid bugs related to the stack:

- Do not shadow a variable like I've done here with count in scope_demo. It leaves you open to subtle and hidden bugs where you *think* you're changing a value but you're actually not.

- Avoid using too many globals, especially if across multiple files. If you have to use them, then use accessor functions like I've done with get_age. This doesn't apply to constants, since those are read-only. I'm talking about variables like THE_SIZE. If you want people to modify or set this variable, then make accessor functions.

- When in doubt, put it on the heap. Don't rely on the semantics of the stack or specialized locations. Just create things with malloc.

- Don't use function static variables like I did in update_ratio. They're rarely useful and end up being a huge pain when you need to make your code concurrent in threads. They're also hard as hell to find compared to a well-done global variable.

- Avoid reusing function parameters. It's confusing as to whether you're just reusing it or if you think you're changing the *caller's* version of it.

As with all things, these rules can be broken when it's practical. In fact, I guarantee you'll run into code that breaks all of these rules and is perfectly fine. The constraints of different platforms even make it necessary sometimes.

How to Break It

For this exercise, try to access or change some things you can't to break the program.

- Try to directly access variables in ex22.c from ex22_main.c that you think you can't access. For example, can you get at ratio inside update_ratio? What if you had a pointer to it?

- Ditch the extern declaration in ex22.h to see what errors or warnings you get.

- Add static or const specifiers to different variables, and then try to change them.

Extra Credit

- Research the concept of pass by value versus pass by reference. Write an example of both.

- Use pointers to gain access to things you shouldn't have access to.

- Use your debugger to see what this kind of access looks like when you do it wrong.

- Write a recursive function that causes a stack overflow. Don't know what a recursive function is? Try calling scope_demo at the bottom of scope_demo itself so that it loops.

- Rewrite the Makefile so that it can build this.

Pass by value
- Function duplicates a variable
  and modifies the duplicate
  leaving original

Pass by reference
- Function receives a reference (ie pointer)
  to variable and directly modifies it.

Meet Duff's Device

This exercise is a brain teaser where I introduce you to one of the most famous hacks in C called Duff's device, named after Tom Duff, its inventor. This little slice of awesome (evil?) has nearly everything you've been learning wrapped in one tiny, little package. Figuring out how it works is also a good, fun puzzle.

> **WARNING!** Part of the fun of C is that you can come up with crazy hacks like this, but this is also what makes C annoying to use. It's good to learn about these tricks because it gives you a deeper understanding of the language and your computer. But you should never use this. Always strive for easy-to-read code.

Discovered by Tom Duff, Duff's device is a trick with the C compiler that actually shouldn't work. I won't tell you what it does yet since this is meant to be a puzzle for you to ponder and try to solve. You'll get this code running and then try to figure out what it does, and *why* it does it this way.

ex23.c

```
1    #include <stdio.h>
2    #include <string.h>
3    #include "dbg.h"
4
5    int normal_copy(char *from, char *to, int count)
6    {
7        int i = 0;
8
9        for (i = 0; i < count; i++) {
10           to[i] = from[i];
11       }
12
13       return i;
14   }
15
16   int duffs_device(char *from, char *to, int count)
17   {
18       {
19           int n = (count + 7) / 8;
```

```
20
21              switch (count % 8) {
22                  case 0:
23                      do {
24                          *to++ = *from++;
25                      case 7:
26                          *to++ = *from++;
27                      case 6:
28                          *to++ = *from++;
29                      case 5:
30                          *to++ = *from++;
31                      case 4:
32                          *to++ = *from++;
33                      case 3:
34                          *to++ = *from++;
35                      case 2:
36                          *to++ = *from++;
37                      case 1:
38                          *to++ = *from++;
39                      } while (--n > 0);
40              }
41          }
42
43      return count;
44  }
45
46  int zeds_device(char *from, char *to, int count)
47  {
48      {
49          int n = (count + 7) / 8;
50
51          switch (count % 8) {
52              case 0:
53  again:      *to++ = *from++;
54
55              case 7:
56              *to++ = *from++;
57              case 6:
58              *to++ = *from++;
```

```
59              case 5:
60          *to++ = *from++;
61              case 4:
62          *to++ = *from++;
63              case 3:
64          *to++ = *from++;
65              case 2:
66          *to++ = *from++;
67              case 1:
68          *to++ = *from++;
69          if (--n > 0)
70              goto again;
71          }
72      }
73
74      return count;
75  }
76
77  int valid_copy(char *data, int count, char expects)
78  {
79      int i = 0;
80      for (i = 0; i < count; i++) {
81          if (data[i] != expects) {
82              log_err("[%d] %c != %c", i, data[i], expects);
83              return 0;
84          }
85      }
86
87      return 1;
88  }
89
90  int main(int argc, char *argv[])
91  {
92      char from[1000] = { 'a' };
93      char to[1000] = { 'c' };
94      int rc = 0;
95
96      // set up the from to have some stuff
97      memset(from, 'x', 1000);
```

```
98          // set it to a failure mode
99          memset(to, 'y', 1000);
100         check(valid_copy(to, 1000, 'y'), "Not initialized right.");
101
102         // use normal copy to
103         rc = normal_copy(from, to, 1000);
104         check(rc == 1000, "Normal copy failed: %d", rc);
105         check(valid_copy(to, 1000, 'x'), "Normal copy failed.");
106
107         // reset
108         memset(to, 'y', 1000);
109
110         // duffs version
111         rc = duffs_device(from, to, 1000);
112         check(rc == 1000, "Duff's device failed: %d", rc);
113         check(valid_copy(to, 1000, 'x'), "Duff's device failed copy.");
114
115         // reset
116         memset(to, 'y', 1000);
117
118         // my version
119         rc = zeds_device(from, to, 1000);
120         check(rc == 1000, "Zed's device failed: %d", rc);
121         check(valid_copy(to, 1000, 'x'), "Zed's device failed copy.");
122
123         return 0;
124     error:
125         return 1;
126     }
```

In this code, I have three versions of a copy function:

normal_copy   This is just a plain for-loop that copies characters from one array to another.

duffs_device   This is called Duff's device, named after Tom Duff, the person to blame for this delicious evil.

zeds_device   A version of Duff's device that just uses a goto so you can clue in to what's happening with the weird do-while placement in duffs_device.

Study these three functions before continuing. Try to explain what's going on to yourself.

What You Should See

There's no output from this program, it just runs and exits. Run it under your debugger to see if you can catch any more errors. Try causing some of your own, as I showed you in Exercise 4.

Solving the Puzzle

The first thing to understand is that C is rather loose regarding some of its syntax. This is why you can put half of a do-while in one part of a switch-statement, then the other half somewhere else, and the code will still work. If you look at my version with the goto again, it's actually more clear what's going on, but make sure you understand how that part works.

The second thing is how the default fallthrough semantics of switch-statements let you jump to a particular case, and then it will just keep running until the end of the switch.

The final clue is the count % 8 and the calculation of n at the top.

Now, to solve how these functions work, do the following:

- Print this code out so that you can write on some paper.
- Write each of the variables in a table as they look when they get initialized right before the switch-statement.
- Follow the logic to the switch, then do the jump to the right case.
- Update the variables, including the to, from, and the arrays they point at.
- When you get to the while part or my goto alternative, check your variables, and then follow the logic either back to the top of the do-while or to where the again label is located.
- Follow through this manual tracing, updating the variables, until you're sure you see how this flows.

Why Bother?

When you've figured out how it actually works, the final question is: Why would you ever want to do this? The purpose of this trick is to manually do loop unrolling. Large, long loops can be slow, so one way to speed them up is to find some fixed chunk of the loop, and then just duplicate the code in the loop that many times sequentially. For example, if you know a loop runs a minimum of 20 times, then you can put the contents of the loop 20 times in the source code.

Duff's device is basically doing this automatically by chunking up the loop into eight iteration chunks. It's clever and actually works, but these days a good compiler will do this for you. You shouldn't need this except in the rare case where you have *proven* it would improve your speed.

Extra Credit

- Never use this again.

- Go look at the Wikipedia entry for Duff's device and see if you can spot the error. Read the article, compare it to the version I have here, and try to understand why the Wikipedia code won't work for you but worked for Tom Duff.

- Create a set of macros that lets you create any length of device like this. For example, what if you wanted to have 32 case statements and didn't want to write out all of them? Can you do a macro that lays down eight at a time?

- Change the `main` to conduct some speed tests to see which one is really the fastest.

- Read about `memcpy`, `memmove`, and `memset`, and also compare their speed.

- Never use this again!

memcpy
Copies value of num bytes from located to by source
directly to memory block pointed to by destination

memmove
Moves value of num bytes to destination from source.
Destination and source can overlap in memory

memset
Fills a block of memory at location with value

Input, Output, Files

You've been using printf to print things, and that's great and all, but you need more. In this exercise, you'll be using the functions fscanf and fgets to build information about a person in a structure. After this simple introduction about reading input, you'll get a full list of the functions that C has for I/O. Some of these you've already seen and used, so this will be another memorization exercise.

ex24.c

```c
#include <stdio.h>
#include "dbg.h"

#define MAX_DATA 100

typedef enum EyeColor {
    BLUE_EYES, GREEN_EYES, BROWN_EYES,
    BLACK_EYES, OTHER_EYES
} EyeColor;

const char *EYE_COLOR_NAMES[] = {
    "Blue", "Green", "Brown", "Black", "Other"
};

typedef struct Person {
    int age;
    char first_name[MAX_DATA];
    char last_name[MAX_DATA];
    EyeColor eyes;
    float income;
} Person;

int main(int argc, char *argv[])
{
    Person you = {.age = 0 };
    int i = 0;
    char *in = NULL;

    printf("What's your First Name? ");
    in = fgets(you.first_name, MAX_DATA - 1, stdin);
    check(in != NULL, "Failed to read first name.");

    printf("What's your Last Name? ");
    in = fgets(you.last_name, MAX_DATA - 1, stdin);
    check(in != NULL, "Failed to read last name.");
```

```
36
37        printf("How old are you? ");
38        int rc = fscanf(stdin, "%d", &you.age);
39        check(rc > 0, "You have to enter a number.");
40
41        printf("What color are your eyes:\n");
42        for (i = 0; i <= OTHER_EYES; i++) {
43            printf("%d) %s\n", i + 1, EYE_COLOR_NAMES[i]);
44        }
45        printf("> ");
46
47        int eyes = -1;
48        rc = fscanf(stdin, "%d", &eyes);
49        check(rc > 0, "You have to enter a number.");
50
51        you.eyes = eyes - 1;
52        check(you.eyes <= OTHER_EYES
53                && you.eyes >= 0, "Do it right, that's not an option.");
54
55        printf("How much do you make an hour? ");
56        rc = fscanf(stdin, "%f", &you.income);
57        check(rc > 0, "Enter a floating point number.");
58
59        printf("----- RESULTS -----\n");
60
61        printf("First Name: %s", you.first_name);
62        printf("Last Name: %s", you.last_name);
63        printf("Age: %d\n", you.age);
64        printf("Eyes: %s\n", EYE_COLOR_NAMES[you.eyes]);
65        printf("Income: %f\n", you.income);
66
67        return 0;
68    error:
69
70        return -1;
71    }
```

This program is deceptively simple, and introduces a function called fscanf, which is the file scanf. The scanf family of functions are the inverse of the printf versions. Where printf printed out data based on a format, scanf reads (or scans) input based on a format.

There's nothing original in the beginning of the file, so here's what the main is doing in the program:

ex24.c:24-28 Sets up some variables we'll need.

ex24.c:30-32 Gets your first name using the fgets function, which reads a string from the input (in this case stdin), but makes sure it doesn't overflow the given buffer.

ex24.c:34-36   Same thing for you.last_name, again using fgets.

ex24.c:38-39   Uses fscanf to read an integer from stdin and put it into you.age. You can see that the same format string is used as printf to print an integer. You should also see that you have to give the *address* of you.age so that fscanf has a pointer to it and can modify it. This is a good example of using a pointer to a piece of data as an out parameter.

ex24.c:41-45   Prints out all of the options available for eye color, with a matching number that works with the EyeColor enum above.

ex24.c:47-50   Using fscanf again, gets a number for the you.eyes, but make sure the input is valid. This is important because someone can enter a value outside the EYE_COLOR_ NAMES array and cause a segmentation fault.

ex24.c:52-53   Gets how much you make as a float for the you.income.

ex24.c:55-61   Prints everything out so you can see if you have it right. Notice that EYE_COLOR_ NAMES is used to print out what the EyeColor enum is actually called.

What You Should See

When you run this program, you should see your inputs being properly converted. Make sure you try to give it bogus input too, so you can see how it protects against the input.

Exercise 24 Session

```
$ make ex24
cc -Wall -g -DNDEBUG     ex24.c    -o ex24
$ ./ex24
What's your First Name? Zed
What's your Last Name? Shaw
How old are you? 37
What color are your eyes:
1) Blue
2) Green
3) Brown
4) Black
5) Other
> 1
How much do you make an hour? 1.2345
----- RESULTS -----
First Name: Zed
Last Name: Shaw
Age: 37
Eyes: Blue
Income: 1.234500
```

How to Break It

This is all fine and good, but the really important part of this exercise is how scanf actually sucks. It's fine for a simple conversion of numbers, but fails for strings because it's difficult to tell scanf how big a buffer is before you read it. There's also a problem with the function gets (not fgets, the non-f version), which we avoided. That function has no idea how big the input buffer is at all and will just trash your program.

To demonstrate the problems with fscanf and strings, change the lines that use fgets so they are fscanf(stdin, "%50s", you.first_name), and then try to use it again. Notice it seems to read too much and then eat your enter key? This doesn't do what you think it does, and rather than deal with weird scanf issues, you should just use fgets.

Next, change the fgets to use gets, then run your debugger on ex24. Do this inside:

```
"run << /dev/urandom"
```

This feeds random garbage into your program. This is called fuzzing your program, and it's a good way to find input bugs. In this case, you're feeding garbage from the /dev/urandom file (device), and then watching it crash. In some platforms, you may have to do this a few times, or even adjust the MAX_DATA define so it's small enough.

The gets function is so bad that some platforms actually warn you when the *program* runs that you're using gets. You should never use this function, ever.

Finally, take the input for you.eyes and remove the check that the number is within the right range. Then, feed it bad numbers like -1 or 1000. Do this under the debugger so you can see what happens there, too.

The I/O Functions

This is a short list of various I/O functions that you should look up. Create flash cards that have the function name and all the variants similar to it.

- fscanf *Read formatted data from stream*
- fgets *Gets string from stream.*
- fopen *Open file*
- freopen *Reopen file w/ different stream/mode*
- fdopen
- fclose *Close file stream*

- fcloseall   *Close all files streams*
- fgetpos   *Cut pos within file*
- fseek   *Go to point in file*
- ftell   *Cut pos within file*
- rewind   *Goto point in file*
- fprintf ⎤ *Formatted print, write, read*
- fwrite   ⎥
- fread   ⎦

Go through these and memorize the different variants and what they do. For example, for the card fscanf, you'll have scanf, sscanf, vscanf, etc., and then what each of those does on the back.

Finally, use man to read the help for each variant to get the information you need for the flash cards. For example, the page for fscanf comes from man fscanf.

Extra Credit

- Rewrite this to not use fscanf at all. You'll need to use functions like atoi to convert the input strings to numbers.

- Change this to use plain scanf instead of fscanf to see what the difference is.

- Fix it so that their input names get stripped of the trailing newline characters and any white space.

- Use scanf to write a function that reads one character at a time and fills in the names but doesn't go past the end. Make this function generic so it can take a size for the string, but just make sure you end the string with '\0' no matter what.

Variable Argument Functions

In C, you can create your own versions of functions like printf and scanf by creating a *variable argument* function, or vararg function. These functions use the header stdarg.h, and with them, you can create nicer interfaces to your library. They are handy for certain types of builder functions, formatting functions, and anything that takes variable arguments.

Understanding vararg functions is *not* essential to creating C programs. I think I've used it maybe 20 times in my code in all of the years I've been programming. However, knowing how a vararg function works will help you debug the programs you use and gives you a better understanding of the computer.

ex25.c

```
 1
 2
 3   #include <stdlib.h>
 4   #include <stdio.h>
 5   #include <stdarg.h>
 6   #include "dbg.h"
 7
 8   #define MAX_DATA 100
 9
10   int read_string(char **out_string, int max_buffer)
11   {
12       *out_string = calloc(1, max_buffer + 1);
13       check_mem(*out_string);
14
15       char *result = fgets(*out_string, max_buffer, stdin);
16       check(result != NULL, "Input error.");
17
18       return 0;
19
20   error:
21       if (*out_string) free(*out_string);
22       *out_string = NULL;
23       return -1;
24   }
25
26   int read_int(int *out_int)
27   {
28       char *input = NULL;
29       int rc = read_string(&input, MAX_DATA);
30       check(rc == 0, "Failed to read number.");
31
32       *out_int = atoi(input);
```

```
33
34          free(input);
35          return 0;
36
37      error:
38          if (input) free(input);
39          return -1;
40      }
41
42      int read_scan(const char *fmt, ...)
43      {
44          int i = 0;
45          int rc = 0;
46          int *out_int = NULL;
47          char *out_char = NULL;
48          char **out_string = NULL;
49          int max_buffer = 0;
50
51          va_list argp;
52          va_start(argp, fmt);
53
54          for (i = 0; fmt[i] != '\0'; i++) {
55              if (fmt[i] == '%') {
56                  i++;
57                  switch (fmt[i]) {
58                      case '\0':
59                          sentinel("Invalid format, you ended with %%.");
60                          break;
61
62                      case 'd':
63                          out_int = va_arg(argp, int *);
64                          rc = read_int(out_int);
65                          check(rc == 0, "Failed to read int.");
66                          break;
67
68                      case 'c':
69                          out_char = va_arg(argp, char *);
70                          *out_char = fgetc(stdin);
71                          break;
72
73                      case 's':
74                          max_buffer = va_arg(argp, int);
75                          out_string = va_arg(argp, char **);
76                          rc = read_string(out_string, max_buffer);
77                          check(rc == 0, "Failed to read string.");
78                          break;
79
80                      default:
81                          sentinel("Invalid format.");
82                  }
```

```
83              } else {
84                  fgetc(stdin);
85              }
86
87              check(!feof(stdin) && !ferror(stdin), "Input error.");
88          }
89
90      va_end(argp);
91      return 0;
92
93  error:
94      va_end(argp);
95      return -1;
96  }
97
98  int main(int argc, char *argv[])
99  {
100     char *first_name = NULL;
101     char initial = ' ';
102     char *last_name = NULL;
103     int age = 0;
104
105     printf("What's your first name? ");
106     int rc = read_scan("%s", MAX_DATA, &first_name);
107     check(rc == 0, "Failed first name.");
108
109     printf("What's your initial? ");
110     rc = read_scan("%c\n", &initial);
111     check(rc == 0, "Failed initial.");
112
113     printf("What's your last name? ");
114     rc = read_scan("%s", MAX_DATA, &last_name);
115     check(rc == 0, "Failed last name.");
116
117     printf("How old are you? ");
118     rc = read_scan("%d", &age);
119
120     printf("---- RESULTS ----\n");
121     printf("First Name: %s", first_name);
122     printf("Initial: '%c'\n", initial);
123     printf("Last Name: %s", last_name);
124     printf("Age: %d\n", age);
125
126     free(first_name);
127     free(last_name);
128     return 0;
129 error:
130     return -1;
131 }
```

This program is similar to the previous exercise, except I have written my own scanf function to handle strings the way I want. The main function should be clear to you, as well as the two functions read_string and read_int, since they do nothing new.

The varargs function is called read_scan, and it does the same thing that scanf is doing using the va_list data structure and supporting macros and functions. Here's how:

- I set as the last parameter of the function the keyword ... to indicate to C that this function will take any number of arguments after the fmt argument. I could put many other arguments before this, but I can't put any more after this.

- After setting up some variables, I create a va_list variable and initialize it with va_start. This configures the gear in stdarg.h that handles variable arguments.

- I then use a for-loop to loop through the format string fmt and process the same kind of formats that scanf has, only much simpler. I just have integers, characters, and strings.

- When I hit a format, I use the switch-statement to figure out what to do.

- Now, to *get* a variable from the va_list argp, I use the macro va_arg(argp, TYPE) where TYPE is the exact type of what I will assign this function parameter to. The downside to this design is that you're flying blind, so if you don't have enough parameters, then oh well, you'll most likely crash.

- The interesting difference from scanf is I'm assuming that people want read_scan to create the strings it reads when it hits an 's' format sequence. When you give this sequence, the function takes two parameters off the va_list argp stack: the max function size to read, and the output character string pointer. Using that information, it just runs read_string to do the real work.

- This makes read_scan more consistent than scanf, since you *always* give an address-of & on variables to have them set appropriately.

- Finally, if the function encounters a character that's not in the correct format, it just reads one char to skip it. It doesn't care what that char is, just that it should skip it.

What You Should See

When you run this one, it's similar to the last one.

Exercise 25 Session

```
$ make ex25
cc -Wall -g -DNDEBUG    ex25.c   -o ex25
$ ./ex25
What's your first name? Zed
What's your initial? A
```

```
What's your last name? Shaw
How old are you? 37
---- RESULTS ----
First Name: Zed
Initial: 'A'
Last Name: Shaw
Age: 37
```

How to Break It

This program should be more robust against buffer overflows, but it doesn't handle the formatted input as well as scanf. To try to break this, change the code so that you forget to pass in the initial size for '%s' formats. Try giving it more data than MAX_DATA, and then see how omitting calloc in read_string changes how it works. Finally, there's a problem where fgets eats the newlines, so try to fix that using fgetc, but leave out the \0 that ends the string.

Extra Credit

- Make double and triple sure that you know what each of the out_ variables is doing. Most importantly, you should know what out_string is and how it's a pointer to a pointer, so that you understand when you're setting the pointer versus the contents is important.

- Write a similar function to printf that uses the varargs system, and rewrite main to use it.

- As usual, read the man page on all of this so that you know what it does on your platform. Some platforms will use macros, others will use functions, and some will have these do nothing. It all depends on the compiler and the platform you use.

Project `logfind`

This is a small project for you to attempt on your own. To be effective at C, you'll need to learn to apply what you know to problems. In this exercise, I describe a tool I want you to implement, and I describe it in a vague way on purpose. This is done so that you will try to implement whatever you can, however you can. When you're done, you can then watch a video for the exercise that shows you how *I* did it, and then you can get the code and compare it to yours.

Think of this project as a real-world puzzle that you might have to solve.

The `logfind` Specification

I want a tool called `logfind` that lets me search through log files for text. This tool is a specialized version of another tool called `grep`, but designed only for log files on a system. The idea is that I can type:

```
logfind zedshaw
```

And, it will search all the common places that log files are stored, and print out every file that has the word "zedshaw" in it.

The `logfind` tool should have these basic features:

1. This tool takes any sequence of words and assumes I mean "and" for them. So `logfind zedshaw smart guy` will find all files that have zedshaw *and* smart *and* guy in them.

2. It takes an optional argument of -o if the parameters are meant to be *or* logic.

3. It loads the list of allowed log files from ~/.`logfind`.

4. The list of file names can be anything that the `glob` function allows. Refer to `man 3 glob` to see how this works. I suggest starting with just a flat list of exact files, and then add `glob` functionality.

5. You should output the matching lines as you scan, and try to match them as fast as possible.

That's the entire description. Remember that this may be *very* hard, so take it a tiny bit at a time. Write some code, test it, write more, test that, and so on in little chunks until you have it working. Start with the simplest thing that gets it working, and then slowly add to it and refine it until every feature is done.

Creative and Defensive Programming

Y ou have now learned most of the basics of C programming and are ready to start becoming a serious programmer. This is where you go from beginner to expert, both with C and hopefully with core computer science concepts. I will be teaching you a few of the core data structures and algorithms that every programmer should know, and then a few very interesting ones I've used in real software for years.

Before I can do that, I have to teach you some basic skills and ideas that will help you make better software. Exercises 27 through 31 will teach you advanced concepts, featuring more talking than coding. After that, you'll apply what you've learned to make a core library of useful data structures.

The first step in getting better at writing C code (and really any language) is to learn a new mind-set called *defensive programming*. Defensive programming assumes that you are going to make many mistakes, and then attempts to prevent them at every possible step. In this exercise, I'm going to teach you how to think about programming defensively.

The Creative Programmer Mind-Set

It's not possible to show you how to be creative in a short exercise like this, but I will tell you that creativity involves taking risks and being open-minded. Fear will quickly kill creativity, so the mind-set I adopt, and many programmers copy, is that accidents are designed to make you unafraid of taking chances and looking like an idiot. Here's my mind-set:

- I can't make a mistake.
- It doesn't matter what people think.
- Whatever my brain comes up with is going to be a great idea.

I only adopt this mind-set temporarily, and even have little tricks to turn it on. By doing this, I can come up with ideas, find creative solutions, open my thoughts to odd connections, and just generally invent weirdness without fear. In this mind-set, I'll typically write a horrible first version of something just to get the idea out.

However, when I've finished my creative prototype, I will throw it out and get serious about making it solid. Where other people make a mistake is carrying the creative mind-set into their implementation phase. This then leads to a very different, destructive mind-set: the dark side of the creative mind-set:

- It's possible to write perfect software.

- My brain tells me the truth, and it can't find any errors: I have therefore written perfect software.

- My code is who I am and people who criticize its perfection are criticizing me.

These are lies. You will frequently run into programmers who feel intense pride about what they've created, which is natural, but this pride gets in the way of their ability to objectively improve their craft. Because of this pride and attachment to what they've written, they can continue to believe that what they write is perfect. As long as they ignore other people's criticism of their code, they can protect their fragile egos and never improve.

The trick to being creative *and* making solid software is the ability to adopt a defensive programming mind-set.

The Defensive Programmer Mind-Set

After you have a working, creative prototype and you're feeling good about the idea, it's time to switch to being a defensive programmer. The defensive programmer basically hates your code and believes these things:

- Software has errors.

- You aren't your software, yet you're responsible for the errors.

- You can never remove the errors, only reduce their probability.

This mind-set lets you be honest about your work and critically analyze it for improvements. Notice that it doesn't say *you* are full of errors? It says your *code* is full of errors. This is a significant thing to understand because it gives you the power of objectivity for the next implementation.

Just like the creative mind-set, the defensive programming mind-set has a dark side, as well. Defensive programmers are paranoid, and this fear prevents them from ever possibly being wrong or making mistakes. That's great when you're trying to be ruthlessly consistent and correct, but it's murder on creative energy and concentration.

The Eight Defensive Programmer Strategies

Once you've adopted this mind-set, you can then rewrite your prototype and follow a set of eight strategies to make your code as solid as possible. While I work on the real version, I ruthlessly follow these strategies and try to remove as many errors as I can, thinking like someone who wants to break the software.

Never Trust Input   Never trust the data you're given and always validate it.

Prevent Errors   If an error is possible, no matter how probable, try to prevent it.

Fail Early and Openly   Fail early, cleanly, and openly, stating what happened, where, and how to fix it.

Document Assumptions   Clearly state the pre-conditions, post-conditions, and invariants.

Prevention over Documentation   Don't do with documentation that which can be done with code or avoided completely.

Automate Everything   Automate everything, especially testing.

Simplify and Clarify   Always simplify the code to the smallest, cleanest form that works without sacrificing safety.

Question Authority   Don't blindly follow or reject rules.

These aren't the only strategies, but they're the core things I feel programmers have to focus on when trying to make good, solid code. Notice that I don't really say exactly how to do these. I'll go into each of these in more detail, and some of the exercises will actually cover them extensively.

Applying the Eight Strategies

These ideas are all as great pop-psychology platitudes, but how do you actually apply them to working code? I'm now going to give you a set of things to always do in this book's code that demonstrates each one with a concrete example. The ideas aren't limited to just these examples, so you should use these as a guide to making your own code more solid.

Never Trust Input

Let's look at an example of bad design and better design. I won't say good design because this could be done even better. Take a look at these two functions that both copy a string and a simple `main` to test out the better one.

ex27_1.c

```
1    #undef NDEBUG
2    #include "dbg.h"
3    #include <stdio.h>
4    #include <assert.h>
5
6    /*
7     * Naive copy that assumes all inputs are always valid
8     * taken from K&R C and cleaned up a bit.
9     */
10   void copy(char to[], char from[])
11   {
12       int i = 0;
13
```

```
14          // while loop will not end if from isn't '\0' terminated
15          while ((to[i] = from[i]) != '\0') {
16              ++i;
17          }
18      }
19
20      /*
21       * A safer version that checks for many common errors using the
22       * length of each string to control the loops and termination.
23       */
24      int safercopy(int from_len, char *from, int to_len, char *to)
25      {
26          assert(from != NULL && to != NULL && "from and to can't be NULL");
27          int i = 0;
28          int max = from_len > to_len - 1 ? to_len - 1 : from_len;
29
30          // to_len must have at least 1 byte
31          if (from_len < 0 || to_len <= 0)
32              return -1;
33
34          for (i = 0; i < max; i++) {
35              to[i] = from[i];
36          }
37
38          to[to_len - 1] = '\0';
39
40          return i;
41      }
42
43      int main(int argc, char *argv[])
44      {
45          // careful to understand why we can get these sizes
46          char from[] = "0123456789";
47          int from_len = sizeof(from);
48
49          // notice that it's 7 chars + \0
50          char to[] = "0123456";
51          int to_len = sizeof(to);
52
53          debug("Copying '%s':%d to '%s':%d", from, from_len, to, to_len);
54
55          int rc = safercopy(from_len, from, to_len, to);
56          check(rc > 0, "Failed to safercopy.");
57          check(to[to_len - 1] == '\0', "String not terminated.");
58
59          debug("Result is: '%s':%d", to, to_len);
60
61          // now try to break it
62          rc = safercopy(from_len * -1, from, to_len, to);
63          check(rc == -1, "safercopy should fail #1");
```

```
64        check(to[to_len - 1] == '\0', "String not terminated.");
65
66        rc = safercopy(from_len, from, 0, to);
67        check(rc == -1, "safercopy should fail #2");
68        check(to[to_len - 1] == '\0', "String not terminated.");
69
70        return 0;
71
72    error:
73        return 1;
74    }
```

The copy function is typical C code and it's the source of a huge number of buffer overflows. It's flawed because it assumes that it will always receive a valid, terminated C string (with '\0'), and just uses a while-loop to process it. Problem is, to ensure that is incredibly difficult, and if it's not handled right, it causes the while-loop to loop infinitely. *A cornerstone of writing solid code is never writing loops that can possibly loop forever.*

The safercopy function tries to solve this by requiring the caller to give the lengths of the two strings it must deal with. By doing this, it can make certain checks about these strings that the copy function can't. It can check that the lengths are right, and that the to string has enough space, and it will *always* terminate. It's impossible for this function to run on forever like the copy function.

This is the idea behind never trusting the inputs you receive. If you assume that your function is going to get a string that's not terminated (which is common), then you can design your function so that it doesn't rely on it to work properly. If you need the arguments to never be NULL, then you should check for that, too. If the sizes should be within sane levels, then check that. You simply assume that whoever is calling you got it wrong, and then try to make it difficult for them to give you another bad state.

This extends to software you write that gets input from the external universe. The famous last words of the programmer are, "Nobody's going to do that." I've seen them say that and then the *next day* someone does exactly that, crashing or hacking their application. If you say nobody is going to do that, just throw in the code to make sure they simply can't hack your application. You'll be glad you did.

There is a diminishing return on this, but here's a list of things I try to do in all of the functions I write in C:

- For each parameter, identify what its preconditions are, and whether the precondition should cause a failure or return an error. If you are writing a library, favor errors over failures.

- Add assert calls at the beginning that check for each failure precondition using assert(test && "message");. This little hack does the test, and when it fails, the OS will typically print the assert line for you that includes that message. This is very helpful when you're trying to figure out why that assert is there.

- For the other preconditions, return the error code or use my check macro to give an error message. I didn't use check in this example since it would confuse the comparison.

- Document *why* these preconditions exist so that when a programmer hits the error, he or she can figure out if they're really necessary or not.

- If you're modifying the inputs, make sure that they are correctly formed when the function exits, or abort if they aren't.

- Always check the error codes of functions you use. For example, people frequently forget to check the return codes from fopen or fread, which causes them to use the resources the return codes give despite the error. This causes your program to crash or open an avenue for an attack.

- You also need to be returning consistent error codes so that you can do this for all of your functions. Once you get in this habit, you'll then understand why my check macros work the way they do.

Just doing these simple things will improve your resource handling and prevent quite a few errors.

Prevent Errors

In response to the previous example, you might hear people say, "Well, it's not very likely someone will use copy wrong." Despite the mountain of attacks made against this very kind of function, some people still believe that the probability of this error is very low. Probability is a funny thing because people are incredibly bad at guessing the probability of any event. People are, however, much better at determining if something is *possible*. They might say the error in copy is not probable, but they can't deny that it's possible.

The key reason is that for something to be probable, it first has to be possible. Determining the possibility is easy, since we can all imagine something happening. What's not so easy is determining its probability after that. Is the chance that someone might use copy wrong 20%, 10%, or 1%? Who knows? You'd need to gather evidence, look at rates of failure in many software packages, and probably survey real programmers about how they use the function.

This means, if you're going to prevent errors, you still need to try to prevent what's possible but first focus your energies on what's most probable. It may not be feasible to handle all of the possible ways your software can be broken, but you have to attempt it. But at the same time, if you don't constrain your efforts to the most probable events, then you'll be wasting time on irrelevant attacks.

Here's a process for determining what to prevent in your software:

- List all the possible errors that can happen, no matter how probable (within reason, of course). No point listing "aliens sucking your memories out to steal your passwords."

- Give each possible error a probability that's a percentage of the operations that can be vulnerable. If you are handling requests from the Internet, then it's the percentage of requests that can cause the error. If they are function calls, then it's what percentage of function calls can cause the error.

- Calculate the effort in number of hours or amount of code to prevent it. You could also just give an easy or hard metric, or any metric that prevents you from working on the impossible when there are easier things to fix still on the list.

- Rank them by effort (lowest to highest), and probability (highest to lowest). This is now your task list.

- Prevent all of the errors you can in this list, aiming for removing the possibility, then reducing the probability if you can't make it impossible.

- If there are errors you can't fix, then document them so someone else can fix them.

This little process will give you a nice list of things to do, but more importantly, keep you from working on useless things when there are other more important things to work on. You can also be more or less formal with this process. If you're doing a full security audit, this will be better done with a whole team and a nice spreadsheet. If you're just writing a function, then simply review the code and scratch these out into some comments. What's important is that you stop assuming that errors don't happen, and you work on removing them when you can without wasting effort.

Fail Early and Openly

If you encounter an error in C you have two choices:

- Return an error code.

- Abort the process.

This is just how it is, so what you need to do is make sure the failures happen quickly, are clearly documented, give an error message, and are easy for the programmer to avoid. This is why the check macros I've given you work the way they do. For every error you find, it prints a message, the file and line number where it happened, and forces a return code. If you just use my macros, you'll end up doing the right thing anyway.

I tend to prefer returning an error code to aborting the program. If it's catastrophic, then I will, but very few errors are truly catastrophic. A good example of when I'll abort a program is if I'm given an invalid pointer, as I did in safercopy. Instead of having the programmer experience a segmentation fault explosion somewhere, I catch it right away and abort. However, if it's common to pass in a NULL, then I'll probably change that to a check instead so that the caller can adapt and keep running.

In libraries, however, I try my hardest to *never* abort. The software using my library can decide if it should abort, and I'll typically abort only if the library is very badly used.

Finally, a big part of being open about errors is not using the same message or error code for more than one possible error. You typically see this with errors in external resources. A library will receive an error on a socket, and then simply report "bad socket." What they should do is return the error on the socket so that it can be properly debugged and fixed. When designing your error reporting, make sure you give a different error message for the different possible errors.

Document Assumptions

If you're following along and using this advice, then what you're doing is building a contract of how your functions expect the world to be. You've created preconditions for each argument, you've handled possible errors, and you're failing elegantly. The next step is to complete the contract and add invariants and postconditions.

An invariant is a condition that must be held true in some state while the function runs. This isn't very common in simple functions, but when you're dealing with complex structures, it becomes more necessary. A good example of an invariant is a condition where a structure is always initialized properly while it's being used. Another example would be that a sorted data structure is always sorted during processing.

A postcondition is a guarantee on the exit value or result of a function running. This can blend together with invariants, but this is something as simple as "function always returns 0 or -1 on error." Usually these are documented, but if your function returns an allocated resource, you can add a postcondition that checks to make sure it's returning something, and not NULL. Or, you can use NULL to indicate an error, so that your postcondition checks that the resource is deallocated on any errors.

In C programming, invariants and postconditions are usually used more in documentation than actual code or assertions. The best way to handle them is to add assert calls for the ones you can, then document the rest. If you do that, when people hit an error they can see what assumptions you made when writing the function.

Prevention over Documentation

A common problem when programmers write code is that they will document a common bug rather than simply fix it. My favorite is when the Ruby on Rails system simply assumed that all months had 30 days. Calendars are hard, so rather than fix it, programmers threw a tiny little comment somewhere that said this was on purpose, and then they refused to fix it for years. Every time someone would complain, they would bluster and yell, "But it's documented!"

Documentation doesn't matter if you can actually fix the problem, and if the function has a fatal flaw, then just don't include it until you can fix it. In the case of Ruby on Rails, not having date functions would have been better than including purposefully broken ones that nobody could use.

As you go through your defensive programming cleanups, try to fix everything you can. If you find yourself documenting more and more problems you can't fix, then consider redesigning the feature or simply removing it. If you *really* have to keep this horribly broken feature, then I suggest you write it, document it, and then find a new job before you are blamed for it.

Automate Everything

You are a programmer, and that means your job is putting other people out of jobs with automation. The pinnacle of this is putting yourself out of a job with your own automation. Obviously, you won't completely eliminate what you do, but if you're spending your whole day rerunning manual tests in your terminal, then your job isn't programming. You are doing QA, and you should automate yourself out of this QA job that you probably don't really want anyway.

The easiest way to do this is to write automated tests, or unit tests. In this book I'm going to get into how to do this easily, but I'll avoid most of the dogma about when you should write tests. I'll focus on how to write them, what to test, and how to be efficient at the testing.

Here are common things programmers fail to automate when they should:

- Testing and validation
- Build processes
- Deployment of software
- System administration
- Error reporting

Try to devote some of your time to automating this and you'll have more time to work on the fun stuff. Or, if this is fun to you, then maybe you should work on software that makes automating these things easier.

Simplify and Clarify

The concept of simplicity is a slippery one to many people, especially smart people. They generally confuse comprehension with simplicity. If they understand it, clearly it's simple. The actual test of simplicity is comparing something with something else that could be simpler. But you'll see people who write code go running to the most complex, obtuse structures possible because they think the simpler version of the same thing is dirty. A love affair with complexity is a programming sickness.

You can fight this disease by first telling yourself, "Simple and clear is not dirty, no matter what everyone else is doing." If everyone else is writing insane visitor patterns involving 19 classes over 12 interfaces, and you can do it with two string operations, then you win. They are wrong, no matter how elegant they think their complex monstrosity is.

Here's the simplest test of which function is better:

- Make sure both functions have no errors. It doesn't matter how fast or simple a function is if it has errors.

- If you can't fix one, then pick the other.

- Do they produce the same result? If not, then pick the one that has the result you need.

- If they produce the same result, then pick the one that either has fewer features, fewer branches, or you just think is simpler.

- Make sure you're not just picking the one that is most impressive. Simple and dirty beats complex and clean any day.

You'll notice that I mostly give up at the end and tell you to use your judgment. Simplicity is ironically a very complex thing, so using your taste as a guide is the best way to go. Just make sure that you adjust your view of what's "good" as you grow and gain more experience.

Question Authority

The final strategy is the most important because it breaks you out of the defensive programming mind-set and lets you transition into the creative mind-set. Defensive programming is authoritarian and can be cruel. The job of this mind-set is to make you follow rules, because without them you'll miss something or get distracted.

This authoritarian attitude has the disadvantage of disabling independent creative thought. Rules are necessary for getting things done, but being a slave to them will kill your creativity.

This final strategy means you should periodically question the rules you follow and assume that they could be wrong, just like the software you are reviewing. What I will typically do is go take a nonprogramming break and let the rules go after a session of defensive programming. Then I'll be ready to do some creative work or more defensive coding if I need to.

Order Is Not Important

The final thing I'll say on this philosophy is that I'm not telling you to do this in a strict order of "CREATE! DEFEND! CREATE! DEFEND!" At first you might want to do that, but I'd actually do either in varying amounts depending on what I wanted to do, and I might even meld them together with no defined boundary.

I also don't think one mind-set is better than another, or that there's a strict separation between them. You need both creativity and strictness to do programming well, so work on both if you want to improve.

Extra Credit

- The code in the book up to this point (and for the rest of it) potentially violates these rules. Go back and apply what you've learned to one exercise to see if you can improve it or find bugs.

- Find an open source project and give some of the files a similar code review. Submit a patch that fixes a bug.

Intermediate Makefiles

In the next three exercises you'll create a skeleton project directory to use in building your C programs later. This skeleton directory will be used for the rest of the book. In this exercise, I'll cover just the Makefile so you can understand it.

The purpose of this structure is to make it easy to build medium-sized programs without having to resort to configure tools. If done right, you can get very far with just GNU make and some small shell scripts.

The Basic Project Structure

The first thing to do is make a c-skeleton directory, and then put a set of basic files and directories in it that many projects have. Here's my starter:

Exercise 28 Session

```
$ mkdir c-skeleton
$ cd c-skeleton/
$ touch LICENSE README.md Makefile
$ mkdir bin src tests
$ cp dbg.h src/   # this is from Ex19
$ ls -l
total 8
-rw-r--r-- 1 zedshaw  staff     0 Mar 31 16:38 LICENSE
-rw-r--r-- 1 zedshaw  staff  1168 Apr  1 17:00 Makefile
-rw-r--r-- 1 zedshaw  staff     0 Mar 31 16:38 README.md
drwxr-xr-x 2 zedshaw  staff    68 Mar 31 16:38 bin
drwxr-xr-x 2 zedshaw  staff    68 Apr  1 10:07 build
drwxr-xr-x 3 zedshaw  staff   102 Apr  3 16:28 src
drwxr-xr-x 2 zedshaw  staff    68 Mar 31 16:38 tests
$ ls -l src
total 8
-rw-r--r-- 1 zedshaw  staff   982 Apr  3 16:28 dbg.h
$
```

At the end you see me do a ls -l so that you can see the final results.

Here's a breakdown:

LICENSE   If you release the source of your projects, you'll want to include a license. If you don't, though, the code is copyright by you and nobody else has rights to it by default.

README.md   Basic instructions for using your project go here. It ends in .md so that it will be interpreted as markdown.

Makefile   The main build file for the project.

bin/   Where programs that users can run go. This is usually empty, and the Makefile will create it if it's not there.

build/   Where libraries and other build artifacts go. Also empty, and the Makefile will create it if it's not there.

src/   Where the source code goes, usually .c and .h files.

tests/   Where automated tests go.

src/dbg.h   I copied the dbg.h from Exercise 19 into src/ for later.

I'll now break down each of the components of this skeleton project so that you can understand how it works.

Makefile

The first thing I'll cover is the Makefile, because from that you can understand how everything else works. The Makefile in this exercise is much more detailed than ones you've used so far, so I'll break it down after you type it in:

Makefile

```
1     CFLAGS=-g -O2 -Wall -Wextra -Isrc -rdynamic -DNDEBUG $(OPTFLAGS)
2     LIBS=-ldl $(OPTLIBS)
3     PREFIX?=/usr/local
4
5     SOURCES=$(wildcard src/**/*.c src/*.c)
6     OBJECTS=$(patsubst %.c,%.o,$(SOURCES))
7
8     TEST_SRC=$(wildcard tests/*_tests.c)
9     TESTS=$(patsubst %.c,%,$(TEST_SRC))
10
11    TARGET=build/libYOUR_LIBRARY.a
12    SO_TARGET=$(patsubst %.a,%.so,$(TARGET))
13
14    # The Target Build
15    all: $(TARGET) $(SO_TARGET) tests
16
17    dev: CFLAGS=-g -Wall -Isrc -Wall -Wextra $(OPTFLAGS)
18    dev: all
19
20    $(TARGET): CFLAGS += -fPIC
21    $(TARGET): build $(OBJECTS)
22        ar rcs $@ $(OBJECTS)
23        ranlib $@
```

```
24    $(SO_TARGET): $(TARGET) $(OBJECTS)
25        $(CC) -shared -o $@ $(OBJECTS)
26
27    build:
28        @mkdir -p build
29        @mkdir -p bin
30
31    # The Unit Tests
32    .PHONY: tests
33    tests: CFLAGS += $(TARGET)
34    tests: $(TESTS)
35        sh ./tests/runtests.sh
36
37    # The Cleaner
38    clean:
39        rm -rf build $(OBJECTS) $(TESTS)
40        rm -f tests/tests.log
41        find . -name "*.gc*" -exec rm {} \;
42        rm -rf `find . -name "*.dSYM" -print`
43
44    # The Install
45    install: all
46        install -d $(DESTDIR)/$(PREFIX)/lib/
47        install $(TARGET) $(DESTDIR)/$(PREFIX)/lib/
48
49    # The Checker
50    check:
51        @echo Files with potentially dangerous functions.
52        @egrep '[^_.>a-zA-Z0-9](str(n?cpy|n?cat|xfrm|n?dup|str|pbrk|tok|_)\
53                |stpn?cpy|a?sn?printf|byte_)' $(SOURCES) || true
```

Remember that you need to consistently indent the Makefile with tab characters. Your text editor should know that and do the right thing. If it doesn't, get a different text editor. No programmer should use an editor that fails at something so simple.

The Header

This Makefile is designed to build a library reliably on almost any platform using special features of GNU make. We'll be working on this library later, so I'll break down each part in sections, starting with the header.

> **Makefile:1**   These are the usual CFLAGS that you set in all of your projects, along with a few others that may be needed to build libraries. *You may need to adjust these for different platforms.* Notice the OPTFLAGS variable at the end that lets people augment the build options as needed.

> **Makefile:2**   These options are used when linking a library. Someone else can then augment the linking options using the OPTLIBS variable.

Makefile:3 This code sets an *optional* variable called PREFIX that will only have this value if the person running the Makefile didn't already give a PREFIX setting. That's what the ?= does.

Makefile:5 This fancy line of awesomeness *dynamically* creates the SOURCES variable by doing a wildcard search for all *.c files in the src/ directory. You have to give both src/**/*.c and src/*.c so that GNU make will include the files in src and the files below it.

Makefile:6 Once you have the list of source files, you can then use the patsubst to take the SOURCES list of *.c files and make a *new* list of all the object files. You do this by telling patsubst to change all %.c extensions to %.o, and then those extensions are assigned to OBJECTS.

Makefile:8 We're using the wildcard again to find all of the test source files for the unit tests. These are separate from the library's source files.

Makefile:9 Then, we're using the same patsubst trick to dynamically get all the TEST targets. In this case, I'm stripping away the .c extension so that a full program will be made with the same name. Previously, I had replaced the .c with {.o} so an object file is created.

Makefile:11 Finally, we say the ultimate target is build/libYOUR_LIBRARY.a, which you will change to be whatever library you're actually trying to build.

This completes the top of the Makefile, but I should explain what I mean by "lets people augment the build." When you run Make, you can do this:

```
# WARNING! Just a demonstration, won't really work right now.
# this installs the library into /tmp
$ make PREFIX=/tmp install
# this tells it to add pthreads
$ make OPTFLAGS=-pthread
```

If you pass in options that match the same kind of variables you have in your Makefile, then those will show up in your build. You can then use this to change how the Makefile runs. The first variable alters the PREFIX so that it installs into /tmp instead. The second one sets OPTFLAGS so that the -pthread option is present.

The Target Build

Continuing with the breakdown of the Makefile, I'm actually building the object files and targets:

Makefile:14 Remember that the first target is what make runs by default when no target is given. In this, it's called all: and it gives $(TARGET) tests as the targets to build.

Look up at the TARGET variable and you see that's the library, so all: will first build the library. The tests target is further down in the Makefile and builds the unit tests.

Makefile:16   Here's another target for making "developer builds" that introduces a technique for changing options for just one target. If I do a "dev build," I want the CFLAGS to include options like –Wextra that are useful for finding bugs. If you place them on the target line as options like this, then give another line that says the original target (in this case all), then it will change the options you set. I use this for setting different flags on different platforms that need it.

Makefile:19   This builds the TARGET library, whatever that is. It also uses the same trick from line 15, giving a target with just options and ways to alter them for this run. In this case, I'm adding –fPIC just for the library build, using the += syntax to add it on.

Makefile:20   Now we see the real target, where I say first make the build directory, and then compile all of the OBJECTS.

Makefile:21   This runs the ar command that actually makes the TARGET. The syntax $@ $(OBJECTS) is a way of saying, "put the target for this Makefile source here and all the OBJECTS after that." In this case, the $@ maps back to the $(TARGET) on line 19, which maps to build/libYOUR_LIBRARY.a. It seems like a lot to keep track of in this indirection, and it can be, but once you get it working, you just change TARGET at the top and build a whole new library.

Makefile:22   Finally, to make the library, you run ranlib on the TARGET and it's built.

Makefile:23-24   This just makes the build/ or bin/ directories if they don't exist. This is then referenced from line 19 when it gives the build target to make sure the build/ directory is made.

You now have all of the stuff you need to build the software, so we'll create a way to build and run unit tests to do automated testing.

The Unit Tests

C is different from other languages because it's easier to create one tiny little program for each thing you're testing. Some testing frameworks try to emulate the module concept other languages have and do dynamic loading, but this doesn't work well in C. It's also unnecessary, because you can just make a single program that's run for each test instead.

I'll cover this part of the Makefile, and then later you'll see the contents of the tests/ directory that make it actually work.

Makefile:29 If you have a target that's not real, but there is a directory or file with that name, then you need to tag the target with .PHONY: so make will ignore the file and always run.

Makefile:30 I use the same trick for modifying the CFLAGS variable to add the TARGET to the build so that each of the test programs will be linked with the TARGET library. In this case, it will add build/libYOUR_LIBRARY.a to the linking.

Makefile:31 Then I have the actual tests: target, which depends on all of the programs listed in the TESTS variable that we created in the header. This one line actually says, "Make, use what you know about building programs and the current CFLAGS settings to build each program in TESTS."

Makefile:32 Finally, when all of the TESTS are built, there's a simple shell script I'll create later that knows how to run them all and report their output. This line actually runs it so you can see the test results.

For the unit testing to work, you'll need to create a little shell script that knows how to run the programs. Go ahead and create this tests/runtests.sh script:

runtests.sh

```
1    echo "Running unit tests:"
2
3    for i in tests/*_tests
4    do
5        if test -f $i
6        then
7            if $VALGRIND ./$i 2>> tests/tests.log
8            then
9                echo $i PASS
10           else
11               echo "ERROR in test $i: here's tests/tests.log"
12               echo "------"
13               tail tests/tests.log
14               exit 1
15           fi
16       fi
17   done
18
19   echo ""
```

I'll be using this later when I cover how unit tests work.

The Cleaner

I now have fully working unit tests, so next up is making things clean when I need to reset everything.

Makefile:38   The `clean:` target starts things off when we need to clean up the project.

Makefile:39-42   This cleans out most of the junk that various compilers and tools leave behind. It also gets rid of the `build/` directory and uses a trick at the end to cleanly erase the weird `*.dSYM` directories that Apple's XCode leaves behind for debugging purposes.

If you run into junk that you need to clean out, simply augment the list of things being deleted in this target.

The Install

After that, I'll need a way to install the project, and for a `Makefile` that's building a library, I just need to put something in the common PREFIX directory, usually `/usr/local/lib`.

Makefile:45   This makes `install:` depend on the `all:` target, so that when you run make `install`, it will be sure to build everything.

Makefile:46   I then use the program `install` to create the target `lib` directory if it doesn't exist. In this case, I'm trying to make the install as flexible as possible by using two variables that are conventions for installers. DESTDIR is handed to make by installers, which do their builds in secure or odd locations, to build packages. PREFIX is used when people want the project to be installed in someplace other than `/usr/local`.

Makefile:47   After that, I'm just using `install` to actually install the library where it needs to go.

The purpose of the `install` program is to make sure things have the right permissions set. When you run make `install`, you usually have to do it as the root user, so the typical build process is make `&& sudo make install`.

The Checker

The very last part of this `Makefile` is a bonus that I include in my C projects to help me dig out any attempts to use the bad functions in C. These are namely the string functions and other un-protected buffer functions.

Makefile:50   This sets a variable that's a big regex looking for bad functions like `strcpy`.

Makefile:51   The `check:` target allows you to run a check whenever you need to.

Makefile:52   This is just a way to print a message, but doing @echo tells make to not print the command, just its output.

Makefile:53 Run the egrep command on the source files to look for any bad patterns. The `||` `true` at the end is a way to prevent make from thinking that egrep failed if it doesn't find errors.

When you run this, it will have the odd effect of returning an error when there's nothing bad going on.

What You Should See

I have two more exercises to go before I'm done building the project skeleton directory, but here's me testing out the features of the Makefile.

Exercise 28 Session

```
$ make clean
rm -rf build
rm -f tests/tests.log
find . -name "*.gc*" -exec rm {} \;
rm -rf `find . -name "*.dSYM" -print`
$ make check
$ make
```

When I run the `clean:` target, it works, but because I don't have any source files in the `src/` directory, none of the other commands really work. I'll finish that up in the next exercises.

Extra Credit

- Try to get the Makefile to actually work by putting a source and header file in `src/` and making the library. You shouldn't need a `main` function in the source file.

- Research what functions the `check:` target is looking for in the BADFUNCS regular expression that it's using.

- If you don't do automated unit testing, then go read about it so you're prepared later.

Libraries and Linking

A central part of any C program is the ability to link it to libraries that your OS provides. Linking is how you get additional features for your program that someone else created and packaged on the system. You've been using some standard libraries that are automatically included, but I'm going to explain the different types of libraries and what they do.

First off, libraries are poorly designed in every programming language. I have no idea why, but it seems language designers think of linking as something they just slap on later. Libraries are usually confusing, hard to deal with, can't do versioning right, and end up being linked differently everywhere.

C is no different, but the way linking and libraries are done in C is an artifact of how the UNIX operating system and executable formats were designed years ago. Learning how C links things helps you understand how your OS works and how it runs your programs.

To start off, there are two basic types of libraries:

static You made one of these when you used `ar` and `ranlib` to create the `libYOUR_LIBRARY.a` in the last exercise. This kind of library is nothing more than a container for a set of `.o` object files and their functions, and you can treat it like one big `.o` file when building your programs.

dynamic These typically end in `.so`, `.dll` or about one million other endings on OS X, depending on the version and who happened to be working that day. Seriously though, OS X adds `.dylib`, `.bundle`, and `.framework` with not much distinction among the three. These files are built and then placed in a common location. When you run your program, the OS dynamically loads these files and links them to your program on the fly.

I tend to like static libraries for small- to medium-sized projects, because they are easier to deal with and work on more operating systems. I also like to put all of the code I can into a static library so that I can then link it to unit tests and to the file programs as needed.

Dynamic libraries are good for larger systems, when space is tight, or if you have a large number of programs that use common functionality. In this case, you don't want to statically link all of the code for the common features to every program, so you put it in a dynamic library so that it is loaded only once for all of them.

In the previous exercise, I laid out how to make a static library (a `.a` file), and that's what I'll use in the rest of the book. In this exercise, I'm going to show you how to make a simple .so library, and how to dynamically load it with the UNIX `dlopen` system. I'll have you do this manually so that you understand everything that's actually happening, then for extra credit you'll use the `c-skeleton` skeleton to create it.

Dynamically Loading a Shared Library

To do this, I will create two source files: One will be used to make a libex29.so library, the other will be a program called ex29 that can load this library and run functions from it.

```
1    #include <stdio.h>
2    #include <ctype.h>
3    #include "dbg.h"
4
5
6    int print_a_message(const char *msg)
7    {
8        printf("A STRING: %s\n", msg);
9
10       return 0;
11   }
12
13
14   int uppercase(const char *msg)
15   {
16       int i = 0;
17
18       // BUG: \0 termination problems
19       for(i = 0; msg[i] != '\0'; i++) {
20           printf("%c", toupper(msg[i]));
21       }
22
23       printf("\n");
24
25       return 0;
26   }
27
28   int lowercase(const char *msg)
29   {
30       int i = 0;
31
32       // BUG: \0 termination problems
33       for(i = 0; msg[i] != '\0'; i++) {
34           printf("%c", tolower(msg[i]));
35       }
36
37       printf("\n");
38
39       return 0;
40   }
41
42   int fail_on_purpose(const char *msg)
43   {
44       return 1;
45   }
```

There's nothing fancy in there, although there are some bugs I'm leaving in on purpose to see if you've been paying attention. You'll fix those later.

What we want to do is use the functions dlopen, dlsym, and dlclose to work with the above functions.

ex29.c

```
1    #include <stdio.h>
2    #include "dbg.h"
3    #include <dlfcn.h>
4
5    typedef int (*lib_function) (const char *data);
6
7    int main(int argc, char *argv[])
8    {
9        int rc = 0;
10       check(argc == 4, "USAGE: ex29 libex29.so function data");
11
12       char *lib_file = argv[1];
13       char *func_to_run = argv[2];
14       char *data = argv[3];
15
16       void *lib = dlopen(lib_file, RTLD_NOW);
17       check(lib != NULL, "Failed to open the library %s: %s", lib_file,
18               dlerror());
19
20       lib_function func = dlsym(lib, func_to_run);
21       check(func != NULL,
22               "Did not find %s function in the library %s: %s", func_to_run,
23               lib_file, dlerror());
24
25       rc = func(data);
26       check(rc == 0, "Function %s return %d for data: %s", func_to_run,
27               rc, data);
28
29       rc = dlclose(lib);
30       check(rc == 0, "Failed to close %s", lib_file);
31
32       return 0;
33
34   error:
35       return 1;
36   }
```

I'll now break this down so you can see what's going on in this small bit of useful code:

> **ex29.c:5**   I'll use this function pointer definition later to call functions in the library. This is nothing new, but make sure you understand what it's doing.

ex29.c:17 After the usual setup for a small program, I use the dlopen function to load up the library that's indicated by lib_file. This function returns a handle that we use later, which works a lot like opening a file.

ex29.c:18 If there's an error, I do the usual check and exit, but notice at then end that I'm using dlerror to find out what the library-related error was.

ex29.c:20 I use dlsym to get a function out of the lib by its *string* name in func_to_run. This is the powerful part, since I'm dynamically getting a pointer to a function based on a string I got from the command line argv.

ex29.c:23 I then call the func function that was returned, and check its return value.

ex29.c:26 Finally, I close the library up just like I would a file. Usually, you keep these open the whole time the program is running, so closing it at the end isn't as useful, but I'm demonstrating it here.

What You Should See

Now that you know what this file does, here's a shell session of me building the libex29.so, ex29 and then working with it. Follow along so you learn how these things are manually built.

Exercise 29 Session

```
# compile the lib file and make the .so
# you may need -fPIC here on some platforms. add that if you get an error
$ cc -c libex29.c -o libex29.o
$ cc -shared -o libex29.so libex29.o

# make the loader program
$ cc -Wall -g -DNDEBUG ex29.c -ldl -o ex29

# try it out with some things that work
$ ex29 ./libex29.so print_a_message "hello there"
-bash: ex29: command not found
$ ./ex29 ./libex29.so print_a_message "hello there"
A STRING: hello there
$ ./ex29 ./libex29.so uppercase "hello there"
HELLO THERE
$ ./ex29 ./libex29.so lowercase "HELLO tHeRe"
hello there
$ ./ex29 ./libex29.so fail_on_purpose "i fail"
[ERROR] (ex29.c:23: errno: None) Function fail_on_purpose return 1 for\
            data: i fail

# try to give it bad args
$ ./ex29 ./libex29.so fail_on_purpose
[ERROR] (ex29.c:11: errno: None) USAGE: ex29 libex29.so function data
```

```
# try calling a function that is not there
$ ./ex29 ./libex29.so adfasfasdf asdfadff
[ERROR] (ex29.c:20: errno: None) Did not find adfasfasdf
    function in the library libex29.so: dlsym(0x1076009b0, adfasfasdf):\
        symbol not found

# try loading a .so that is not there
$ ./ex29 ./libex.so adfasfasdf asdfadfas
[ERROR] (ex29.c:17: errno: No such file or directory) Failed to open
    the library libex.so: dlopen(libex.so, 2): image not found
$
```

One thing that you may run into is that every OS, every version of every OS, and every compiler on every version of every OS, seems to want to change the way you build a shared library every time some new programmer thinks it's wrong. If the line I use to make the libex29.so file is wrong, then let me know and I'll add some comments for other platforms.

WARNING! Sometimes you'll do what you think is normal, and run this command cc -Wall -g -DNDEBUG -ldl ex29.c -o ex29 thinking everything will work, but nope. You see, on some platforms the order of where libraries go makes them work or not, and for no real reason. In Debian or Ubuntu, you have to do cc -Wall -g -DNDEBUG ex29.c -ldl -o ex29 for no reason at all. It's just the way it is. So since this works on OS X I'm doing it here, but in the future, if you link against a dynamic library and it can't find a function, try shuffling things around.

The irritation here is there's an actual platform difference on nothing more than the order of command line arguments. On no rational planet should putting an -ldl at one position be different from another. It's an option, and having to know these things is incredibly annoying.

How to Break It

Open libex29.so and edit it with an editor that can handle binary files. Change a couple of bytes, then close itlibex29.so. Try to see if you can get the dlopen function to load it even though you've corrupted it.

Extra Credit

- Were you paying attention to the bad code I have in the libex29.c functions? Do you see how, even though I use a for-loop they still check for '\0' endings? Fix this so that the functions always take a length for the string to work with inside the function.

- Take the c-skeleton skeleton, and create a new project for this exercise. Put the libex29.c file in the src/ directory. Change the Makefile so that it builds this as build/libex29.so.

- Take the ex29.c file and put it in tests/ex29_tests.c so that it runs as a unit test. Make this all work, which means that you'll have to change it so that it loads the build/libex29.so file and runs tests similar to what I did manually above.

- Read the man dlopen documentation and read about all of the related functions. Try some of the other options to dlopen beside RTLD_NOW.

Automated Testing

Automated testing is used frequently in other languages like Python and Ruby, but rarely used in C. Part of the reason comes from the difficulty of automatically loading and testing pieces of C code. In this chapter, we'll create a very small testing framework and get your skeleton directory to build an example test case.

The framework I'm going to use, and you'll include in your c-skeleton skeleton, is called *minunit* which started with a tiny snippet of code by Jera Design. I evolved it further, to be this:

minunit.h

```
1    #undef NDEBUG
2    #ifndef _minunit_h
3    #define _minunit_h
4
5    #include <stdio.h>
6    #include <dbg.h>
7    #include <stdlib.h>
8
9    #define mu_suite_start() char *message = NULL
10
11   #define mu_assert(test, message) if (!(test)) {\
12       log_err(message); return message; }
13   #define mu_run_test(test) debug("\n-----%s", " " #test); \
14       message = test(); tests_run++; if (message) return message;
15
16   #define RUN_TESTS(name) int main(int argc, char *argv[]) {\
17       argc = 1; \
18       debug("----- RUNNING: %s", argv[0]);\
19       printf("----\nRUNNING: %s\n", argv[0]);\
20       char *result = name();\
21       if (result != 0) {\
22           printf("FAILED: %s\n", result);\
23       }\
24       else {\
25           printf("ALL TESTS PASSED\n");\
26       }\
27       printf("Tests run: %d\n", tests_run);\
28       exit(result != 0);\
29   }
30
31   int tests_run;
32
33   #endif
```

There's practically nothing left of the original, since now I'm using the dbg.h macros and a large macro that I created at the end for the boilerplate test runner. Even with this tiny amount of code, we'll create a fully functioning unit test system that you can use in your C code once it's combined with a shell script to run the tests.

Wiring Up the Test Framework

To continue this exercise, you should have your src/libex29.c working. You should have also completed the Exercise 29 Extra Credit to get the ex29.c loader program to properly run. In Exercise 29, I ask you to make it work like a unit test, but I'm going to start over and show you how to do that with minunit.h.

The first thing to do is create a simple empty unit test name, tests/libex29_tests.c with this in it:

ex30.c

```
 1    #include "minunit.h"
 2
 3    char *test_dlopen()
 4    {
 5
 6        return NULL;
 7    }
 8
 9    char *test_functions()
10    {
11
12        return NULL;
13    }
14
15    char *test_failures()
16    {
17
18        return NULL;
19    }
20
21    char *test_dlclose()
22    {
23
24        return NULL;
25    }
26
27    char *all_tests()
28    {
29        mu_suite_start();
30
31        mu_run_test(test_dlopen);
```

```
32        mu_run_test(test_functions);
33        mu_run_test(test_failures);
34        mu_run_test(test_dlclose);
35
36        return NULL;
37    }
38
39    RUN_TESTS(all_tests);
```

This code is demonstrating the RUN_TESTS macro in tests/minunit.h and how to use the other test runner macros. I have the actual test functions stubbed out so that you can see how to structure a unit test. I'll break this file down first:

libex29_tests.c:1   This includes the minunit.h framework.

libex29_tests.c:3-7   A first test. Tests are structured so that they take no arguments and return a char * that's NULL on *success*. This is important because the other macros will be used to return an error message to the test runner.

libex29_tests.c:9-25   These are more tests that are the same as the first.

libex29_tests.c:27   The runner function that will control all of the other tests. It has the same form as any other test case, but it gets configured with some additional gear.

libex29_tests.c:28   This sets up some common stuff for a test with mu_suite_start.

libex29_tests.c:30   This is how you say what tests to run, using the mu_run_test macro.

libex29_tests.c:35   After you say what tests to run, you then return NULL just like a normal test function.

libex29_tests.c:38   Finally, you just use the big RUN_TESTS macro to wire up the main method with all of the goodies, and tell it to run the all_tests starter.

That's all there is to running a test, and now you should try getting just this to run within the project skeleton. Here's what it looks like when I do it:

Exercise 30 Session

---

not printable

I first did a make clean and then I ran the build, which remade the template libYOUR_LIBRARY .a and libYOUR_LIBRARY.so files. Remember that you did this in the Extra Credit for Exercise 29, but just in case you didn't get it, here's the diff for the Makefile I'm using now:

ex30.Makefile.diff

```
diff --git a/code/c-skeleton/Makefile b/code/c-skeleton/Makefile
index 135d538..21b92bf 100644
--- a/code/c-skeleton/Makefile
+++ b/code/c-skeleton/Makefile
```

```
@@ -9,9 +9,10 @@ TEST_SRC=$(wildcard tests/*_tests.c)
 TESTS=$(patsubst %.c,%,$(TEST_SRC))

 TARGET=build/libYOUR_LIBRARY.a
+SO_TARGET=$(patsubst %.a,%.so,$(TARGET))

 # The Target Build
-all: $(TARGET) tests
+all: $(TARGET) $(SO_TARGET) tests

 dev: CFLAGS=-g -Wall -Isrc -Wall -Wextra $(OPTFLAGS)
 dev: all
@@ -21,6 +22,9 @@ $(TARGET): build $(OBJECTS)
     ar rcs $@ $(OBJECTS)
     ranlib $@

+$(SO_TARGET): $(TARGET) $(OBJECTS)
+ $(CC) -shared -o $@ $(OBJECTS)
+
 build:
     @mkdir -p build
     @mkdir -p bin
```

With those changes you should now be building everything and finally be able to fill in the remaining unit test functions:

libex29_tests.c

```c
1    #include "minunit.h"
2    #include <dlfcn.h>
3
4    typedef int (*lib_function) (const char *data);
5    char *lib_file = "build/libYOUR_LIBRARY.so";
6    void *lib = NULL;
7
8    int check_function(const char *func_to_run, const char *data,
9            int expected)
10   {
11       lib_function func = dlsym(lib, func_to_run);
12       check(func != NULL,
13               "Did not find %s function in the library %s: %s", func_to_run,
14               lib_file, dlerror());
15
16       int rc = func(data);
17       check(rc == expected, "Function %s return %d for data: %s",
18               func_to_run, rc, data);
19
20       return 1;
21   error:
22       return 0;
23   }
24
25   char *test_dlopen()
```

```
26    {
27        lib = dlopen(lib_file, RTLD_NOW);
28        mu_assert(lib != NULL, "Failed to open the library to test.");
29
30        return NULL;
31    }
32
33    char *test_functions()
34    {
35        mu_assert(check_function("print_a_message", "Hello", 0),
36                "print_a_message failed.");
37        mu_assert(check_function("uppercase", "Hello", 0),
38                "uppercase failed.");
39        mu_assert(check_function("lowercase", "Hello", 0),
40                "lowercase failed.");
41
42        return NULL;
43    }
44
45    char *test_failures()
46    {
47        mu_assert(check_function("fail_on_purpose", "Hello", 1),
48                "fail_on_purpose should fail.");
49
50        return NULL;
51    }
52
53    char *test_dlclose()
54    {
55        int rc = dlclose(lib);
56        mu_assert(rc == 0, "Failed to close lib.");
57
58        return NULL;
59    }
60
61    char *all_tests()
62    {
63        mu_suite_start();
64
65        mu_run_test(test_dlopen);
66        mu_run_test(test_functions);
67        mu_run_test(test_failures);
68        mu_run_test(test_dlclose);
69
70        return NULL;
71    }
72
73    RUN_TESTS(all_tests);
```

Hopefully by now you can figure out what's going on, since there's nothing new in this except for the check_function function. This is a common pattern where I use a chunk of code repeatedly, and then simply automate it by either creating a function or a macro for it. In this case, I'm going to run functions in the `.so` that I load, so I just made a little function to do it.

Extra Credit

- This works but it's probably a bit messy. Clean the c-skeleton directory up so that it has all of these files, but remove any of the code related to Exercise 29. You should be able to copy this directory over and kick-start new projects without much editing.

- Study the `runtests.sh`, and then go read about bash syntax so you know what it does. Do you think you could write a C version of this script?

Common Undefined Behavior

At this point in the book, it's time to introduce you to the most common kinds of UB that you will encounter. C has 191 behaviors that the standards committee has decided aren't defined by the standard, and therefore anything goes. Some of these behaviors are legitimately not the compiler's job, but the vast majority are simply lazy capitulations by the standards committee that cause annoyances, or worse, defects. An example of laziness:

An unmatched "or" character is encountered on a logical source line during tokenization.

In this instance, the C99 standard actually allows a compiler writer to fail at a parsing task that a junior in college could get right. Why is this? Who knows, but most likely someone on the standards committee was working on a C compiler with this defect and managed to get this in the standard rather than fix their compiler. Or, as I said, simple laziness.

The crux of the issue with UB is the difference between the C abstract machine, defined in the standard and real computers. The C standard describes the C language according to a strictly defined abstract machine. This is a perfectly valid way to design a language, except where the C standard goes wrong: It doesn't require compilers to implement this abstract machine and enforce its specification. Instead, a compiler writer can completely ignore the abstract machine in 191 instances of the standard. It should really be called an "abstract machine, but", as in, "It's a strictly defined abstract machine, but..."

This allows the standards committee and compiler implementers to have their cake and eat it, too. They can have a standard that is full of omissions, lax specification, and errors, but when *you* encounter one of these, they can point at the abstract machine and simply say in their best robot voice, "THE ABSTRACT MACHINE IS ALL THAT MATTERS. YOU DO NOT CONFORM!" Yet, in 191 instances that compiler writers don't have to conform, you do. You are a second class citizen, even though the language is really written for you to use.

This means that *you*, not the compiler writer, are left to enforce the rules of an abstract computational machine, and when you inevitably fail, it's your fault. The compiler doesn't have to flag the UB, do anything reasonable, and it's your fault for not memorizing all 191 rules that should be avoided. You are just stupid for not memorizing 191 complex potholes on the road to C. This is a wonderful situation for the classic know-it-all type who can memorize these 191 finer points of annoyance with which to beat beginners to intellectual death.

There's an additional hypocrisy with UB that is doubly infuriating. If you show a C fanatic code that properly uses C strings but can overwrite the string terminator, they will say, "That's UB. It's not the C language's fault!" However, if you show them UB that has `while(x)  x  <<=  1` in it, they will say, "That's UB idiot! Fix your damn code!" This lets the C fanatic simultaneously use UB to defend the purity of C's design, and also beat you up for being an idiot who writes bad code. Some UB is meant as, "you can ignore the security of this since it's not C's fault", and other UB is meant as, "you are an idiot for writing this code," and the distinction between the two is not specified in the standard.

As you can see, I am *not* a fan of the huge list of UB. I had to memorize all of these before the C99 standard, and just didn't bother to memorize the changes. I'd simply moved on to a way and found a way to avoid as much UB as I possibly could, trying to stay within the abstract machine specification while also working with real machines. This turns out to be almost impossible, so I just don't write new code in C anymore because of its glaringly obvious problems.

WARNING! The technical explanation as to why C UB is wrong comes from Alan Turing:

1.   C UB contains behaviors that are lexical, semantic, and execution based.

2.   The lexical and semantic behaviors can be detected by the compiler.

3.   The execution-based behaviors fall into Turing's definition of the *halting problem*, and are therefore NP-complete.

4.   This means that to avoid C UB, it requires solving one of the oldest proven unsolvable problems in computer science, making UB effectively impossible for a computer to avoid.

To put it more succinctly: "If the only way to know that you've violated the abstract machine with UB is to run your C program, then you will never be able to completely avoid UB."

UB 20

Because of this, I'm going to list the top 20 undefined behaviors in C, and tell you how to avoid them as best I can. In general, the way to avoid UB is to write clean code, but some of these behaviors are impossible to avoid. For example, writing past the end of a C string is an undefined behavior, yet it's easily done by accident and externally accessible to an attacker. This list will also include related UB that all fall into the same category but with differing contexts.

Common UBs

1.   An object is referred to outside of its lifetime (6.2.4).

   • The value of a pointer to an object whose lifetime has ended is used (6.2.4).

   • The value of an object with automatic storage duration is used while it is indeterminate (6.2.4, 6.7.8, 6.8).

2. Conversion to or from an integer type produces a value outside the range that can be represented (6.3.1.4).

    - Demotion of one real floating type to another produces a value outside the range that can be represented (6.3.1.5).

3. Two declarations of the same object or function specify types that are not compatible (6.2.7).

4. An lvalue having array type is converted to a pointer to the initial element of the array, and the array object has register storage class (6.3.2.1).

    - An attempt is made to use the value of a void expression, or an implicit or explicit conversion (except to void) is applied to a void expression (6.3.2.2).

    - Conversion of a pointer to an integer type produces a value outside the range that can be represented (6.3.2.3).

    - Conversion between two pointer types produces a result that is incorrectly aligned (6.3.2.3).

    - A pointer is used to call a function whose type is not compatible with the pointed-to type (6.3.2.3).

    - The operand of the unary * operator has an invalid value (6.5.3.2).

    - A pointer is converted to other than an integer or pointer type (6.5.4).

    - Addition or subtraction of a pointer into, or just beyond, an array object and an integer type produces a result that does not point into, or just beyond, the same array object (6.5.6).

    - Addition or subtraction of a pointer into, or just beyond, an array object and an integer type produces a result that points just beyond the array object and is used as the operand of a unary * operator that is evaluated (6.5.6).

    - Pointers that do not point into, or just beyond, the same array object are subtracted (6.5.6).

    - An array subscript is out of range, even if an object is apparently accessible with the given subscript (as in the lvalue expression a[1][7] given the declaration int a[4][5]) (6.5.6).

    - The result of subtracting two pointers is not representable in an object of type ptrdiff_t (6.5.6).

    - Pointers that do not point to the same aggregate or union (nor just beyond the same array object) are compared using relational operators (6.5.8).

    - An attempt is made to access, or generate a pointer to just past, a flexible array member of a structure when the referenced object provides no elements for that array (6.7.2.1).

- Two pointer types that are required to be compatible are not identically qualified, or are not pointers to compatible types (6.7.5.1).

- The size expression in an array declaration is not a constant expression and evaluates at program execution time to a nonpositive value (6.7.5.2).

- The pointer passed to a library function array parameter does not have a value such that all address computations and object accesses are valid (7.1.4).

5.   The program attempts to modify a string literal (6.4.5).

6.   An object has its stored value accessed other than by an lvalue of an allowable type (6.5).

7.   An attempt is made to modify the result of a function call, a conditional operator, an assignment operator, or a comma operator, or to access it after the next sequence point (6.5.2.2, 6.5.15, 6.5.16, 6.5.17).

8.   The value of the second operand of the / or % operator is zero (6.5.5).

9.   An object is assigned to an inexactly overlapping object or to an exactly overlapping object with incompatible type (6.5.16.1).

10. A constant expression in an initializer is not, or does not evaluate to, one of the following: an arithmetic constant expression, a null pointer constant, an address constant, or an address constant for an object type plus or minus an integer constant expression (6.6).

- An arithmetic constant expression does not have arithmetic type; has operands that are not integer constants, floating constants, enumeration constants, character constants, or sizeof expressions; or contains casts (outside operands to sizeof operators) other than conversions of arithmetic types to arithmetic types (6.6).

11. An attempt is made to modify an object defined with a const-qualified type through use of an lvalue with non-const-qualified type (6.7.3).

12. A function with external linkage is declared with an inline function specifier, but is not also defined in the same translation unit (6.7.4).

13. The value of an unnamed member of a structure or union is used (6.7.8).

14. The } that terminates a function is reached, and the value of the function call is used by the caller (6.9.1).

15. A file with the same name as one of the standard headers, not provided as part of the implementation, is placed in any of the standard places that are searched for included source files (7.1.2).

16. The value of an argument to a character handling function is neither equal to the value of EOF nor representable as an unsigned char (7.4).

17. The value of the result of an integer arithmetic or conversion function cannot be represented (7.8.2.1, 7.8.2.2, 7.8.2.3, 7.8.2.4, 7.20.6.1, 7.20.6.2, 7.20.1).

18. The value of a pointer to a FILE object is used after the associated file is closed (7.19.3).

    - The stream for the `fflush` function points to an input stream or to an update stream in which the most recent operation was input (7.19.5.2).

    - The string pointed to by the mode argument in a call to the `fopen` function does not exactly match one of the specified character sequences (7.19.5.3).

    - An output operation on an update stream is followed by an input operation without an intervening call to the `fflush` function or a file positioning function, or an input operation on an update stream is followed by an output operation with an intervening call to a file positioning function (7.19.5.3).

19. A conversion specification for a formatted output function uses a # or 0 flag with a conversion specifier other than those described (7.19.6.1, 7.24.2.1). * An s conversion specifier is encountered by one of the formatted output functions, and the argument is missing the null terminator (unless a precision is specified that does not require null termination) (7.19.6.1, 7.24.2.1). * The contents of the array supplied in a call to the `fgets`, `gets`, or `fgetws` function are used after a read error occurred (7.19.7.2, 7.19.7.7, 7.24.3.2).

20. A non-null pointer returned by a call to the `calloc`, `malloc`, or `realloc` function with a zero requested size is used to access an object (7.20.3). * The value of a pointer that refers to space deallocated by a call to the `free` or `realloc` function is used (7.20.3). * The pointer argument to the `free` or `realloc` function does not match a pointer earlier returned by `calloc`, `malloc`, or `realloc`, or the space has been deallocated by a call to `free` or `realloc` (7.20.3.2, 7.20.3.4).

There are many more, but these seem to be the ones that I run into the most often or that come up the most often in C code. They are also the most difficult to avoid, so if you at least remember these, you'll be able to avoid the major ones.

Double Linked Lists

The purpose of this book is to teach you how your computer really works, and included in that is how various data structures and algorithms function. Computers by themselves don't do a lot of useful processing. To make them do useful things, you need to structure the data and then organize the processing of these structures. Other programming languages either include libraries that implement all of these structures, or they have direct syntax for them. C makes you implement all of the data structures that you need yourself, which makes it the perfect language to learn how they actually work.

My goal is to help you do three things:

- Understand what's really going on in Python, Ruby, or JavaScript code like this: data = {"name": "Zed"}

- Get even better at C code by using data structures to apply what you know to a set of solved problems.

- Learn a core set of data structures and algorithms so that you are better informed about what works best in certain situations.

What Are Data Structures

The name *data structure* is self-explanatory. It's an organization of data that fits a certain model. Maybe the model is designed to allow processing the data in a new way. Maybe it's just organized to store it on disk efficiently. In this book, I'll follow a simple pattern for making data structures that work reliably:

- Define a structure for the main outer structure.

- Define a structure for the contents, usually nodes with links between them.

- Create functions that operate on these two structures.

There are other styles of data structures in C, but this pattern works well and is consistent for making most data structures.

Making the Library

For the rest of this book, you'll be creating a library that you can use when you're done. This library will have the following elements:

- Header (.h) files for each data structure.

- Implementation (.c) files for the algorithms.

- Unit tests that test all of them to make sure they keep working.

- Documentation that we'll auto-generate from the header files.

You already have the c-skeleton, so use it to create a liblcthw project:

```
$ cp -r c-skeleton liblcthw
$ cd liblcthw/
$ ls
LICENSE      Makefile      README.md     bin   build     src   tests
$ vim Makefile
$ ls src/
dbg.h                libex29.c        libex29.o
$ mkdir src/lcthw
$ mv src/dbg.h src/lcthw
$ vim tests/minunit.h
$ rm src/libex29.* tests/libex29*
$ make clean
rm -rf build   tests/libex29_tests
rm -f tests/tests.log
find . -name "*.gc*" -exec rm {} \;
rm -rf `find . -name "*.dSYM" -print`
$ ls tests/
minunit.h runtests.sh
$
```

In this session I do the following:

- Copy the c-skeleton over.

- Edit the Makefile to change libYOUR_LIBRARY.a to liblcthw.a as the new TARGET.

- Make the src/lcthw directory, where we'll put our code.

- Move the src/dbg.h into this new directory.

- Edit tests/minunit.h so that it uses #include <lcthw/dbg.h> as the include.

- Get rid of the source and test files that we don't need for libex29.*.

- Clean up everything that's left over.

Now that you're ready to start building the library, the first data structure that I'll build is the doubly linked list.

Doubly Linked Lists

The first data structure that we'll add to liblcthw is a doubly linked list. This is the simplest data structure you can make, and it has useful properties for certain operations. A linked list works by nodes having pointers to their next or previous element. A doubly linked list contains pointers to both, while a singly linked list only points at the next element.

Because each node has pointers to the next and previous elements, and because you keep track of the first and last elements of the list, you can do some operations very quickly with doubly linked lists. Anything that involves inserting or deleting an element will be very fast. They're also easy to implement by most programmers.

The main disadvantage of a linked list is that traversing it involves processing every single pointer along the way. This means that searching, most sorting, and iterating over the elements will be slow. It also means that you can't really jump to random parts of the list. If you had an array of elements, you could just index right into the middle of the list, but a linked list uses a stream of pointers. That means if you want the tenth element, you have to go through the first nine elements.

Definition

As I said in the introduction to this exercise, first write a header file with the right C structure statements in it.

list.h

```
#ifndef lcthw_List_h
#define lcthw_List_h

#include <stdlib.h>

struct ListNode;

typedef struct ListNode {
    struct ListNode *next;
    struct ListNode *prev;
    void *value;
} ListNode;

typedef struct List {
    int count;
    ListNode *first;
    ListNode *last;
} List;

List *List_create();
void List_destroy(List * list);
void List_clear(List * list);
void List_clear_destroy(List * list);

#define List_count(A) ((A)->count)
#define List_first(A) ((A)->first != NULL ? (A)->first->value : NULL)
#define List_last(A) ((A)->last != NULL ? (A)->last->value : NULL)

void List_push(List * list, void *value);
void *List_pop(List * list);
```

```
void List_unshift(List * list, void *value);
void *List_shift(List * list);

void *List_remove(List * list, ListNode * node);

#define LIST_FOREACH(L, S, M, V) ListNode *_node = NULL;\
                                   ListNode *V = NULL;\
    for(V = _node = L->S; _node != NULL; V = _node = _node->M)

#endif
```

The first thing I do is create two structures for the ListNode and the List that will contain those nodes. This creates the data structure, which I'll use in the functions and macros that I define after that. If you read these functions, you'll see that they're rather simple. I'll be explaining them when I cover the implementation, but hopefully you can guess what they do.

Each ListNode has three components within the data structure:

- A value, which is a pointer to anything, and stores the thing we want to put in the list.

- A ListNode *next pointer, which points at another ListNode that holds the next element in the list.

- A ListNode *prev that holds the previous element. Complex, right? Calling the previous thing "previous." I could have used "anterior" and "posterior," but only a jerk would do that.

The List struct is then nothing more than a container for these ListNode structs that have been linked together in a chain. It keeps track of the count, first, and last elements of the list.

Finally, take a look at src/lcthw/list.h:37 where I define the LIST_FOREACH macro. This is a common programming idiom where you make a macro that generates iteration code so people can't mess it up. Getting this kind of processing right can be difficult with data structures, so writing macros helps people out. You'll see how I use this when I talk about the implementation.

Implementation

You should mostly understand how a doubly linked list works. It's nothing more than nodes with two pointers to the next and previous elements of the list. You can then write the src/lcthw/list.c code to see how each operation is implemented.

list.c

```
1    #include <lcthw/list.h>
2    #include <lcthw/dbg.h>
3
4    List *List_create()
```

```
 5    {
 6        return calloc(1, sizeof(List));
 7    }
 8
 9    void List_destroy(List * list)
10    {
11        LIST_FOREACH(list, first, next, cur) {
12            if (cur->prev) {
13                free(cur->prev);
14            }
15        }
16
17        free(list->last);
18        free(list);
19    }
20
21    void List_clear(List * list)
22    {
23        LIST_FOREACH(list, first, next, cur) {
24            free(cur->value);
25        }
26    }
27
28    void List_clear_destroy(List * list)
29    {
30        List_clear(list);
31        List_destroy(list);
32    }
33
34    void List_push(List * list, void *value)
35    {
36        ListNode *node = calloc(1, sizeof(ListNode));
37        check_mem(node);
38
39        node->value = value;
40
41        if (list->last == NULL) {
42            list->first = node;
43            list->last = node;
44        } else {
45            list->last->next = node;
46            node->prev = list->last;
47            list->last = node;
48        }
49
50        list->count++;
51
52    error:
53        return;
54    }
```

```
55
56    void *List_pop(List * list)
57    {
58        ListNode *node = list->last;
59        return node != NULL ? List_remove(list, node) : NULL;
60    }
61
62    void List_unshift(List * list, void *value)
63    {
64        ListNode *node = calloc(1, sizeof(ListNode));
65        check_mem(node);
66
67        node->value = value;
68
69        if (list->first == NULL) {
70            list->first = node;
71            list->last = node;
72        } else {
73            node->next = list->first;
74            list->first->prev = node;
75            list->first = node;
76        }
77
78        list->count++;
79
80    error:
81        return;
82    }
83
84    void *List_shift(List * list)
85    {
86        ListNode *node = list->first;
87        return node != NULL ? List_remove(list, node) : NULL;
88    }
89
90    void *List_remove(List * list, ListNode * node)
91    {
92        void *result = NULL;
93
94        check(list->first && list->last, "List is empty.");
95        check(node, "node can't be NULL");
96
97        if (node == list->first && node == list->last) {
98            list->first = NULL;
99            list->last = NULL;
100       } else if (node == list->first) {
101           list->first = node->next;
102           check(list->first != NULL,
103                   "Invalid list, somehow got a first that is NULL.");
104           list->first->prev = NULL;
```

```
105              } else if (node == list->last) {
106                  list->last = node->prev;
107                  check(list->last != NULL,
108                          "Invalid list, somehow got a next that is NULL.");
109                  list->last->next = NULL;
110              } else {
111                  ListNode *after = node->next;
112                  ListNode *before = node->prev;
113                  after->prev = before;
114                  before->next = after;
115              }
116
117          list->count--;
118          result = node->value;
119          free(node);
120
121      error:
122          return result;
123      }
```

I then implement all of the operations on a doubly linked list that can't be done with simple macros. Rather than cover every tiny, little line of this file, I'm going to give a high-level overview of every operation in both the list.h and list.c files, and then leave you to read the code.

list.h:List_count   Returns the number of elements in the list, which is maintained as elements are added and removed.

list.h:List_first   Returns the first element of the list, but doesn't remove it.

list.h:List_last   Returns the last element of the list, but doesn't remove it.

list.h:LIST_FOREACH   Iterates over the elements in the list.

list.c:List_create   Simply creates the main List struct.

list.c:List_destroy   Destroys a List and any elements it might have.

list.c:List_clear   A convenient function for freeing the *values* in each node, not the nodes.

list.c:List_clear_destroy   Clears and destroys a list. It's not very efficient since it loops through them twice.

list.c:List_push   The first operation that demonstrates the advantage of a linked list. It adds a new element to the end of the list, and because that's just a couple of pointer assignments, it does it very fast.

list.c:List_pop   The inverse of List_push, this takes the last element off and returns it.

list.c:List_unshift   The other thing you can easily do to a linked list is add elements to the *front* of the list very quickly. In this case, I call that List_unshift for lack of a better term.

list.c:List_shift   Just like List_pop, this removes the first element and returns it.

list.c:List_remove   This is actually doing all of the removal when you do List_pop or List_shift. Something that seems to always be difficult in data structures is removing things, and this function is no different. It has to handle quite a few conditions depending on if the element being removed is at the front, the end, both the front and the end, or the middle.

Most of these functions are nothing special, and you should be able to easily digest this and understand it from just the code. You should definitely focus on how the LIST_FOREACH macro is used in List_destroy so that you can understand how much it simplifies this common operation.

Tests

After you have those compiling, it's time to create the test that makes sure they operate correctly.

list_tests.c

```
1    #include "minunit.h"
2    #include <lcthw/list.h>
3    #include <assert.h>
4
5    static List *list = NULL;
6    char *test1 = "test1 data";
7    char *test2 = "test2 data";
8    char *test3 = "test3 data";
9
10   char *test_create()
11   {
12       list = List_create();
13       mu_assert(list != NULL, "Failed to create list.");
14
15       return NULL;
16   }
17
18   char *test_destroy()
19   {
20       List_clear_destroy(list);
21
22       return NULL;
23
24   }
25
26   char *test_push_pop()
27   {
28       List_push(list, test1);
29       mu_assert(List_last(list) == test1, "Wrong last value.");
30
```

```
31       List_push(list, test2);
32       mu_assert(List_last(list) == test2, "Wrong last value");
33
34       List_push(list, test3);
35       mu_assert(List_last(list) == test3, "Wrong last value.");
36       mu_assert(List_count(list) == 3, "Wrong count on push.");
37
38       char *val = List_pop(list);
39       mu_assert(val == test3, "Wrong value on pop.");
40
41       val = List_pop(list);
42       mu_assert(val == test2, "Wrong value on pop.");
43
44       val = List_pop(list);
45       mu_assert(val == test1, "Wrong value on pop.");
46       mu_assert(List_count(list) == 0, "Wrong count after pop.");
47
48       return NULL;
49   }
50
51   char *test_unshift()
52   {
53       List_unshift(list, test1);
54       mu_assert(List_first(list) == test1, "Wrong first value.");
55
56       List_unshift(list, test2);
57       mu_assert(List_first(list) == test2, "Wrong first value");
58
59       List_unshift(list, test3);
60       mu_assert(List_first(list) == test3, "Wrong last value.");
61       mu_assert(List_count(list) == 3, "Wrong count on unshift.");
62
63       return NULL;
64   }
65
66   char *test_remove()
67   {
68       // we only need to test the middle remove case since push/shift
69       // already tests the other cases
70
71       char *val = List_remove(list, list->first->next);
72       mu_assert(val == test2, "Wrong removed element.");
73       mu_assert(List_count(list) == 2, "Wrong count after remove.");
74       mu_assert(List_first(list) == test3, "Wrong first after remove.");
75       mu_assert(List_last(list) == test1, "Wrong last after remove.");
76
77       return NULL;
78   }
79
80   char *test_shift()
```

```
81    {
82        mu_assert(List_count(list) != 0, "Wrong count before shift.");
83
84        char *val = List_shift(list);
85        mu_assert(val == test3, "Wrong value on shift.");
86
87        val = List_shift(list);
88        mu_assert(val == test1, "Wrong value on shift.");
89        mu_assert(List_count(list) == 0, "Wrong count after shift.");
90
91        return NULL;
92    }
93
94    char *all_tests()
95    {
96        mu_suite_start();
97
98        mu_run_test(test_create);
99        mu_run_test(test_push_pop);
100       mu_run_test(test_unshift);
101       mu_run_test(test_remove);
102       mu_run_test(test_shift);
103       mu_run_test(test_destroy);
104
105       return NULL;
106   }
107
108   RUN_TESTS(all_tests);
```

This test simply goes through every operation and makes sure it works. I use a simplification in the test where I create just one List *list for the whole program, and then have the tests work on it. This saves the trouble of building a List for every test, but it could mean that some tests only pass because of how the previous test ran. In this case, I try to make each test keep the list clear or actually use the results from the previous test.

What You Should See

If you did everything right, then when you do a build and run the unit tests, it should look like this:

Exercise 32.build Session

```
$ make
cc -g -O2 -Wall -Wextra -Isrc -rdynamic -DNDEBUG  -fPIC   -c -o\
    src/lcthw/list.o src/lcthw/list.c
ar rcs build/liblcthw.a src/lcthw/list.o
ranlib build/liblcthw.a
cc -shared -o build/liblcthw.so src/lcthw/list.o
cc -g -O2 -Wall -Wextra -Isrc -rdynamic -DNDEBUG  build/liblcthw.a
```

```
        tests/list_tests.c    -o tests/list_tests
sh ./tests/runtests.sh
Running unit tests:
----
RUNNING: ./tests/list_tests
ALL TESTS PASSED
Tests run: 6
tests/list_tests PASS
$
```

Make sure six tests ran, it builds without warnings or errors, and it's making the build /liblcthw.a and build/liblcthw.so files.

How to Improve It

Instead of breaking this, I'm going to tell you how to improve the code:

- You can make List_clear_destroy more efficient by using LIST_FOREACH and doing both free calls inside one loop.

- You can add asserts for preconditions so that the program isn't given a NULL value for the List *list parameters.

- You can add invariants that check that the list's contents are always correct, such as count is never < 0, and if count > 0, then first isn't NULL.

- You can add documentation to the header file in the form of comments before each struct, function, and macro that describes what it does.

These improvements speak to the defensive programming practices I talked about earlier, hardening this code against flaws and improving usability. Go ahead and do these things, and then find as many other ways to improve the code as you can.

Extra Credit

- Research doubly versus singly linked lists and when one is preferred over the other.

- Research the limitations of a doubly linked list. For example, while they are efficient for inserting and deleting elements, they are very slow for iterating over them all.

- What operations are missing that you can imagine needing? Some examples are copying, joining, and splitting. Implement these operations and write the unit tests for them.

Linked List Algorithms

I'm going to cover two algorithms for a linked list that involve sorting. I'm going to warn you first that if you need to sort the data, then don't use a linked list. These are horrible for sorting things, and there are much better data structures you can use if that's a requirement. I'm covering these two algorithms because they are slightly difficult to pull off with a linked list, and to get you thinking about how to efficiently manipulate them.

In the interest of writing this book, I'm going to put the algorithms in two different files `list_algos.h` and `list_algos.c` then write a test in `list_algos_test.c`. For now, just follow my structure, since it keeps things clean, but if you ever work on other libraries, remember that this isn't a common structure.

In this exercise, I'm also going to give you an extra challenge and I want you to try not to cheat. I'm going to give you the *unit test* first, and I want you to type it in. Then, I want you to try and implement the two algorithms based on their descriptions in Wikipedia before seeing if your code looks like my code.

Bubble and Merge Sorts

You know what's awesome about the Internet? I can just refer you to the "bubble sort" and "merge sort" pages on Wikipedia and tell you to read those. Man, that saves me a boatload of typing. Now I can tell you how to actually implement each of these using the pseudo-code they have there. Here's how you can tackle an algorithm like this:

- Read the description and look at any visualizations it has.

- Either draw the algorithm on paper using boxes and lines, or actually take a deck of playing cards (or cards with numbers) and try to do the algorithm manually. This gives you a concrete demonstration of how the algorithm works.

- Create the skeleton functions in your `list_algos.c` file and make a working `list_algos.h` file, then set up your test harness.

- Write your first failing test and get everything to compile.

- Go back to the Wikipedia page and copy-paste the pseudo-code (not the C code!) into the guts of the first function that you're making.

- Translate this pseudo-code into good C code the way I've taught you, using your unit test to make sure it's working.

- Fill out some more tests for edge cases like empty lists, already sorted lists, and the like.

- Repeat this for the next algorithm and test it.

I just gave you the secret to figuring out most of the algorithms out there—until you get to some of the more insane ones, that is. In this case, you're just doing the bubble and merge sorts from Wikipedia, but those will be good starters.

The Unit Test

Here is the unit test you should use for the pseudo-code:

list_algos_tests.c

```
1   #include "minunit.h"
2   #include <lcthw/list_algos.h>
3   #include <assert.h>
4   #include <string.h>
5
6   char *values[] = { "XXXX", "1234", "abcd", "xjvef", "NDSS" };
7
8   #define NUM_VALUES 5
9
10  List *create_words()
11  {
12      int i = 0;
13      List *words = List_create();
14
15      for (i = 0; i < NUM_VALUES; i++) {
16          List_push(words, values[i]);
17      }
18
19      return words;
20  }
21
22  int is_sorted(List * words)
23  {
24      LIST_FOREACH(words, first, next, cur) {
25          if (cur->next && strcmp(cur->value, cur->next->value) > 0) {
26              debug("%s %s", (char *)cur->value,
27                      (char *)cur->next->value);
28              return 0;
29          }
30      }
31
32      return 1;
33  }
34
35  char *test_bubble_sort()
```

```
36    {
37        List *words = create_words();
38
39        // should work on a list that needs sorting
40        int rc = List_bubble_sort(words, (List_compare) strcmp);
41        mu_assert(rc == 0, "Bubble sort failed.");
42        mu_assert(is_sorted(words),
43                "Words are not sorted after bubble sort.");
44
45        // should work on an already sorted list
46        rc = List_bubble_sort(words, (List_compare) strcmp);
47        mu_assert(rc == 0, "Bubble sort of already sorted failed.");
48        mu_assert(is_sorted(words),
49                "Words should be sort if already bubble sorted.");
50
51        List_destroy(words);
52
53        // should work on an empty list
54        words = List_create(words);
55        rc = List_bubble_sort(words, (List_compare) strcmp);
56        mu_assert(rc == 0, "Bubble sort failed on empty list.");
57        mu_assert(is_sorted(words), "Words should be sorted if empty.");
58
59        List_destroy(words);
60
61        return NULL;
62    }
63
64    char *test_merge_sort()
65    {
66        List *words = create_words();
67
68        // should work on a list that needs sorting
69        List *res = List_merge_sort(words, (List_compare) strcmp);
70        mu_assert(is_sorted(res), "Words are not sorted after merge sort.");
71
72        List *res2 = List_merge_sort(res, (List_compare) strcmp);
73        mu_assert(is_sorted(res),
74                "Should still be sorted after merge sort.");
75        List_destroy(res2);
76        List_destroy(res);
77
78        List_destroy(words);
79        return NULL;
80    }
81
82    char *all_tests()
83    {
84        mu_suite_start();
85
```

```
86          mu_run_test(test_bubble_sort);
87          mu_run_test(test_merge_sort);
88
89          return NULL;
90    }
91
92    RUN_TESTS(all_tests);
```

I suggest that you start with the bubble sort and get that working, and then move on to the merge sort. What I would do is lay out the function prototypes and skeletons that get all three files compiling, but not passing the test. Then, I'd just fill in the implementation until it starts working.

The Implementation

Are you cheating? In future exercises, I'll just give you a unit test and tell you to implement it, so it's good practice for you to not look at this code until you get your own working. Here's the code for the list_algos.c and list_algos.h:

list_algos.h

```
#ifndef lcthw_List_algos_h
#define lcthw_List_algos_h

#include <lcthw/list.h>

typedef int (*List_compare) (const void *a, const void *b);

int List_bubble_sort(List * list, List_compare cmp);

List *List_merge_sort(List * list, List_compare cmp);

#endif
```

list_algos.c

```
1    #include <lcthw/list_algos.h>
2    #include <lcthw/dbg.h>
3
4    inline void ListNode_swap(ListNode * a, ListNode * b)
5    {
6        void *temp = a->value;
7        a->value = b->value;
8        b->value = temp;
9    }
10
11   int List_bubble_sort(List * list, List_compare cmp)
12   {
13       int sorted = 1;
```

```
14
15          if (List_count(list) <= 1) {
16              return 0;                 // already sorted
17          }
18
19          do {
20              sorted = 1;
21              LIST_FOREACH(list, first, next, cur) {
22                  if (cur->next) {
23                      if (cmp(cur->value, cur->next->value) > 0) {
24                          ListNode_swap(cur, cur->next);
25                          sorted = 0;
26                      }
27                  }
28              }
29          } while (!sorted);
30
31          return 0;
32      }
33
34      inline List *List_merge(List * left, List * right, List_compare cmp)
35      {
36          List *result = List_create();
37          void *val = NULL;
38
39          while (List_count(left) > 0 || List_count(right) > 0) {
40              if (List_count(left) > 0 && List_count(right) > 0) {
41                  if (cmp(List_first(left), List_first(right)) <= 0) {
42                      val = List_shift(left);
43                  } else {
44                      val = List_shift(right);
45                  }
46
47                  List_push(result, val);
48              } else if (List_count(left) > 0) {
49                  val = List_shift(left);
50                  List_push(result, val);
51              } else if (List_count(right) > 0) {
52                  val = List_shift(right);
53                  List_push(result, val);
54              }
55          }
56
57          return result;
58      }
59
60      List *List_merge_sort(List * list, List_compare cmp)
61      {
62          if (List_count(list) <= 1) {
63              return list;
```

```
64          }
65
66          List *left = List_create();
67          List *right = List_create();
68          int middle = List_count(list) / 2;
69
70          LIST_FOREACH(list, first, next, cur) {
71              if (middle > 0) {
72                  List_push(left, cur->value);
73              } else {
74                  List_push(right, cur->value);
75              }
76
77              middle--;
78          }
79
80          List *sort_left = List_merge_sort(left, cmp);
81          List *sort_right = List_merge_sort(right, cmp);
82
83          if (sort_left != left)
84              List_destroy(left);
85          if (sort_right != right)
86              List_destroy(right);
87
88          return List_merge(sort_left, sort_right, cmp);
89      }
```

The bubble sort isn't too hard to figure out, although it's really slow. The merge sort is much more complicated, and honestly, I could probably spend a bit more time optimizing this code if I wanted to sacrifice clarity.

There is another way to implement a merge sort using a bottom-up method, but it's a little harder to understand, so I didn't do it. As I've already said, sorting algorithms on linked lists are entirely pointless. You could spend all day trying to make this faster and it will still be slower than almost any other sortable data structure. Simply don't use linked lists if you need to sort things.

What You Should See

If everything works, then you should get something like this:

Exercise 33 Session

```
$ make clean all
rm -rf build src/lcthw/list.o src/lcthw/list_algos.o\
        tests/list_algos_tests tests/list_tests
rm -f tests/tests.log
find . -name "*.gc*" -exec rm {} \;
rm -rf `find . -name "*.dSYM" -print`
```

```
cc -g -O2 -Wall -Wextra -Isrc -rdynamic -DNDEBUG  -fPIC   -c -o\
     src/lcthw/list.o src/lcthw/list.c
cc -g -O2 -Wall -Wextra -Isrc -rdynamic -DNDEBUG  -fPIC   -c -o\
     src/lcthw/list_algos.o src/lcthw/list_algos.c
ar rcs build/liblcthw.a src/lcthw/list.o src/lcthw/list_algos.o
ranlib build/liblcthw.a
cc -shared -o build/liblcthw.so src/lcthw/list.o src/lcthw/list_algos.o
cc -g -O2 -Wall -Wextra -Isrc -rdynamic -DNDEBUG  build/liblcthw.a\
     tests/list_algos_tests.c   -o tests/list_algos_tests
cc -g -O2 -Wall -Wextra -Isrc -rdynamic -DNDEBUG  build/liblcthw.a\
     tests/list_tests.c   -o tests/list_tests
sh ./tests/runtests.sh
Running unit tests:
----
RUNNING: ./tests/list_algos_tests
ALL TESTS PASSED
Tests run: 2
tests/list_algos_tests PASS
----
RUNNING: ./tests/list_tests
ALL TESTS PASSED
Tests run: 6
tests/list_tests PASS
$
```

After this exercise, I'm not going to show you this output unless it's necessary to show you how it works. From now on, you should know that I ran the tests and that they all passed and everything compiled.

How to Improve It

Going back to the description of the algorithms, there are several ways to improve these implementations. Here are a few obvious ones:

- The merge sort does a crazy amount of copying and creating lists, so find ways to reduce this.
- The bubble sort description in Wikipedia mentions a few optimizations. Try to implement them.
- Can you use the List_split and List_join (if you implemented them) to improve merge sort?
- Go through all of the defensive programming checks and improve the robustness of this implementation, protecting against bad NULL pointers, and then create an optional debug level invariant that works like is_sorted does after a sort.

Extra Credit

- Create a unit test that compares the performance of the two algorithms. You'll want to look at man 3 time for a basic timer function, and run enough iterations to at least have a few seconds of samples.

- Play with the amount of data in the lists that need to be sorted and see if that changes your timing.

- Find a way to simulate filling different sized random lists, measuring how long they take. Then, graph the result to see how it compares to the description of the algorithm.

- Try to explain why sorting linked lists is a really bad idea.

- Implement a List_insert_sorted that will take a given value, and using the List_compare, insert the element at the right position so that the list is always sorted. How does using this method compare to sorting a list after you've built it?

- Try implementing the bottom-up merge sort described on the Wikipedia page. The code there is already C, so it should be easy to recreate, but try to understand how it's working compared to the slower one I have here.

Dynamic Array

This is an array that grows on its own and has most of the same features as a linked list. It will usually take up less space, run faster, and has other beneficial properties. This exercise will cover a few of the disadvantages, like very slow removal from the front, with a solution to just do it at the end.

A dynamic array is simply an array of void ** pointers that's pre-allocated in one shot and that point at the data. In the linked list, you had a full structure that stored the void *value pointer, but in a dynamic array, there's just a single array with all of them. This means you don't need any other pointers for next and previous records since you can just index into the dynamic array directly.

To start, I'll give you the header file you should type in for the implementation:

darray.h

```
#ifndef _DArray_h
#define _DArray_h
#include <stdlib.h>
#include <assert.h>
#include <lcthw/dbg.h>

typedef struct DArray {
    int end;
    int max;
    size_t element_size;
    size_t expand_rate;
    void **contents;
} DArray;

DArray *DArray_create(size_t element_size, size_t initial_max);

void DArray_destroy(DArray * array);

void DArray_clear(DArray * array);

int DArray_expand(DArray * array);

int DArray_contract(DArray * array);

int DArray_push(DArray * array, void *el);

void *DArray_pop(DArray * array);

void DArray_clear_destroy(DArray * array);
```

```
#define DArray_last(A) ((A)->contents[(A)->end - 1])
#define DArray_first(A) ((A)->contents[0])
#define DArray_end(A) ((A)->end)
#define DArray_count(A) DArray_end(A)
#define DArray_max(A) ((A)->max)

#define DEFAULT_EXPAND_RATE 300

static inline void DArray_set(DArray * array, int i, void *el)
{
    check(i < array->max, "darray attempt to set past max");
    if (i > array->end)
        array->end = i;
    array->contents[i] = el;
error:
    return;
}

static inline void *DArray_get(DArray * array, int i)
{
    check(i < array->max, "darray attempt to get past max");
    return array->contents[i];
error:
    return NULL;
}

static inline void *DArray_remove(DArray * array, int i)
{
    void *el = array->contents[i];

    array->contents[i] = NULL;

    return el;
}

static inline void *DArray_new(DArray * array)
{
    check(array->element_size > 0,
            "Can't use DArray_new on 0 size darrays.");

    return calloc(1, array->element_size);

error:
    return NULL;
}

#define DArray_free(E) free((E))

#endif
```

This header file is showing you a new technique where I put `static inline` functions right in the header. These function definitions will work similarly to the #define macros that you've been making, but they're cleaner and easier to write. If you need to create a block of code for a macro and you don't need code generation, then use a `static inline` function.

Compare this technique to the LIST_FOREACH that *generates* a proper for-loop for a list. This would be impossible to do with a `static inline` function because it actually has to generate the inner block of code for the loop. The only way to do that is with a callback function, but that's not as fast and it's harder to use.

I'll then change things up and have you create the unit test for DArray:

darray_tests.c

```
1    #include "minunit.h"
2    #include <lcthw/darray.h>
3
4    static DArray *array = NULL;
5    static int *val1 = NULL;
6    static int *val2 = NULL;
7
8    char *test_create()
9    {
10       array = DArray_create(sizeof(int), 100);
11       mu_assert(array != NULL, "DArray_create failed.");
12       mu_assert(array->contents != NULL, "contents are wrong in darray");
13       mu_assert(array->end == 0, "end isn't at the right spot");
14       mu_assert(array->element_size == sizeof(int),
15               "element size is wrong.");
16       mu_assert(array->max == 100, "wrong max length on initial size");
17
18       return NULL;
19    }
20
21    char *test_destroy()
22    {
23       DArray_destroy(array);
24
25       return NULL;
26    }
27
28    char *test_new()
29    {
30       val1 = DArray_new(array);
31       mu_assert(val1 != NULL, "failed to make a new element");
32
33       val2 = DArray_new(array);
34       mu_assert(val2 != NULL, "failed to make a new element");
35
```

```
36            return NULL;
37        }
38
39        char *test_set()
40        {
41            DArray_set(array, 0, val1);
42            DArray_set(array, 1, val2);
43
44            return NULL;
45        }
46
47        char *test_get()
48        {
49            mu_assert(DArray_get(array, 0) == val1, "Wrong first value.");
50            mu_assert(DArray_get(array, 1) == val2, "Wrong second value.");
51
52            return NULL;
53        }
54
55        char *test_remove()
56        {
57            int *val_check = DArray_remove(array, 0);
58            mu_assert(val_check != NULL, "Should not get NULL.");
59            mu_assert(*val_check == *val1, "Should get the first value.");
60            mu_assert(DArray_get(array, 0) == NULL, "Should be gone.");
61            DArray_free(val_check);
62
63            val_check = DArray_remove(array, 1);
64            mu_assert(val_check != NULL, "Should not get NULL.");
65            mu_assert(*val_check == *val2, "Should get the first value.");
66            mu_assert(DArray_get(array, 1) == NULL, "Should be gone.");
67            DArray_free(val_check);
68
69            return NULL;
70        }
71
72        char *test_expand_contract()
73        {
74            int old_max = array->max;
75            DArray_expand(array);
76            mu_assert((unsigned int)array->max == old_max + array->expand_rate,
77                    "Wrong size after expand.");
78
79            DArray_contract(array);
80            mu_assert((unsigned int)array->max == array->expand_rate + 1,
81                    "Should stay at the expand_rate at least.");
82
83            DArray_contract(array);
84            mu_assert((unsigned int)array->max == array->expand_rate + 1,
85                    "Should stay at the expand_rate at least.");
```

```
86
87          return NULL;
88      }
89
90      char *test_push_pop()
91      {
92          int i = 0;
93          for (i = 0; i < 1000; i++) {
94              int *val = DArray_new(array);
95              *val = i * 333;
96              DArray_push(array, val);
97          }
98
99          mu_assert(array->max == 1201, "Wrong max size.");
100
101          for (i = 999; i >= 0; i--) {
102              int *val = DArray_pop(array);
103              mu_assert(val != NULL, "Shouldn't get a NULL.");
104              mu_assert(*val == i * 333, "Wrong value.");
105              DArray_free(val);
106          }
107
108          return NULL;
109      }
110
111      char *all_tests()
112      {
113          mu_suite_start();
114
115          mu_run_test(test_create);
116          mu_run_test(test_new);
117          mu_run_test(test_set);
118          mu_run_test(test_get);
119          mu_run_test(test_remove);
120          mu_run_test(test_expand_contract);
121          mu_run_test(test_push_pop);
122          mu_run_test(test_destroy);
123
124          return NULL;
125      }
126
127      RUN_TESTS(all_tests);
```

This shows you how all of the operations are used, which then makes implementing the DArray much easier:

darray.c

```
1       #include <lcthw/darray.h>
2       #include <assert.h>
3
```

```
 4    DArray *DArray_create(size_t element_size, size_t initial_max)
 5    {
 6        DArray *array = malloc(sizeof(DArray));
 7        check_mem(array);
 8        array->max = initial_max;
 9        check(array->max > 0, "You must set an initial_max > 0.");
10
11        array->contents = calloc(initial_max, sizeof(void *));
12        check_mem(array->contents);
13
14        array->end = 0;
15        array->element_size = element_size;
16        array->expand_rate = DEFAULT_EXPAND_RATE;
17
18        return array;
19
20    error:
21        if (array)
22            free(array);
23        return NULL;
24    }
25
26    void DArray_clear(DArray * array)
27    {
28        int i = 0;
29        if (array->element_size > 0) {
30            for (i = 0; i < array->max; i++) {
31                if (array->contents[i] != NULL) {
32                    free(array->contents[i]);
33                }
34            }
35        }
36    }
37
38    static inline int DArray_resize(DArray * array, size_t newsize)
39    {
40        array->max = newsize;
41        check(array->max > 0, "The newsize must be > 0.");
42
43        void *contents = realloc(
44                array->contents, array->max * sizeof(void *));
45        // check contents and assume realloc doesn't harm the original on error
46
47        check_mem(contents);
48
49        array->contents = contents;
50
51        return 0;
52    error:
53        return -1;
```

```
54      }
55
56      int DArray_expand(DArray * array)
57      {
58          size_t old_max = array->max;
59          check(DArray_resize(array, array->max + array->expand_rate) == 0,
60                  "Failed to expand array to new size: %d",
61                  array->max + (int)array->expand_rate);
62
63          memset(array->contents + old_max, 0, array->expand_rate + 1);
64          return 0;
65
66      error:
67          return -1;
68      }
69
70      int DArray_contract(DArray * array)
71      {
72          int new_size = array->end < (int)array->expand_rate ?
73                  (int)array->expand_rate : array->end;
74
75          return DArray_resize(array, new_size + 1);
76      }
77
78      void DArray_destroy(DArray * array)
79      {
80          if (array) {
81              if (array->contents)
82                  free(array->contents);
83              free(array);
84          }
85      }
86
87      void DArray_clear_destroy(DArray * array)
88      {
89          DArray_clear(array);
90          DArray_destroy(array);
91      }
92
93      int DArray_push(DArray * array, void *el)
94      {
95          array->contents[array->end] = el;
96          array->end++;
97
98          if (DArray_end(array) >= DArray_max(array)) {
99              return DArray_expand(array);
100         } else {
101             return 0;
102         }
103     }
```

```
104
105    void *DArray_pop(DArray * array)
106    {
107        check(array->end - 1 >= 0, "Attempt to pop from empty array.");
108
109        void *el = DArray_remove(array, array->end - 1);
110        array->end--;
111
112        if (DArray_end(array) > (int)array->expand_rate
113                && DArray_end(array) % array->expand_rate) {
114            DArray_contract(array);
115        }
116
117        return el;
118    error:
119        return NULL;
120    }
```

This shows you another way to tackle complex code. Instead of diving right into the .c implementation, look at the header file, and then read the unit test. This gives you an abstract-to-concrete understanding of how the pieces work together, making it easier to remember.

Advantages and Disadvantages

A DArray is better when you need to optimize these operations:

- Iteration: You can just use a basic for-loop and DArray_count with DArray_get, and you're done. No special macros needed, and it's faster because you aren't walking through pointers.

- Indexing: You can use DArray_get and DArray_set to access any element at random, but with a List you have to go through N elements to get to N+1.

- Destroying: You can just free the struct and the contents in two operations. A List requires a series of free calls and walking every element.

- Cloning: You can also clone it in just two operations (plus whatever it's storing) by copying the struct and contents. Again, a list requires walking through the whole thing and copying every ListNode plus its value.

- Sorting: As you saw, List is horrible if you need to keep the data sorted. A DArray opens up a whole class of great sorting algorithms, because now you can access elements randomly.

- Large Data: If you need to keep around a lot of data, then a DArray wins since its base, contents, takes up less memory than the same number of ListNode structs.

However, the List wins on these operations:

- Insert and remove on the front (what I called shift): A DArray needs special treatment to be able to do this efficiently, and usually it has to do some copying.

- Splitting or joining: A List can just copy some pointers and it's done, but with a DArray, you have copy all of the arrays involved.

- Small Data: If you only need to store a few elements, then typically the storage will be smaller in a List than a generic DArray. This is because the DArray needs to expand the backing store to accommodate future inserts, while a List only makes what it needs.

With this, I prefer to use a DArray for most of the things you see other people use a List for. I reserve using List for any data structure that requires a small number of nodes to be added and removed from either end. I'll show you two similar data structures called a Stack and Queue where this is important.

How to Improve It

As usual, go through each function and operation and add the defensive programming checks, pre-conditions, invariants, and anything else you can find to make the implementation more bulletproof.

Extra Credit

- Improve the unit tests to cover more of the operations, and test them using a for-loop to ensure that they work.

- Research what it would take to implement bubble sort and merge sort for DArray, but don't do it yet. I'll be implementing DArray algorithms next, so you'll do this then.

- Write some performance tests for common operations and compare them to the same operations in List. You did some of this already, but this time, write a unit test that repeatedly does the operation in question and then, in the main runner, do the timing.

- Look at how the DArray_expand is implemented using a constant increase (size + 300). Typically, dynamic arrays are implemented with a multiplicative increase (size × 2), but I've found this to cost needless memory for no real performance gain. Test my assertion and see when you'd want a multiplicative increase instead of a constant increase.

Sorting and Searching

In this exercise, I'm going to cover four sorting algorithms and one search algorithm. The sorting algorithms are going to be quick sort, heap sort, merge sort, and radix sort. I'm then going to show you how do a to binary search after you've done a radix sort.

However, I'm a lazy guy, and in most standard C libraries you have existing implementations of the heapsort, quicksort, and merge sort algorithms. Here's how you use them:

darray_algos.c

```
1    #include <lcthw/darray_algos.h>
2    #include <stdlib.h>
3
4    int DArray_qsort(DArray * array, DArray_compare cmp)
5    {
6        qsort(array->contents, DArray_count(array), sizeof(void *), cmp);
7        return 0;
8    }
9
10   int DArray_heapsort(DArray * array, DArray_compare cmp)
11   {
12       return heapsort(array->contents, DArray_count(array),
13               sizeof(void *), cmp);
14   }
15
16   int DArray_mergesort(DArray * array, DArray_compare cmp)
17   {
18       return mergesort(array->contents, DArray_count(array),
19               sizeof(void *), cmp);
20   }
```

That's the whole implementation of the darray_algos.c file, and it should work on most modern UNIX systems. What each of these does is sort the contents store of void pointers using the DArray_compare that you give it. I'll show you the header file for this, too:

darray_algos.h

```
#ifndef darray_algos_h
#define darray_algos_h

#include <lcthw/darray.h>

typedef int (*DArray_compare) (const void *a, const void *b);

int DArray_qsort(DArray * array, DArray_compare cmp);
```

```
int DArray_heapsort(DArray * array, DArray_compare cmp);

int DArray_mergesort(DArray * array, DArray_compare cmp);

#endif
```

It's about the same size and should be what you expect. Next, you can see how these functions are used in the unit test for these three:

darray_algos_tests.c

```
1    #include "minunit.h"
2    #include <lcthw/darray_algos.h>
3
4    int testcmp(char **a, char **b)
5    {
6        return strcmp(*a, *b);
7    }
8
9    DArray *create_words()
10   {
11       DArray *result = DArray_create(0, 5);
12       char *words[] = { "asdfasfd",
13           "werwar", "13234", "asdfasfd", "oioj" };
14       int i = 0;
15
16       for (i = 0; i < 5; i++) {
17           DArray_push(result, words[i]);
18       }
19
20       return result;
21   }
22
23   int is_sorted(DArray * array)
24   {
25       int i = 0;
26
27       for (i = 0; i < DArray_count(array) - 1; i++) {
28           if (strcmp(DArray_get(array, i), DArray_get(array, i + 1)) > 0) {
29               return 0;
30           }
31       }
32
33       return 1;
34   }
35
36   char *run_sort_test(int (*func) (DArray *, DArray_compare),
37       const char *name)
38   {
39       DArray *words = create_words();
```

```
40          mu_assert(!is_sorted(words), "Words should start not sorted.");
41
42          debug("--- Testing %s sorting algorithm", name);
43          int rc = func(words, (DArray_compare) testcmp);
44          mu_assert(rc == 0, "sort failed");
45          mu_assert(is_sorted(words), "didn't sort it");
46
47          DArray_destroy(words);
48
49          return NULL;
50      }
51
52      char *test_qsort()
53      {
54          return run_sort_test(DArray_qsort, "qsort");
55      }
56
57      char *test_heapsort()
58      {
59          return run_sort_test(DArray_heapsort, "heapsort");
60      }
61
62      char *test_mergesort()
63      {
64          return run_sort_test(DArray_mergesort, "mergesort");
65      }
66
67      char *all_tests()
68      {
69          mu_suite_start();
70
71          mu_run_test(test_qsort);
72          mu_run_test(test_heapsort);
73          mu_run_test(test_mergesort);
74
75          return NULL;
76      }
77
78      RUN_TESTS(all_tests);
```

The thing to notice, and actually what tripped me up for a whole day, is the definition of testcmp on line 4. You have to use a char ** and *not* a char * because qsort gives you a pointer to *the pointers* in the contents array. The function qsort and friends are scanning the array, and handing *pointers* to each element in the array to your comparison function. Since what I have in the contents array are pointers, that means you get a pointer to a pointer.

With that out of the way, you have just implemented three difficult sorting algorithms in about 20 lines of code. You could stop there, but part of this book is learning how these algorithms work, so the Extra Credit section is going to involve implementing each of these.

Radix Sort and Binary Search

Since you're going to implement quicksort, heapsort, and merge sort on your own, I'm going to show you a funky algorithm called radix sort. It has a slightly narrow usefulness in sorting arrays of integers, but seems to work like magic. In this case, I'm going to create a special data structure called a RadixMap that's used to map one integer to another.

Here's the header file for the new algorithm, which is both algorithm and data structure in one:

radixmap.h

```
#ifndef _radixmap_h
#include <stdint.h>

typedef union RMElement {
    uint64_t raw;
    struct {
        uint32_t key;
        uint32_t value;
    } data;
} RMElement;

typedef struct RadixMap {
    size_t max;
    size_t end;
    uint32_t counter;
    RMElement *contents;
    RMElement *temp;
} RadixMap;

RadixMap *RadixMap_create(size_t max);

void RadixMap_destroy(RadixMap * map);

void RadixMap_sort(RadixMap * map);

RMElement *RadixMap_find(RadixMap * map, uint32_t key);

int RadixMap_add(RadixMap * map, uint32_t key, uint32_t value);

int RadixMap_delete(RadixMap * map, RMElement * el);

#endif
```

You see that I have a lot of the same operations as in a Dynamic Array or a List data structure, but the difference is I'm working only with fixed size 32-bit uint32_t integers. I'm also introducing you to a new C concept called the union here.

C Unions

A union is a way to refer to the same piece of memory in a number of different ways. You define it like a struct, except every element is sharing the same space with all of the others. You can think of a union as a picture of the memory, and the elements in the union as different colored lenses to view the picture.

What they are used for is to either save memory or convert chunks of memory between formats. The first usage is typically done with variant types, where you create a structure that has tag for the type, and then a union inside it for each type. When used for converting between formats of memory, you can simply define the two structures, and then access the right one.

First, let me show you how to make a variant type with C unions:

ex35.c

```
1    #include <stdio.h>
2
3    typedef enum {
4        TYPE_INT,
5        TYPE_FLOAT,
6        TYPE_STRING,
7    } VariantType;
8
9    struct Variant {
10       VariantType type;
11       union {
12           int as_integer;
13           float as_float;
14           char *as_string;
15       } data;
16   };
17
18   typedef struct Variant Variant;
19
20   void Variant_print(Variant * var)
21   {
22       switch (var->type) {
23           case TYPE_INT:
24               printf("INT: %d\n", var->data.as_integer);
25               break;
26           case TYPE_FLOAT:
27               printf("FLOAT: %f\n", var->data.as_float);
28               break;
29           case TYPE_STRING:
30               printf("STRING: %s\n", var->data.as_string);
31               break;
32           default:
33               printf("UNKNOWN TYPE: %d", var->type);
34       }
35   }
```

```
36
37    int main(int argc, char *argv[])
38    {
39        Variant a_int = {.type = TYPE_INT, .data.as_integer = 100 };
40        Variant a_float = {.type = TYPE_FLOAT, .data.as_float = 100.34 };
41        Variant a_string = {.type = TYPE_STRING,
42            .data.as_string = "YO DUDE!" };
43
44        Variant_print(&a_int);
45        Variant_print(&a_float);
46        Variant_print(&a_string);
47
48        // here's how you access them
49        a_int.data.as_integer = 200;
50        a_float.data.as_float = 2.345;
51        a_string.data.as_string = "Hi there.";
52
53        Variant_print(&a_int);
54        Variant_print(&a_float);
55        Variant_print(&a_string);
56
57        return 0;
58    }
```

You find this in many implementations of dynamic languages. The language will define some base variant type with tags for all the base types of the language, and then usually there's a generic object tag for the types you can create. The advantage of doing this is that the Variant only takes up as much space as the VariantType type tag and the largest member of the union. This is because C is layering each element of the Variant.data union together, so they overlap. To do that, C sizes the union big enough to hold the largest element.

In the radixmap.h file, I have the RMElement union, which demonstrates using a union to convert blocks of memory between types. In this case, I want to store a uint64_t-sized integer for sorting purposes, but I want two uint32_t integers for the data to represent a key and value pair. By using a union, I'm able to cleanly access the same block of memory in the two different ways I need.

The Implementation

I next have the actual RadixMap implementation for each of these operations:

radixmap.c

```
1    /*
2     * Based on code by Andre Reinald then heavily modified by Zed A. Shaw.
3     */
4
5    #include <stdio.h>
6    #include <stdlib.h>
```

```
 7    #include <assert.h>
 8    #include <lcthw/radixmap.h>
 9    #include <lcthw/dbg.h>
10
11    RadixMap *RadixMap_create(size_t max)
12    {
13        RadixMap *map = calloc(sizeof(RadixMap), 1);
14        check_mem(map);
15
16        map->contents = calloc(sizeof(RMElement), max + 1);
17        check_mem(map->contents);
18
19        map->temp = calloc(sizeof(RMElement), max + 1);
20        check_mem(map->temp);
21
22        map->max = max;
23        map->end = 0;
24
25        return map;
26    error:
27        return NULL;
28    }
29
30    void RadixMap_destroy(RadixMap * map)
31    {
32        if (map) {
33            free(map->contents);
34            free(map->temp);
35            free(map);
36        }
37    }
38
39    #define ByteOf(x,y) (((uint8_t *)x)[(y)])
40
41    static inline void radix_sort(short offset, uint64_t max,
42            uint64_t * source, uint64_t * dest)
43    {
44        uint64_t count[256] = { 0 };
45        uint64_t *cp = NULL;
46        uint64_t *sp = NULL;
47        uint64_t *end = NULL;
48        uint64_t s = 0;
49        uint64_t c = 0;
50
51        // count occurences of every byte value
52        for (sp = source, end = source + max; sp < end; sp++) {
53            count[ByteOf(sp, offset)]++;
54        }
55
56        // transform count into index by summing
```

```
57          // elements and storing into same array
58          for (s = 0, cp = count, end = count + 256; cp < end; cp++) {
59              c = *cp;
60              *cp = s;
61              s += c;
62          }
63
64          // fill dest with the right values in the right place
65          for (sp = source, end = source + max; sp < end; sp++) {
66              cp = count + ByteOf(sp, offset);
67              dest[*cp] = *sp;
68              ++(*cp);
69          }
70      }
71
72      void RadixMap_sort(RadixMap * map)
73      {
74          uint64_t *source = &map->contents[0].raw;
75          uint64_t *temp = &map->temp[0].raw;
76
77          radix_sort(0, map->end, source, temp);
78          radix_sort(1, map->end, temp, source);
79          radix_sort(2, map->end, source, temp);
80          radix_sort(3, map->end, temp, source);
81      }
82
83      RMElement *RadixMap_find(RadixMap * map, uint32_t to_find)
84      {
85          int low = 0;
86          int high = map->end - 1;
87          RMElement *data = map->contents;
88
89          while (low <= high) {
90              int middle = low + (high - low) / 2;
91              uint32_t key = data[middle].data.key;
92
93              if (to_find < key) {
94                  high = middle - 1;
95              } else if (to_find > key) {
96                  low = middle + 1;
97              } else {
98                  return &data[middle];
99              }
100         }
101
102         return NULL;
103     }
104
105     int RadixMap_add(RadixMap * map, uint32_t key, uint32_t value)
106     {
```

```
107        check(key < UINT32_MAX, "Key can't be equal to UINT32_MAX.");
108
109        RMElement element = {.data = {.key = key,.value = value} };
110        check(map->end + 1 < map->max, "RadixMap is full.");
111
112        map->contents[map->end++] = element;
113
114        RadixMap_sort(map);
115
116        return 0;
117
118    error:
119        return -1;
120    }
121
122    int RadixMap_delete(RadixMap * map, RMElement * el)
123    {
124        check(map->end > 0, "There is nothing to delete.");
125        check(el != NULL, "Can't delete a NULL element.");
126
127        el->data.key = UINT32_MAX;
128
129        if (map->end > 1) {
130            // don't bother resorting a map of 1 length
131            RadixMap_sort(map);
132        }
133
134        map->end--;
135
136        return 0;
137    error:
138        return -1;
139    }
```

As usual, enter this in and get it working, along with the unit test, and then I'll explain what's happening. Take *special care* with the radix_sort function since it's very particular in how it's implemented.

radixmap_tests.c

```
1    #include "minunit.h"
2    #include <lcthw/radixmap.h>
3    #include <time.h>
4
5    static int make_random(RadixMap * map)
6    {
7        size_t i = 0;
8
9        for (i = 0; i < map->max - 1; i++) {
10            uint32_t key = (uint32_t) (rand() | (rand() << 16));
11            check(RadixMap_add(map, key, i) == 0, "Failed to add key %u.",
```

```
12                      key);
13          }
14
15          return i;
16
17      error:
18          return 0;
19      }
20
21      static int check_order(RadixMap * map)
22      {
23          RMElement d1, d2;
24          unsigned int i = 0;
25
26          // only signal errors if any (should not be)
27          for (i = 0; map->end > 0 && i < map->end - 1; i++) {
28              d1 = map->contents[i];
29              d2 = map->contents[i + 1];
30
31              if (d1.data.key > d2.data.key) {
32                  debug("FAIL:i=%u, key: %u, value: %u, equals max? %d\n", i,
33                          d1.data.key, d1.data.value,
34                          d2.data.key == UINT32_MAX);
35                  return 0;
36              }
37          }
38
39          return 1;
40      }
41
42      static int test_search(RadixMap * map)
43      {
44          unsigned i = 0;
45          RMElement *d = NULL;
46          RMElement *found = NULL;
47
48          for (i = map->end / 2; i < map->end; i++) {
49              d = &map->contents[i];
50              found = RadixMap_find(map, d->data.key);
51              check(found != NULL, "Didn't find %u at %u.", d->data.key, i);
52              check(found->data.key == d->data.key,
53                      "Got the wrong result: %p:%u looking for %u at %u", found,
54                      found->data.key, d->data.key, i);
55          }
56
57          return 1;
58      error:
59          return 0;
60      }
61
```

```
62     // test for big number of elements
63     static char *test_operations()
64     {
65         size_t N = 200;
66
67         RadixMap *map = RadixMap_create(N);
68         mu_assert(map != NULL, "Failed to make the map.");
69         mu_assert(make_random(map), "Didn't make a random fake radix map.");
70
71         RadixMap_sort(map);
72         mu_assert(check_order(map),
73                 "Failed to properly sort the RadixMap.");
74
75         mu_assert(test_search(map), "Failed the search test.");
76         mu_assert(check_order(map),
77                 "RadixMap didn't stay sorted after search.");
78
79         while (map->end > 0) {
80             RMElement *el = RadixMap_find(map,
81                     map->contents[map->end / 2].data.key);
82             mu_assert(el != NULL, "Should get a result.");
83
84             size_t old_end = map->end;
85
86             mu_assert(RadixMap_delete(map, el) == 0, "Didn't delete it.");
87             mu_assert(old_end - 1 == map->end, "Wrong size after delete.");
88
89             // test that the end is now the old value,
90             // but uint32 max so it trails off
91             mu_assert(check_order(map),
92                     "RadixMap didn't stay sorted after delete.");
93         }
94
95         RadixMap_destroy(map);
96
97         return NULL;
98     }
99
100    char *all_tests()
101    {
102        mu_suite_start();
103        srand(time(NULL));
104
105        mu_run_test(test_operations);
106
107        return NULL;
108    }
109
110    RUN_TESTS(all_tests);
```

I shouldn't have to explain too much about the test. It's simply simulating placing random integers into the RadixMap, and then making sure it can get them out reliably. Not too interesting.

In the radixmap.c file, most of the operations are easy to understand if you read the code. Here's a description of what the basic functions are doing and how they work:

RadixMap_create   As usual, I'm allocating all of the memory needed for the structures defined in radixmap.h. I'll be using the temp and contents later when I talk about radix_sort.

RadixMap_destroy   Again, I'm just destroying what was created.

radix_sort   Here's the meat of the data structure, but I'll explain what it's doing in the next section.

RadixMap_sort   This uses the radix_sort function to actually sort the contents. It does this by sorting between the contents and temp until finally contents is sorted. You'll see how this works when I describe radix_sort later.

RadixMap_find   This is using a binary search algorithm to find a key you give it. I'll explain how this works shortly.

RadixMap_add   Using the RadixMap_sort function, this will add the key and value you request at the end, then simply sort it again so that everything is in the right place. Once everything is sorted, the RadixMap_find will work properly because it's a binary search.

RadixMap_delete   This works the same as RadixMap_add, except it deletes elements of the structure by setting their values to the max for a unsigned 32-bit integer, UINT32_MAX. This means that you can't use that value as an key value, but it makes deleting elements easy. Simply set it to that and then sort, and it'll get moved to the end. Now it's deleted.

Study the code for the functions I described. That just leaves RadixMap_sort, radix_sort, and RadixMap_find to understand.

RadixMap_find and Binary Search

I'll start with how the binary search is implemented. Binary search is a simple algorithm that most people can understand intuitively. In fact, you could take a deck of playing cards and do this manually. Here's how this function works, and how a binary search is done, step by step:

- Set a high and low mark based on the size of the array.
- Get the middle element between the low and high marks.

- If the key is less-than, then the key must be below the middle. Set high to one less than middle.

- If the key is greater-than, then the key must be above the middle. Set the low mark one greater than the middle.

- If it's equal, you found it. Stop.

- Keep looping until low and high pass each other. You won't find it if you exit the loop.

What you're effectively doing is guessing where the key might be by picking the middle and comparing it to the high and low marks. Since the data is sorted, you know that the the key has to be above or below your guess. If it's below, then you just divided the search space in half. You keep going until you either find it or you overlap the boundaries and exhaust the search space.

RadixMap_sort and radix_sort

A radix sort is easy to understand if you try to do it manually first. What this algorithm does is exploit the fact that numbers are stored with a sequence of digits that go from least significant to most significant. It then takes the numbers and buckets them by the digit, and when it has processed all of the digits, the numbers come out sorted. At first it seems like magic, and honestly, looking at the code sure seems like it is, so try doing it manually once.

To do this algorithm, write out a bunch of three-digit numbers in a random order. Let's say we do 223, 912, 275, 100, 633, 120, and 380.

- Place the number in buckets by the ones digit: [380, 100, 120], [912], [633, 223], [275].

- I now have to go through each of these buckets in order, and then sort it by the tens digit: [100], [912], [120, 223], [633], [275], [380].

- Now each bucket contains numbers that are sorted by the ones digit and then the tens digit. I need to then go through these in order and fill in the final hundreds digit: [100, 120], [223, 275], [380], [633], [912].

- At this point each bucket is sorted by hundreds, tens and ones, and if I take each bucket in order, I get the final sorted list: 100, 120, 223, 275, 380, 633, 912.

Make sure you do this a few times so you understand how it works. It really is a slick little algorithm. Most importantly, it will work on numbers of arbitrary size, so you can sort really huge numbers because you're just doing them 1 byte at a time.

In my situation, the digits (also called place values) are individual 8-bit bytes, so I need 256 buckets to store the distribution of the numbers by their digits. I also need a way to store them such that I don't use too much space. If you look at radix_sort, you'll see that the first thing I do is build a count histogram so I know how many occurrences of each digit there are for the given offset.

Once I know the counts for each digit (all 256 of them), I can then use them as distribution points into a target array. For example, if I have 10 bytes that are 0x00, then I know I can place them in the first ten slots of the target array. This gives me an index for where they go in the target array, which is the second for-loop in radix_sort.

Finally, once I know where they can go in the target array I simply go through all of the digits in the source array for this offset, and place the numbers in their slots in order. Using the ByteOf macro helps keep the code clean, since there's a bit of pointer hackery to make it work. However, the end result is that all of the integers will be placed in the bucket for their digit when the final for-loop is done.

What becomes interesting is how I use this in RadixMap_sort to sort these 64-bit integers by just the first 32 bits. Remember how I have the key and value in a union for the RMElement type? That means that to sort this array by the key, I only need to sort the first 4 bytes (32 bits / 8 bits per byte) of every integer.

If you look at the RadixMap_sort, you see that I grab a quick pointer to the contents and temp for source and target arrays, and then I call radix_sort four times. Each time I call it, I alternate source and target, and do the next byte. When I'm done, the radix_sort has done its job and the final copy has been sorted into the contents.

How to Improve It

There is a big disadvantage to this implementation because it has to process the entire array four times on every insertion. It does do it fast, but it'd be better if you could limit the amount of sorting by the size of what needs to be sorted.

There are two ways you can improve this implementation:

- Use a binary search to find the minimum position for the new element, then only sort from there to the end. You find the minimum, put the new element on the end, and then just sort from the minimum on. This will cut your sort space down considerably most of the time.

- Keep track of the biggest key currently being used, and then only sort enough digits to handle that key. You can also keep track of the smallest number, and then only sort the digits necessary for the range. To do this, you'll have to start caring about CPU integer ordering (endianness).

Try these optimizations, but only after you augment the unit test with some timing information so you can see if you're actually improving the speed of the implementation.

Extra Credit

- Implement quicksort, heapsort, and merge sort and then provide a #define that lets you pick among the three, or create a second set of functions you can call. Use the technique I taught you to read the Wikipedia page for the algorithm, and then implement it with the pseudo-code.

- Compare the performance of your optimizations to the original implementations.

- Use these sorting functions to create a DArray_sort_add that adds elements to the DArray but sorts the array afterward.

- Write a DArray_find that uses the binary search algorithm from RadixMap_find and the DArray_compare to find elements in a sorted DArray.

Safer Strings

This exercise is designed to get you using bstring from now on, explain why C's strings are an incredibly bad idea, and then have you change the liblcthw code to use bstring.

Why C Strings Were a Horrible Idea

When people talk about problems with C, they say its concept of a string is one of the top flaws. You've been using these extensively, and I've talked about the kinds of flaws they have, but there isn't much that explains exactly why C strings are flawed and always will be. I'll try to explain that right now, and after decades of using C's strings, there's enough evidence for me to say that they are just a bad idea.

It's impossible to confirm that any given C string is valid:

- A C string is invalid if it doesn't end in '\0'.

- Any loop that processes an invalid C string will loop infinitely (or just create a buffer overflow).

- C strings don't have a known length, so the only way to check if they're terminated correctly is to loop through them.

- Therefore, it isn't possible to validate a C string without possibly looping infinitely.

This is simple logic. You can't write a loop that checks if a C string is valid because invalid C strings cause loops to never terminate. That's it, and the only solution is to *include the size*. Once you know the size, you can avoid the infinite loop problem. If you look at the two functions I showed you from Exercise 27, you see this:

ex36.c

```
1    void copy(char to[], char from[])
2    {
3        int i = 0;
4
5        // while loop will not end if from isn't '\0' terminated
6        while ((to[i] = from[i]) != '\0') {
7            ++i;
8        }
9    }
```

```
10
11    int safercopy(int from_len, char *from, int to_len, char *to)
12    {
13        int i = 0;
14        int max = from_len > to_len - 1 ? to_len - 1 : from_len;
15
16        // to_len must have at least 1 byte
17        if (from_len < 0 || to_len <= 0)
18            return -1;
19
20        for (i = 0; i < max; i++) {
21            to[i] = from[i];
22        }
23
24        to[to_len - 1] = '\0';
25
26        return i;
27    }
```

Imagine that you want to add a check to the copy function to confirm that the from string is valid. How would you do that? You'd write a loop that checked that the string ended in '\0'. Oh wait. If the string doesn't end in '\0', then how does the checking loop end? It doesn't. Checkmate.

No matter what you do, you can't check that a C string is valid without knowing the length of the underlying storage, and in this case, the safercopy includes those lengths. This function doesn't have the same problem since its loops will always terminate, and even if you lie to it about the size, you still have to give it a finite size.

What the Better String Library does is create a structure that always includes the length of the string's storage. Because the length is always available to a bstring, then all of its operations can be safer. The loops will terminate, the contents can be validated, and it won't have this major flaw. The library also comes with a ton of operations you need with strings, like splitting, formatting, and searching, and they're most likely done right and are safer.

There could be flaws in bstring, but it's been around a long time, so those are probably minimal. They still find flaws in glibc, so what's a programmer to do, right?

Using bstrlib

There are quite a few improved string libraries, but I like bstrlib because it fits in one file for the basics, and has most of the stuff you need to deal with strings. In this exercise you'll need to get two files, bstrlib.c and bstrlib.h, from the Better String Library.

Here's me doing this in the `liblcthw` project directory:

```
$ mkdir bstrlib
$ cd bstrlib/
$ unzip ~/Downloads/bstrlib-05122010.zip
Archive:  /Users/zedshaw/Downloads/bstrlib-05122010.zip
...
$ ls
bsafe.c           bstraux.c       bstrlib.h
bstrwrap.h        license.txt     test.cpp
bsafe.h           bstraux.h       bstrlib.txt
cpptest.cpp       porting.txt     testaux.c
bstest.c bstrlib.c        bstrwrap.cpp
gpl.txt           security.txt
$ mv bstrlib.h bstrlib.c ../src/lcthw/
$ cd ../
$ rm -rf bstrlib
# make the edits
$ vim src/lcthw/bstrlib.c
$ make clean all
...
$
```

On line 14, you see me edit the `bstrlib.c` file to move it to a new location and fix a bug on OS X. Here's the diff file:

```
25c25
< #include "bstrlib.h"
---
> #include <lcthw/bstrlib.h>
2759c2759
< #ifdef __GNUC__
---
> #if defined(__GNUC__) && !defined(__APPLE__)
```

Here I change the `include` to be `<lcthw/bstrlib.h>`, and then fix one of the `ifdef` at line 2759.

Learning the Library

This exercise is short, and it's meant to simply get you ready for the remaining exercises that use the Better String Library. In the next two exercises, I'll use `bstrlib.c` to create a hashmap data structure.

You should now get familiar with this library by reading the header file and the implementations, and then write a tests/bstr_tests.c that tests out the following functions:

bfromcstr   Create a bstring from a C style constant.

blk2bstr   Do the same thing, but give the length of the buffer.

bstrcpy   Copy a bstring.

bassign   Set one bstring to another.

bassigncstr   Set a bstring to a C string's contents.

bassignblk   Set a bstring to a C string but give the length.

bdestroy   Destroy a bstring.

bconcat   Concatenate one bstring onto another.

bstricmp   Compare two bstrings returning the same result as strcmp.

biseq   Test if two bstrings are equal.

binstr   Tell if one bstring is in another.

bfindreplace   Find one bstring in another, then replace it with a third.

bsplit   Split a bstring into a bstrList.

bformat   Do a format string, which is super handy.

blength   Get the length of a bstring.

bdata   Get the data from a bstring.

bchar   Get a char from a bstring.

Your test should try out all of these operations, and a few more that you find interesting from the header file.

Hashmaps

Hash maps (hashmaps, hashes, or sometimes dictionaries) are used frequently in dynamic programming for storing key/value data. A hashmap works by performing a hashing calculation on the keys to produce an integer, then uses that integer to find a bucket to get or set the value. It's a very fast, practical data structure because it works on nearly any data and is easy to implement.

Here's an example of using a hashmap (aka, dictionary) in Python:

ex37.py

```python
fruit_weights = {'Apples': 10, 'Oranges': 100, 'Grapes': 1.0}

for key, value in fruit_weights.items():
    print key, "=", value
```

Almost every modern language has something like this, so many people end up writing code and never understand how this actually works. By creating the Hashmap data structure in C, I'll show you how this works. I'll start with the header file so I can talk about the data structure.

hashmap.h

```c
#ifndef _lcthw_Hashmap_h
#define _lcthw_Hashmap_h

#include <stdint.h>
#include <lcthw/darray.h>

#define DEFAULT_NUMBER_OF_BUCKETS 100

typedef int (*Hashmap_compare) (void *a, void *b);
typedef uint32_t(*Hashmap_hash) (void *key);

typedef struct Hashmap {
    DArray *buckets;
    Hashmap_compare compare;
    Hashmap_hash hash;
} Hashmap;

typedef struct HashmapNode {
    void *key;
    void *data;
    uint32_t hash;
} HashmapNode;

typedef int (*Hashmap_traverse_cb) (HashmapNode * node);
```

```
Hashmap *Hashmap_create(Hashmap_compare compare, Hashmap_hash);
void Hashmap_destroy(Hashmap * map);

int Hashmap_set(Hashmap * map, void *key, void *data);
void *Hashmap_get(Hashmap * map, void *key);

int Hashmap_traverse(Hashmap * map, Hashmap_traverse_cb traverse_cb);

void *Hashmap_delete(Hashmap * map, void *key);

#endif
```

The structure consists of a Hashmap that contains any number of HashmapNode structs. Looking at Hashmap, you can see that it's structured like this:

DArray *buckets   A dynamic array that will be set to a fixed size of 100 buckets. Each bucket will in turn contain a DArray that will hold HashmapNode pairs.

Hashmap_compare compare   This is a comparison function that the Hashmap uses to find elements by their key. It should work like all of the other compare functions, and it defaults to using bstrcmp so that keys are just bstrings.

Hashmap_hash hash   This is the hashing function, and it's responsible for taking a key, processing its contents, and producing a single uint32_t index number. You'll see the default one soon.

This almost tells you how the data is stored, but the buckets DArray hasn't been created yet. Just remember that it's kind of a two-level mapping:

- There are 100 buckets that make up the first level, and things are in these buckets based on their hash.

- Each bucket is a DArray that contains HashmapNode structs that are simply appended to the end as they're added.

The HashmapNode is then composed of these three elements:

void *key   The key for this key=value pair.

void *value   The value.

uint32_t hash   The calculated hash, which makes finding this node quicker. We can just check the hash and skip any that don't match, only checking the key if it's equal.

The rest of the header file is nothing new, so now I can show you the implementation `hashmap.c` file:

hashmap.c

```
1    #undef NDEBUG
2    #include <stdint.h>
3    #include <lcthw/hashmap.h>
4    #include <lcthw/dbg.h>
5    #include <lcthw/bstrlib.h>
6
7    static int default_compare(void *a, void *b)
8    {
9        return bstrcmp((bstring) a, (bstring) b);
10   }
11
12   /**
13    * Simple Bob Jenkins's hash algorithm taken from the
14    * wikipedia description.
15    */
16   static uint32_t default_hash(void *a)
17   {
18       size_t len = blength((bstring) a);
19       char *key = bdata((bstring) a);
20       uint32_t hash = 0;
21       uint32_t i = 0;
22
23       for (hash = i = 0; i < len; ++i) {
24           hash += key[i];
25           hash += (hash << 10);
26           hash ^= (hash >> 6);
27       }
28
29       hash += (hash << 3);
30       hash ^= (hash >> 11);
31       hash += (hash << 15);
32
33       return hash;
34   }
35
36   Hashmap *Hashmap_create(Hashmap_compare compare, Hashmap_hash hash)
37   {
38       Hashmap *map = calloc(1, sizeof(Hashmap));
39       check_mem(map);
40
41       map->compare = compare == NULL ? default_compare : compare;
42       map->hash = hash == NULL ? default_hash : hash;
43       map->buckets = DArray_create(
```

```
44                     sizeof(DArray *), DEFAULT_NUMBER_OF_BUCKETS);
45          map->buckets->end = map->buckets->max;  // fake out expanding it
46          check_mem(map->buckets);
47
48          return map;
49
50      error:
51          if (map) {
52              Hashmap_destroy(map);
53          }
54
55          return NULL;
56      }
57
58      void Hashmap_destroy(Hashmap * map)
59      {
60          int i = 0;
61          int j = 0;
62
63          if (map) {
64              if (map->buckets) {
65                  for (i = 0; i < DArray_count(map->buckets); i++) {
66                      DArray *bucket = DArray_get(map->buckets, i);
67                      if (bucket) {
68                          for (j = 0; j < DArray_count(bucket); j++) {
69                              free(DArray_get(bucket, j));
70                          }
71                          DArray_destroy(bucket);
72                      }
73                  }
74                  DArray_destroy(map->buckets);
75              }
76
77              free(map);
78          }
79      }
80
81      static inline HashmapNode *Hashmap_node_create(int hash, void *key,
82              void *data)
83      {
84          HashmapNode *node = calloc(1, sizeof(HashmapNode));
85          check_mem(node);
86
87          node->key = key;
88          node->data = data;
89          node->hash = hash;
90
91          return node;
92
93      error:
```

```
94          return NULL;
95      }
96
97      static inline DArray *Hashmap_find_bucket(Hashmap * map, void *key,
98              int create,
99              uint32_t * hash_out)
100     {
101         uint32_t hash = map->hash(key);
102         int bucket_n = hash % DEFAULT_NUMBER_OF_BUCKETS;
103         check(bucket_n >= 0, "Invalid bucket found: %d", bucket_n);
104         // store it for the return so the caller can use it
105         *hash_out = hash;
106
107         DArray *bucket = DArray_get(map->buckets, bucket_n);
108
109         if (!bucket && create) {
110             // new bucket, set it up
111             bucket = DArray_create(
112                     sizeof(void *), DEFAULT_NUMBER_OF_BUCKETS);
113             check_mem(bucket);
114             DArray_set(map->buckets, bucket_n, bucket);
115         }
116
117         return bucket;
118
119     error:
120         return NULL;
121     }
122
123     int Hashmap_set(Hashmap * map, void *key, void *data)
124     {
125         uint32_t hash = 0;
126         DArray *bucket = Hashmap_find_bucket(map, key, 1, &hash);
127         check(bucket, "Error can't create bucket.");
128
129         HashmapNode *node = Hashmap_node_create(hash, key, data);
130         check_mem(node);
131
132         DArray_push(bucket, node);
133
134         return 0;
135
136     error:
137         return -1;
138     }
139
140     static inline int Hashmap_get_node(Hashmap * map, uint32_t hash,
141             DArray * bucket, void *key)
142     {
143         int i = 0;
```

```
144
145         for (i = 0; i < DArray_end(bucket); i++) {
146             debug("TRY: %d", i);
147             HashmapNode *node = DArray_get(bucket, i);
148             if (node->hash == hash && map->compare(node->key, key) == 0) {
149                 return i;
150             }
151         }
152
153         return -1;
154     }
155
156     void *Hashmap_get(Hashmap * map, void *key)
157     {
158         uint32_t hash = 0;
159         DArray *bucket = Hashmap_find_bucket(map, key, 0, &hash);
160         if (!bucket) return NULL;
161
162         int i = Hashmap_get_node(map, hash, bucket, key);
163         if (i == -1) return NULL;
164
165         HashmapNode *node = DArray_get(bucket, i);
166         check(node != NULL,
167                 "Failed to get node from bucket when it should exist.");
168
169         return node->data;
170
171     error:                      // fallthrough
172         return NULL;
173     }
174
175     int Hashmap_traverse(Hashmap * map, Hashmap_traverse_cb traverse_cb)
176     {
177         int i = 0;
178         int j = 0;
179         int rc = 0;
180
181         for (i = 0; i < DArray_count(map->buckets); i++) {
182             DArray *bucket = DArray_get(map->buckets, i);
183             if (bucket) {
184                 for (j = 0; j < DArray_count(bucket); j++) {
185                     HashmapNode *node = DArray_get(bucket, j);
186                     rc = traverse_cb(node);
187                     if (rc != 0)
188                         return rc;
189                 }
190             }
191         }
192
193         return 0;
```

```
194    }
195
196    void *Hashmap_delete(Hashmap * map, void *key)
197    {
198        uint32_t hash = 0;
199        DArray *bucket = Hashmap_find_bucket(map, key, 0, &hash);
200        if (!bucket)
201            return NULL;
202
203        int i = Hashmap_get_node(map, hash, bucket, key);
204        if (i == -1)
205            return NULL;
206
207        HashmapNode *node = DArray_get(bucket, i);
208        void *data = node->data;
209        free(node);
210
211        HashmapNode *ending = DArray_pop(bucket);
212
213        if (ending != node) {
214            // alright looks like it's not the last one, swap it
215            DArray_set(bucket, i, ending);
216        }
217
218        return data;
219    }
```

There's nothing very complicated in the implementation, but the default_hash and Hashmap_find_bucket functions will need some explanation. When you use Hashmap_create, you can pass in any compare and hash functions you want, but if you don't, it uses the default_compare and default_hash functions.

The first thing to look at is how default_hash does its thing. This is a simple hash function called a Jenkins hash after Bob Jenkins. I got the algorithm from the "Jenkins hash" page on Wikipedia. It simply goes through each byte of the key to hash (a bstring), and then it works the bits so that the end result is a single uint32_t. It does this with some adding and exclusive or (XOR) operations.

There are many different hash functions, all with different properties, but once you have one, you need a way to use it to find the right buckets. The Hashmap_find_bucket does it like this:

- First, it calls map->hash(key) to get the hash for the key.
- It then finds the bucket using hash % DEFAULT_NUMBER_OF_BUCKETS, so every hash will always find some bucket no matter how big it is.
- It then gets the bucket, which is also a DArray, and if it's not there, it will create the bucket. However, that depends on if the create variable says to do so.

- Once it has found the DArray bucket for the right hash, it returns it, and the hash_out variable is used to give the caller the hash that was found.

All of the other functions then use Hashmap_find_bucket to do their work:

- Setting a key/value involves finding the bucket, making a HashmapNode, and then adding it to the bucket.

- Getting a key involves finding the bucket, and then finding the HashmapNode that matches the hash and key that you want.

- Deleting an item finds the bucket, finds where the requested node is, and then removes it by swapping the last node into its place.

The only other function that you should study is the Hashmap_traverse. This simply walks through every bucket, and for any bucket that has possible values, it calls the traverse_cb on each value. This is how you scan a whole Hashmap for its values.

The Unit Test

Finally, you have the unit test to test all of these operations:

hashmap_tests.c

```
1    #include "minunit.h"
2    #include <lcthw/hashmap.h>
3    #include <assert.h>
4    #include <lcthw/bstrlib.h>
5
6    Hashmap *map = NULL;
7    static int traverse_called = 0;
8    struct tagbstring test1 = bsStatic("test data 1");
9    struct tagbstring test2 = bsStatic("test data 2");
10   struct tagbstring test3 = bsStatic("xest data 3");
11   struct tagbstring expect1 = bsStatic("THE VALUE 1");
12   struct tagbstring expect2 = bsStatic("THE VALUE 2");
13   struct tagbstring expect3 = bsStatic("THE VALUE 3");
14
15   static int traverse_good_cb(HashmapNode * node)
16   {
17       debug("KEY: %s", bdata((bstring) node->key));
18       traverse_called++;
19       return 0;
20   }
21
22   static int traverse_fail_cb(HashmapNode * node)
23   {
24       debug("KEY: %s", bdata((bstring) node->key));
```

```
25          traverse_called++;
26
27          if (traverse_called == 2) {
28              return 1;
29          } else {
30              return 0;
31          }
32      }
33
34      char *test_create()
35      {
36          map = Hashmap_create(NULL, NULL);
37          mu_assert(map != NULL, "Failed to create map.");
38
39          return NULL;
40      }
41
42      char *test_destroy()
43      {
44          Hashmap_destroy(map);
45
46          return NULL;
47      }
48
49      char *test_get_set()
50      {
51          int rc = Hashmap_set(map, &test1, &expect1);
52          mu_assert(rc == 0, "Failed to set &test1");
53          bstring result = Hashmap_get(map, &test1);
54          mu_assert(result == &expect1, "Wrong value for test1.");
55
56          rc = Hashmap_set(map, &test2, &expect2);
57          mu_assert(rc == 0, "Failed to set test2");
58          result = Hashmap_get(map, &test2);
59          mu_assert(result == &expect2, "Wrong value for test2.");
60
61          rc = Hashmap_set(map, &test3, &expect3);
62          mu_assert(rc == 0, "Failed to set test3");
63          result = Hashmap_get(map, &test3);
64          mu_assert(result == &expect3, "Wrong value for test3.");
65
66          return NULL;
67      }
68
69      char *test_traverse()
70      {
71          int rc = Hashmap_traverse(map, traverse_good_cb);
72          mu_assert(rc == 0, "Failed to traverse.");
73          mu_assert(traverse_called == 3, "Wrong count traverse.");
74
```

```
75          traverse_called = 0;
76          rc = Hashmap_traverse(map, traverse_fail_cb);
77          mu_assert(rc == 1, "Failed to traverse.");
78          mu_assert(traverse_called == 2, "Wrong count traverse for fail.");
79
80          return NULL;
81      }
82
83      char *test_delete()
84      {
85          bstring deleted = (bstring) Hashmap_delete(map, &test1);
86          mu_assert(deleted != NULL, "Got NULL on delete.");
87          mu_assert(deleted == &expect1, "Should get test1");
88          bstring result = Hashmap_get(map, &test1);
89          mu_assert(result == NULL, "Should delete.");
90
91          deleted = (bstring) Hashmap_delete(map, &test2);
92          mu_assert(deleted != NULL, "Got NULL on delete.");
93          mu_assert(deleted == &expect2, "Should get test2");
94          result = Hashmap_get(map, &test2);
95          mu_assert(result == NULL, "Should delete.");
96
97          deleted = (bstring) Hashmap_delete(map, &test3);
98          mu_assert(deleted != NULL, "Got NULL on delete.");
99          mu_assert(deleted == &expect3, "Should get test3");
100         result = Hashmap_get(map, &test3);
101         mu_assert(result == NULL, "Should delete.");
102
103         return NULL;
104     }
105
106     char *all_tests()
107     {
108         mu_suite_start();
109
110         mu_run_test(test_create);
111         mu_run_test(test_get_set);
112         mu_run_test(test_traverse);
113         mu_run_test(test_delete);
114         mu_run_test(test_destroy);
115
116         return NULL;
117     }
118
119     RUN_TESTS(all_tests);
```

The only thing to learn about this unit test is that at the top I use a feature of bstring to create static strings to work within the tests. I use the tagbstring and bsStatic to create them on lines 7–13.

How to Improve It

This is a very simple implementation of Hashmap, as are most of the other data structures in this book. My goal isn't to give you insanely great, hyper-speed, well-tuned data structures. Usually those are much too complicated to discuss and only distract you from the real, basic data structure at work. My goal is to give you an understandable starting point to then improve upon or better understand the implementation.

In this case, there are some things you can do with this implementation:

- You can use a sort on each bucket so that they're always sorted. This increases your insert time but decreases your find time, because you can then use a binary search to find each node. Right now, it's looping through all of the nodes in a bucket just to find one.
- You can dynamically size the number of buckets, or let the caller specify the number for each Hashmap created.
- You can use a better default_hash. There are tons of them.
- This (and nearly every Hashmap) is vulnerable to someone picking keys that will fill only one bucket, and then tricking your program into processing them. This then makes your program run slower because it changes from processing a Hashmap to effectively processing a single DArray. If you sort the nodes in the bucket, this helps, but you can also use better hashing functions, and for the really paranoid programmer, add a random salt so that keys can't be predicted.
- You could have it delete buckets that are empty of nodes to save space, or put empty buckets into a cache so you can save on time lost creating and destroying them.
- Right now, it just adds elements even if they already exist. Write an alternative set method that only adds an element if it isn't set already.

As usual, you should go through each function and make it bulletproof. The Hashmap could also use a debug setting for doing an invariant check.

Extra Credit

- Research the Hashmap implementation in your favorite programming language to see what features it has.
- Find out what the major disadvantages of a Hashmap are and how to avoid them. For example, it doesn't preserve order without special changes, nor does it work when you need to find things based on parts of keys.
- Write a unit test that demonstrates the defect of filling a Hashmap with keys that land in the same bucket, then test how this impacts performance. A good way to do this is to just reduce the number of buckets to something stupid, like five.

Hashmap Algorithms

There are three hash functions that you'll implement in this exercise:

FNV-1a   Named after the creators Glenn Fowler, Phong Vo, and Landon Curt Noll, this hash produces good numbers and is reasonably fast.

Adler-32   Named after Mark Adler, this is a horrible hash algorithm, but it's been around a long time and it's good for studying.

DJB Hash   This hash algorithm is attributed to Dan J. Bernstein (DJB), but it's difficult to find his discussion of the algorithm. It's shown to be fast, but possibly not great numbers.

You've already seen the Jenkins hash as the default hash for the Hashmap data structure, so this exercise will be looking at these three new hash functions. The code for them is usually small, and it's not optimized at all. As usual, I'm going for understanding and not blinding speed.

The header file is very simple, so I'll start with that:

hashmap_algos.h

```
#ifndef hashmap_algos_h
#define hashmap_algos_h

#include <stdint.h>

uint32_t Hashmap_fnv1a_hash(void *data);

uint32_t Hashmap_adler32_hash(void *data);

uint32_t Hashmap_djb_hash(void *data);

#endif
```

I'm just declaring the three functions I'll implement in the hashmap_algos.c file:

hashmap_algos.c

```
1   #include <lcthw/hashmap_algos.h>
2   #include <lcthw/bstrlib.h>
3
4   // settings taken from
5   // http://www.isthe.com/chongo/tech/comp/fnv/index.html#FNV-param
6   const uint32_t FNV_PRIME = 16777619;
7   const uint32_t FNV_OFFSET_BASIS = 2166136261;
```

```
 8
 9    uint32_t Hashmap_fnv1a_hash(void *data)
10    {
11        bstring s = (bstring) data;
12        uint32_t hash = FNV_OFFSET_BASIS;
13        int i = 0;
14
15        for (i = 0; i < blength(s); i++) {
16            hash ^= bchare(s, i, 0);
17            hash *= FNV_PRIME;
18        }
19
20        return hash;
21    }
22
23    const int MOD_ADLER = 65521;
24
25    uint32_t Hashmap_adler32_hash(void *data)
26    {
27        bstring s = (bstring) data;
28        uint32_t a = 1, b = 0;
29        int i = 0;
30
31        for (i = 0; i < blength(s); i++) {
32            a = (a + bchare(s, i, 0)) % MOD_ADLER;
33            b = (b + a) % MOD_ADLER;
34        }
35
36        return (b << 16) | a;
37    }
38
39    uint32_t Hashmap_djb_hash(void *data)
40    {
41        bstring s = (bstring) data;
42        uint32_t hash = 5381;
43        int i = 0;
44
45        for (i = 0; i < blength(s); i++) {
46            hash = ((hash << 5) + hash) + bchare(s, i, 0); /* hash * 33 + c */
47        }
48
49        return hash;
50    }
```

This file, then, has the three hash algorithms. You should notice that I'm just using a bstring for the key, but I'm using the bchare function to get a character from the bstring, but returning 0 if that character is outside the string's length.

Each of these algorithms are found online, so go search for them and read about them. Again, I primarily used Wikipedia and then followed it to other sources.

I then have a unit test that tests out each algorithm, but it also tests whether it will distribute well across a number of buckets:

hashmap_algos_tests.c

```
1    #include <lcthw/bstrlib.h>
2    #include <lcthw/hashmap.h>
3    #include <lcthw/hashmap_algos.h>
4    #include <lcthw/darray.h>
5    #include "minunit.h"
6
7    struct tagbstring test1 = bsStatic("test data 1");
8    struct tagbstring test2 = bsStatic("test data 2");
9    struct tagbstring test3 = bsStatic("xest data 3");
10
11   char *test_fnv1a()
12   {
13       uint32_t hash = Hashmap_fnv1a_hash(&test1);
14       mu_assert(hash != 0, "Bad hash.");
15
16       hash = Hashmap_fnv1a_hash(&test2);
17       mu_assert(hash != 0, "Bad hash.");
18
19       hash = Hashmap_fnv1a_hash(&test3);
20       mu_assert(hash != 0, "Bad hash.");
21
22       return NULL;
23   }
24
25   char *test_adler32()
26   {
27       uint32_t hash = Hashmap_adler32_hash(&test1);
28       mu_assert(hash != 0, "Bad hash.");
29
30       hash = Hashmap_adler32_hash(&test2);
31       mu_assert(hash != 0, "Bad hash.");
32
33       hash = Hashmap_adler32_hash(&test3);
34       mu_assert(hash != 0, "Bad hash.");
35
36       return NULL;
37   }
38
39   char *test_djb()
40   {
41       uint32_t hash = Hashmap_djb_hash(&test1);
42       mu_assert(hash != 0, "Bad hash.");
43
44       hash = Hashmap_djb_hash(&test2);
45       mu_assert(hash != 0, "Bad hash.");
46
47       hash = Hashmap_djb_hash(&test3);
```

```
48           mu_assert(hash != 0, "Bad hash.");
49
50           return NULL;
51       }
52
53       #define BUCKETS 100
54       #define BUFFER_LEN 20
55       #define NUM_KEYS BUCKETS * 1000
56       enum { ALGO_FNV1A, ALGO_ADLER32, ALGO_DJB };
57
58       int gen_keys(DArray * keys, int num_keys)
59       {
60           int i = 0;
61           FILE *urand = fopen("/dev/urandom", "r");
62           check(urand != NULL, "Failed to open /dev/urandom");
63
64           struct bStream *stream = bsopen((bNread) fread, urand);
65           check(stream != NULL, "Failed to open /dev/urandom");
66
67           bstring key = bfromcstr("");
68           int rc = 0;
69
70           // FNV1a histogram
71           for (i = 0; i < num_keys; i++) {
72               rc = bsread(key, stream, BUFFER_LEN);
73               check(rc >= 0, "Failed to read from /dev/urandom.");
74
75               DArray_push(keys, bstrcpy(key));
76           }
77
78           bsclose(stream);
79           fclose(urand);
80           return 0;
81
82       error:
83           return -1;
84       }
85
86       void destroy_keys(DArray * keys)
87       {
88           int i = 0;
89           for (i = 0; i < NUM_KEYS; i++) {
90               bdestroy(DArray_get(keys, i));
91           }
92
93           DArray_destroy(keys);
94       }
95
96       void fill_distribution(int *stats, DArray * keys,
97               Hashmap_hash hash_func)
```

```
98      {
99          int i = 0;
100         uint32_t hash = 0;
101
102         for (i = 0; i < DArray_count(keys); i++) {
103             hash = hash_func(DArray_get(keys, i));
104             stats[hash % BUCKETS] += 1;
105         }
106
107     }
108
109     char *test_distribution()
110     {
111         int i = 0;
112         int stats[3][BUCKETS] = { {0} };
113         DArray *keys = DArray_create(0, NUM_KEYS);
114
115         mu_assert(gen_keys(keys, NUM_KEYS) == 0,
116                 "Failed to generate random keys.");
117
118         fill_distribution(stats[ALGO_FNV1A], keys, Hashmap_fnv1a_hash);
119         fill_distribution(stats[ALGO_ADLER32], keys, Hashmap_adler32_hash);
120         fill_distribution(stats[ALGO_DJB], keys, Hashmap_djb_hash);
121
122         fprintf(stderr, "FNV\tA32\tDJB\n");
123
124         for (i = 0; i < BUCKETS; i++) {
125             fprintf(stderr, "%d\t%d\t%d\n",
126                     stats[ALGO_FNV1A][i],
127                     stats[ALGO_ADLER32][i], stats[ALGO_DJB][i]);
128         }
129
130         destroy_keys(keys);
131
132         return NULL;
133     }
134
135     char *all_tests()
136     {
137         mu_suite_start();
138
139         mu_run_test(test_fnv1a);
140         mu_run_test(test_adler32);
141         mu_run_test(test_djb);
142         mu_run_test(test_distribution);
143
144         return NULL;
145     }
146
147     RUN_TESTS(all_tests);
```

I have the number of BUCKETS in this code set fairly high, since I have a fast enough computer, but if it runs slow, just lower it and NUM_KEYS. What this test lets me do is run the test and then look at the distribution of keys for each hash function using a bit of analysis with a language called R.

I do this by crafting a big list of keys using the gen_keys function. These keys are taken out of the /dev/urandom device and are random byte keys. I then use these keys to have the fill_distribution function fill up the stats array with where those keys would hash in a theoretical set of buckets. All this function does is go through all of the keys, do the hash, then do what the Hashmap would do to find its bucket.

Finally, I'm simply printing out a three-column table with the final count for each bucket, showing how many keys managed to get into each bucket randomly. I can then look at these numbers to see if the hash functions are distributing keys evenly.

What You Should See

Teaching you R is outside the scope of this book, but if you want to get it and try this, it can be found at www.r-project.org.

Here is an abbreviated shell session that shows me running tests/hashmap_algos_test to get the table produced by test_distribution (not shown here), and then using R to see what the summary statistics are.

Exercise 38 Session

```
$ tests/hashmap_algos_tests
# copy-paste the table it prints out
$ vim hash.txt
$ R
> hash <- read.table("hash.txt", header=T)
> summary(hash)
      FNV              A32              DJB
 Min.   : 945    Min.   : 908.0    Min.   : 927
 1st Qu.: 980    1st Qu.: 980.8    1st Qu.: 979
 Median : 998    Median :1000.0    Median : 998
 Mean   :1000    Mean   :1000.0    Mean   :1000
 3rd Qu.:1016    3rd Qu.:1019.2    3rd Qu.:1021
 Max.   :1072    Max.   :1075.0    Max.   :1082
>
```

First, I just run the test, which on your screen will print the table. Then, I just copy-paste it out of my terminal and use vim hash.txt to save the data. If you look at the data, it has the header FNV A32 DJB for each of the three algorithms.

Secondly, I run R and load the data using the read.table command. This is a smart function that works with this kind of tab-delimited data, and I only have to tell it header=T for it to know that the data has a header.

Finally, I have the data loaded and can use summary to print out its summary statistics for each column. Here you can see that each function actually does alright with this random data. Here's what each of these rows means:

Min. This is the minimum value found for the data in that column. FNV-1a seems to win on this run since it has the largest number, meaning it has a tighter range at the low end.

1st Qu. This is the point where the first quarter of the data ends.

Median This is the number that's in the middle if you sorted them. Median is most useful when compared to mean.

Mean Mean is the average most people think of, and it's the sum divided by the count of the data. If you look, all of them are 1,000, which is great. If you compare this to the median, you see that all three have really close medians to the mean. What this means is the data isn't skewed in one direction, so you can trust the mean.

3rd Qu. This is the point where the last quarter of the data starts and represents the tail end of the numbers.

Max. This is the maximum number of the data, and presents the upper bound on all of them.

Looking at this data, you see that all of these hashes seem to do well on random keys, and the means match the NUM_KEYS setting that I made. What I'm looking for is this: If I make 1,000 keys per bucket (BUCKETS × 1000), then on average each bucket should have 1,000 keys in it. If the hash function isn't working, then you'll see these summary statistics show a mean that's not 1,000, and really high ranges at the first and third quarters. A good hash function should have a dead-on 1,000 mean, and as tight a range as possible.

You should also know that you'll get different numbers from mine, and even between different runs of this unit test.

How to Break It

I'm finally going to have you do some breaking in this exercise. I want you to write the worst hash function you can, and then use the data to prove that it's really bad. You can use R to do the statistics, just like I did, but maybe you have another tool that you can use to give you the same summary statistics.

The goal is to make a hash function that seems normal to an untrained eye, but when actually run, it has a bad mean and is all over the place. That means you can't just have it return 1. You have to give a stream of numbers that seem alright but aren't, and they're loading up some buckets too much.

Extra points if you can make a minimal change to one of the four hash algorithms that I gave you to do this.

The purpose of this exercise is to imagine that some friendly coder comes to you and offers to improve your hash function, but actually just makes a nice little back door that really screws up your Hashmap.

As the Royal Society says, "*Nullius in verba.*"

Extra Credit

- Take the `default_hash` out of the `hashmap.c`, make it one of the algorithms in `hashmap_algos.c`, and then make all of the tests work again.

- Add the `default_hash` to the `hashmap_algos_tests.c` test and compare its statistics to the other hash functions.

- Find a few more hash functions and add them, too. You can never have too many hash functions!

String Algorithms

In this exercise, I'm going to show you a supposedly faster string search algorithm, called `binstr`, and compare it to the one that exists in `bstrlib.c`. The documentation for `binstr` says that it uses a simple "brute force" string search to find the first instance. The one that I'll implement will use the Boyer-Moore-Horspool (BMH) algorithm, which is supposed to be faster if you analyze the theoretical time. Assuming my implementation isn't flawed, you'll see that the practical time for BMH is much worse than the simple brute force of `binstr`.

The point of this exercise isn't really to explain the algorithm, because it's simple enough for you to read the "Boyer-Moore-Horspool algorithm" page on Wikipedia. The gist of this algorithm is that it calculates a *skip characters* list as a first operation, then it uses this list to quickly scan through the string. It's supposed to be faster than brute force, so let's get the code into the right files and see.

First, I have the header:

string_algos.h

```
#ifndef string_algos_h
#define string_algos_h

#include <lcthw/bstrlib.h>
#include <lcthw/darray.h>

typedef struct StringScanner {
    bstring in;
    const unsigned char *haystack;
    ssize_t hlen;
    const unsigned char *needle;
    ssize_t nlen;
    size_t skip_chars[UCHAR_MAX + 1];
} StringScanner;

int String_find(bstring in, bstring what);

StringScanner *StringScanner_create(bstring in);

int StringScanner_scan(StringScanner * scan, bstring tofind);

void StringScanner_destroy(StringScanner * scan);

#endif
```

In order to see the effects of this skip characters list, I'm going to make two versions of the BMH algorithm:

String_find   This simply finds the first instance of one string in another, doing the entire algorithm in one shot.

StringScanner_scan   This uses a `StringScanner` state structure to separate the skip list build from the actual find. This will let me see what impact that has on performance. This model also gives me the advantage of incrementally scanning for one string in another and quickly finding all instances.

Once you have that, here's the implementation:

string_algos.c

```
1    #include <lcthw/string_algos.h>
2    #include <limits.h>
3
4    static inline void String_setup_skip_chars(size_t * skip_chars,
5            const unsigned char *needle,
6            ssize_t nlen)
7    {
8        size_t i = 0;
9        size_t last = nlen - 1;
10
11       for (i = 0; i < UCHAR_MAX + 1; i++) {
12           skip_chars[i] = nlen;
13       }
14
15       for (i = 0; i < last; i++) {
16           skip_chars[needle[i]] = last - i;
17       }
18   }
19
20   static inline const unsigned char *String_base_search(const unsigned
21           char *haystack,
22           ssize_t hlen,
23           const unsigned
24           char *needle,
25           ssize_t nlen,
26           size_t *
27           skip_chars)
28   {
29       size_t i = 0;
30       size_t last = nlen - 1;
31
32       assert(haystack != NULL && "Given bad haystack to search.");
33       assert(needle != NULL && "Given bad needle to search for.");
34
```

```
35          check(nlen > 0, "nlen can't be <= 0");
36          check(hlen > 0, "hlen can't be <= 0");
37
38          while (hlen >= nlen) {
39              for (i = last; haystack[i] == needle[i]; i--) {
40                  if (i == 0) {
41                      return haystack;
42                  }
43              }
44
45              hlen -= skip_chars[haystack[last]];
46              haystack += skip_chars[haystack[last]];
47          }
48
49      error:                    // fallthrough
50          return NULL;
51      }
52
53      int String_find(bstring in, bstring what)
54      {
55          const unsigned char *found = NULL;
56
57          const unsigned char *haystack = (const unsigned char *)bdata(in);
58          ssize_t hlen = blength(in);
59          const unsigned char *needle = (const unsigned char *)bdata(what);
60          ssize_t nlen = blength(what);
61          size_t skip_chars[UCHAR_MAX + 1] = { 0 };
62
63          String_setup_skip_chars(skip_chars, needle, nlen);
64
65          found = String_base_search(haystack, hlen,
66                      needle, nlen, skip_chars);
67
68          return found != NULL ? found - haystack : -1;
69      }
70
71      StringScanner *StringScanner_create(bstring in)
72      {
73          StringScanner *scan = calloc(1, sizeof(StringScanner));
74          check_mem(scan);
75
76          scan->in = in;
77          scan->haystack = (const unsigned char *)bdata(in);
78          scan->hlen = blength(in);
79
80          assert(scan != NULL && "fuck");
81          return scan;
82
83      error:
84          free(scan);
```

```
85          return NULL;
86      }
87
88      static inline void StringScanner_set_needle(StringScanner * scan,
89              bstring tofind)
90      {
91          scan->needle = (const unsigned char *)bdata(tofind);
92          scan->nlen = blength(tofind);
93
94          String_setup_skip_chars(scan->skip_chars, scan->needle, scan->nlen);
95      }
96
97      static inline void StringScanner_reset(StringScanner * scan)
98      {
99          scan->haystack = (const unsigned char *)bdata(scan->in);
100         scan->hlen = blength(scan->in);
101     }
102
103     int StringScanner_scan(StringScanner * scan, bstring tofind)
104     {
105         const unsigned char *found = NULL;
106         ssize_t found_at = 0;
107
108         if (scan->hlen <= 0) {
109             StringScanner_reset(scan);
110             return -1;
111         }
112
113         if ((const unsigned char *)bdata(tofind) != scan->needle) {
114             StringScanner_set_needle(scan, tofind);
115         }
116
117         found = String_base_search(scan->haystack, scan->hlen,
118                 scan->needle, scan->nlen,
119                 scan->skip_chars);
120
121         if (found) {
122             found_at = found - (const unsigned char *)bdata(scan->in);
123             scan->haystack = found + scan->nlen;
124             scan->hlen -= found_at - scan->nlen;
125         } else {
126             // done, reset the setup
127             StringScanner_reset(scan);
128             found_at = -1;
129         }
130
131         return found_at;
132     }
133
134     void StringScanner_destroy(StringScanner * scan)
```

```
135    {
136        if (scan) {
137            free(scan);
138        }
139    }
```

The entire algorithm is in two static inline functions called String_setup_skip_chars and String_base_search. These are then used in the other functions to actually implement the searching styles I want. Study these first two functions and compare them to the Wikipedia description so that you know what's going on.

The String_find then just uses these two functions to do a find and return the position found. It's very simple, and I'll use it to see how this build skip_chars phase impacts real, practical performance. Keep in mind that you could maybe make this faster, but I'm teaching you how to confirm theoretical speed after you implement an algorithm.

The StringScanner_scan function then follows the common pattern I use of create, scan, and destroy, and is used to incrementally scan a string for another string. You'll see how this is used when I show you the unit test that will test this out.

Finally, I have the unit test that first confirms that this is all working, then it runs simple performance tests for all three, finding algorithms in a *commented out section*.

string_algos_tests.c

```
1    #include "minunit.h"
2    #include <lcthw/string_algos.h>
3    #include <lcthw/bstrlib.h>
4    #include <time.h>
5
6    struct tagbstring IN_STR = bsStatic(
7            "I have ALPHA beta ALPHA and oranges ALPHA");
8    struct tagbstring ALPHA = bsStatic("ALPHA");
9    const int TEST_TIME = 1;
10
11   char *test_find_and_scan()
12   {
13       StringScanner *scan = StringScanner_create(&IN_STR);
14       mu_assert(scan != NULL, "Failed to make the scanner.");
15
16       int find_i = String_find(&IN_STR, &ALPHA);
17       mu_assert(find_i > 0, "Failed to find 'ALPHA' in test string.");
18
19       int scan_i = StringScanner_scan(scan, &ALPHA);
20       mu_assert(scan_i > 0, "Failed to find 'ALPHA' with scan.");
21       mu_assert(scan_i == find_i, "find and scan don't match");
22
23       scan_i = StringScanner_scan(scan, &ALPHA);
24       mu_assert(scan_i > find_i,
```

```
25                      "should find another ALPHA after the first");
26
27          scan_i = StringScanner_scan(scan, &ALPHA);
28          mu_assert(scan_i > find_i,
29                      "should find another ALPHA after the first");
30
31          mu_assert(StringScanner_scan(scan, &ALPHA) == -1,
32                      "shouldn't find it");
33
34          StringScanner_destroy(scan);
35
36          return NULL;
37      }
38
39      char *test_binstr_performance()
40      {
41          int i = 0;
42          int found_at = 0;
43          unsigned long find_count = 0;
44          time_t elapsed = 0;
45          time_t start = time(NULL);
46
47          do {
48              for (i = 0; i < 1000; i++) {
49                  found_at = binstr(&IN_STR, 0, &ALPHA);
50                  mu_assert(found_at != BSTR_ERR, "Failed to find!");
51                  find_count++;
52              }
53
54              elapsed = time(NULL) - start;
55          } while (elapsed <= TEST_TIME);
56
57          debug("BINSTR COUNT: %lu, END TIME: %d, OPS: %f",
58                  find_count, (int)elapsed, (double)find_count / elapsed);
59          return NULL;
60      }
61
62      char *test_find_performance()
63      {
64          int i = 0;
65          int found_at = 0;
66          unsigned long find_count = 0;
67          time_t elapsed = 0;
68          time_t start = time(NULL);
69
70          do {
71              for (i = 0; i < 1000; i++) {
72                  found_at = String_find(&IN_STR, &ALPHA);
73                  find_count++;
74              }
```

```
75
76            elapsed = time(NULL) - start;
77        } while (elapsed <= TEST_TIME);
78
79        debug("FIND COUNT: %lu, END TIME: %d, OPS: %f",
80                find_count, (int)elapsed, (double)find_count / elapsed);
81
82        return NULL;
83    }
84
85    char *test_scan_performance()
86    {
87        int i = 0;
88        int found_at = 0;
89        unsigned long find_count = 0;
90        time_t elapsed = 0;
91        StringScanner *scan = StringScanner_create(&IN_STR);
92
93        time_t start = time(NULL);
94
95        do {
96            for (i = 0; i < 1000; i++) {
97                found_at = 0;
98
99                do {
100                    found_at = StringScanner_scan(scan, &ALPHA);
101                    find_count++;
102                } while (found_at != -1);
103            }
104
105            elapsed = time(NULL) - start;
106        } while (elapsed <= TEST_TIME);
107
108        debug("SCAN COUNT: %lu, END TIME: %d, OPS: %f",
109                find_count, (int)elapsed, (double)find_count / elapsed);
110
111        StringScanner_destroy(scan);
112
113        return NULL;
114    }
115
116    char *all_tests()
117    {
118        mu_suite_start();
119
120        mu_run_test(test_find_and_scan);
121
122        // this is an idiom for commenting out sections of code
123    #if 0
124        mu_run_test(test_scan_performance);
```

```
125        mu_run_test(test_find_performance);
126        mu_run_test(test_binstr_performance);
127   #endif
128
129        return NULL;
130   }
131
132   RUN_TESTS(all_tests);
```

I have it written here with #if 0, which is a way to use the CPP to comment out a section of code. Type it in like this, and then remove it and the #endif so that you can see these performance tests run. As you continue with the book, simply comment these out so that the test doesn't waste development time.

There's nothing amazing in this unit test; it just runs each of the different functions in loops that last long enough to get a few seconds of sampling. The first test (test_find_and_scan) just confirms that what I've written works, because there's no point in testing the speed of something that doesn't work. Then, the next three functions run a large number of searches, using each of the three functions.

The trick to notice is that I grab the starting time in start, and then I loop until at least TEST_TIME seconds have passed. This makes sure that I get enough samples to work with while comparing the three. I'll then run this test with different TEST_TIME settings and analyze the results.

What You Should See

When I run this test on my laptop, I get numbers that look like this:

Exercise 39.1 Session

```
$ ./tests/string_algos_tests
DEBUG tests/string_algos_tests.c:124: ----- RUNNING:
    ./tests/string_algos_tests
----
RUNNING: ./tests/string_algos_tests
DEBUG tests/string_algos_tests.c:116:
----- test_find_and_scan
DEBUG tests/string_algos_tests.c:117:
----- test_scan_performance
DEBUG tests/string_algos_tests.c:105: SCAN COUNT:\
        110272000, END TIME: 2, OPS: 55136000.000000
DEBUG tests/string_algos_tests.c:118:
----- test_find_performance
DEBUG tests/string_algos_tests.c:76: FIND COUNT:\
        12710000, END TIME: 2, OPS: 6355000.000000
DEBUG tests/string_algos_tests.c:119:
----- test_binstr_performance
```

```
DEBUG tests/string_algos_tests.c:54: BINSTR COUNT:\
       72736000, END TIME: 2, OPS: 36368000.000000
ALL TESTS PASSED
Tests run: 4
$
```

I look at this and I want to do more than 2 seconds for each run. I want to run this many times, and then use R to check it out like I did before. Here's what I get for ten samples for about 10 seconds each:

```
scan find binstr
71195200 6353700 37110200
75098000 6358400 37420800
74910000 6351300 37263600
74859600 6586100 37133200
73345600 6365200 37549700
74754400 6358000 37162400
75343600 6630400 37075000
73804800 6439900 36858700
74995200 6384300 36811700
74781200 6449500 37383000
```

The way I got this is using a little bit of shell help, and then editing the output:

Exercise 39.2 Session

```
$ for i in 1 2 3 4 5 6 7 8 9 10
> do echo "RUN --- $i" >> times.log
> ./tests/string_algos_tests 2>&1 | grep COUNT >> times.log
> done
$ less times.log
$ vim times.log
```

Right away, you can see that the scanning system beats the pants off both of the others, but I'll open this in R and confirm the results:

Exercise 39.3 Session

```
> times <- read.table("times.log", header=T)
> summary(times)
      scan              find             binstr
 Min.   :71195200   Min.   :6351300   Min.   :36811700
 1st Qu.:74042200   1st Qu.:6358100   1st Qu.:37083800
 Median :74820400   Median :6374750   Median :37147800
 Mean   :74308760   Mean   :6427680   Mean   :37176830
 3rd Qu.:74973900   3rd Qu.:6447100   3rd Qu.:37353150
 Max.   :75343600   Max.   :6630400   Max.   :37549700
>
```

To understand why I'm getting the summary statistics, I have to explain some statistics for you. What I'm looking for in these numbers is simply this: "Are these three functions (scan, find, bsinter) actually different?" I know that each time I run my tester function, I get slightly different numbers, and those numbers can cover a certain range. You see here that the first and third quarters do that for each sample.

What I look at first is the mean, and I want to see if each sample's mean is different from the others. I can see that, and clearly the scan beats binstr, which also beats find. However, I have a problem. If I use just the mean, there's a *chance* that the ranges of each sample might overlap.

What if I have means that are different, but the first and third quarters overlap? In that case, I could say that if I ran the samples again there's a chance that the means might not be different. The more overlap I have in the ranges, the higher probability that my two samples (and my two functions) are *not* actually different. Any difference that I'm seeing in the two (in this case three) is just random chance.

There are many tools that you can use to solve this problem, but in our case, I can just look at the first and third quarters and the mean for all three samples. If the means are different, and the quarters are way off with no possibility of overlapping, then it's alright to say that they are different.

In my three samples, I can say that scan, find, and binstr are different, don't overlap in range, and I can trust the sample (for the most part).

Analyzing the Results

Looking at the results, I can see that String_find is much slower than the other two. In fact, it's so slow that I'd think there's something wrong with how I implemented it. However, when I compare it to StringScanner_scan, I can see that it's most likely the part that builds the skip list that's costing the time. Not only is find slower, it's also doing *less* than scan because it's just finding the first string while scan finds all of them.

I can also see that scan beats binstr, as well, and by quite a large margin. Again, not only does scan do more than both of these, but it's also much faster.

There are a few caveats with this analysis:

- I may have messed up this implementation or the test. At this point I would go research all of the possible ways to do a BMH algorithm and try to improve it. I would also confirm that I'm doing the test right.

- If you alter the time the test runs, you'll get different results. There is a warm-up period that I'm not investigating.

- The test_scan_performance unit test isn't quite the same as the others, but it's doing more than the other tests, so it's probably alright.

- I'm only doing the test by searching for one string in another. I could randomize the strings to find their position and length as a confounding factor.

- Maybe `binstr` is implemented better than simple brute force.

- I could be running these in an unfortunate order. Maybe randomizing which test runs first will give better results.

One thing to gather from this is that you need to confirm real performance even if you implement an algorithm correctly. In this case, the claim is that the BMH algorithm should have beaten the `binstr` algorithm, but a simple test proved it didn't. Had I not done this, I would have been using an inferior algorithm implementation without knowing it. With these metrics, I can start to tune my implementation, or simply scrap it and find another one.

Extra Credit

- See if you can make the `Scan_find` faster. Why is my implementation here slow?

- Try some different scan times and see if you get different numbers. What impact does the length of time that you run the test have on the `scan` times? What can you say about that result?

- Alter the unit test so that it runs each function for a short burst in the beginning to clear out any warm-up period, and then start the timing portion. Does that change the dependence on the length of time the test runs? Does it change how many operations per second are possible?

- Make the unit test randomize the strings to find and then measure the performance you get. One way to do this is to use the `bsplit` function from `bstrlib.h` to split the IN_STR on spaces. Then, you can use the `bstrList` struct that you get to access each string it returns. This will also teach you how to use `bstrList` operations for string processing.

- Try some runs with the tests in different orders to see if you get different results.

Binary Search Trees

The binary tree is the simplest tree-based data structure, and even though it's been replaced by hash maps in many languages, it's still useful for many applications. Variants on the binary tree exist for very useful things like database indexes, search algorithm structures, and even graphics.

I'm calling my binary tree a BSTree for binary search tree, and the best way to describe it is that it's another way to do a Hashmap style key/value store. The difference is that instead of hashing the key to find a location, the BSTree compares the key to nodes in a tree, and then walks through the tree to find the best place to store it, based on how it compares to other nodes.

Before I really explain how this works, let me show you the bstree.h header file so that you can see the data structures, and then I can use that to explain how it's built.

bstree.h

```
#ifndef _lcthw_BSTree_h
#define _lcthw_BSTree_h

typedef int (*BSTree_compare) (void *a, void *b);

typedef struct BSTreeNode {
    void *key;
    void *data;

    struct BSTreeNode *left;
    struct BSTreeNode *right;
    struct BSTreeNode *parent;
} BSTreeNode;

typedef struct BSTree {
    int count;
    BSTree_compare compare;
    BSTreeNode *root;
} BSTree;

typedef int (*BSTree_traverse_cb) (BSTreeNode * node);

BSTree *BSTree_create(BSTree_compare compare);
void BSTree_destroy(BSTree * map);

int BSTree_set(BSTree * map, void *key, void *data);
void *BSTree_get(BSTree * map, void *key);

int BSTree_traverse(BSTree * map, BSTree_traverse_cb traverse_cb);

void *BSTree_delete(BSTree * map, void *key);

#endif
```

This follows the same pattern that I've been using this whole time where I have a base container named BSTree, which has nodes named BSTreeNode that make up the actual contents. Bored yet? Good, there's no reason to be clever with this kind of structure.

The important thing is how the BSTreeNode is configured, and how it gets used to do each operation: set, get, and delete. I'll cover get first since it's the easiest operation, and I'll pretend I'm doing it manually against the data structure:

- I take the key you're looking for and I start at the root. First thing I do is compare your key with that node's key.
- If your key is less than the node.key, then I traverse down the tree using the left pointer.
- If your key is greater than the node.key, then I go down with right.
- I repeat steps 2 and 3 until I either find a matching node.key or get to a node that has no left and right. In the first case, I return the node.data. In the second, I return NULL.

That's all there is to get, so now on to set. It's nearly the same thing, except you're looking for where to put a new node:

- If there is no BSTree.root, then I just make it and we're done. That's the first node.
- After that, I compare your key to node.key, starting at the root.
- If your key is less than or equal to the node.key, then I want to go left. If your key is greater than and not equal to the node.key, then I want to go right.
- I keep repeating step 3 until I reach a node where left or right doesn't exist, but that's the direction I need to go.
- Once there, I set that direction (left or right) to a new node for the key and data I want, and then set this new node's parent to the previous node I came from. I'll use the parent node when I do delete.

This also makes sense given how get works. If finding a node involves going left or right depending on how the key compares, then setting a node involves the same thing until I can set the left or right for a new node.

Take some time to draw out a few trees on paper and go through setting and getting nodes so you understand how this works. After that, you're ready to look at the implementation, and I can explain delete. Deleting in trees is a *major* pain, and so it's best explained by doing a line-by-line code breakdown.

bstree.c

```
1    #include <lcthw/dbg.h>
2    #include <lcthw/bstree.h>
3    #include <stdlib.h>
4    #include <lcthw/bstrlib.h>
```

```
5
6    static int default_compare(void *a, void *b)
7    {
8        return bstrcmp((bstring) a, (bstring) b);
9    }
10
11   BSTree *BSTree_create(BSTree_compare compare)
12   {
13       BSTree *map = calloc(1, sizeof(BSTree));
14       check_mem(map);
15
16       map->compare = compare == NULL ? default_compare : compare;
17
18       return map;
19
20   error:
21       if (map) {
22           BSTree_destroy(map);
23       }
24       return NULL;
25   }
26
27   static int BSTree_destroy_cb(BSTreeNode * node)
28   {
29       free(node);
30       return 0;
31   }
32
33   void BSTree_destroy(BSTree * map)
34   {
35       if (map) {
36           BSTree_traverse(map, BSTree_destroy_cb);
37           free(map);
38       }
39   }
40
41   static inline BSTreeNode *BSTreeNode_create(BSTreeNode * parent,
42           void *key, void *data)
43   {
44       BSTreeNode *node = calloc(1, sizeof(BSTreeNode));
45       check_mem(node);
46
47       node->key = key;
48       node->data = data;
49       node->parent = parent;
50       return node;
51
52   error:
53       return NULL;
54   }
```

```
55
56      static inline void BSTree_setnode(BSTree * map, BSTreeNode * node,
57              void *key, void *data)
58      {
59          int cmp = map->compare(node->key, key);
60
61          if (cmp <= 0) {
62              if (node->left) {
63                  BSTree_setnode(map, node->left, key, data);
64              } else {
65                  node->left = BSTreeNode_create(node, key, data);
66              }
67          } else {
68              if (node->right) {
69                  BSTree_setnode(map, node->right, key, data);
70              } else {
71                  node->right = BSTreeNode_create(node, key, data);
72              }
73          }
74      }
75
76      int BSTree_set(BSTree * map, void *key, void *data)
77      {
78          if (map->root == NULL) {
79              // first so just make it and get out
80              map->root = BSTreeNode_create(NULL, key, data);
81              check_mem(map->root);
82          } else {
83              BSTree_setnode(map, map->root, key, data);
84          }
85
86          return 0;
87      error:
88          return -1;
89      }
90
91      static inline BSTreeNode *BSTree_getnode(BSTree * map,
92              BSTreeNode * node, void *key)
93      {
94          int cmp = map->compare(node->key, key);
95
96          if (cmp == 0) {
97              return node;
98          } else if (cmp < 0) {
99              if (node->left) {
100                 return BSTree_getnode(map, node->left, key);
101             } else {
102                 return NULL;
103             }
104         } else {
```

```
105                if (node->right) {
106                    return BSTree_getnode(map, node->right, key);
107                } else {
108                    return NULL;
109                }
110            }
111        }
112
113    void *BSTree_get(BSTree * map, void *key)
114    {
115        if (map->root == NULL) {
116            return NULL;
117        } else {
118            BSTreeNode *node = BSTree_getnode(map, map->root, key);
119            return node == NULL ? NULL : node->data;
120        }
121    }
122
123    static inline int BSTree_traverse_nodes(BSTreeNode * node,
124            BSTree_traverse_cb traverse_cb)
125    {
126        int rc = 0;
127
128        if (node->left) {
129            rc = BSTree_traverse_nodes(node->left, traverse_cb);
130            if (rc != 0)
131                return rc;
132        }
133
134        if (node->right) {
135            rc = BSTree_traverse_nodes(node->right, traverse_cb);
136            if (rc != 0)
137                return rc;
138        }
139
140        return traverse_cb(node);
141    }
142
143    int BSTree_traverse(BSTree * map, BSTree_traverse_cb traverse_cb)
144    {
145        if (map->root) {
146            return BSTree_traverse_nodes(map->root, traverse_cb);
147        }
148
149        return 0;
150    }
151
152    static inline BSTreeNode *BSTree_find_min(BSTreeNode * node)
153    {
154        while (node->left) {
```

```
155                    node = node->left;
156            }
157
158            return node;
159    }
160
161    static inline void BSTree_replace_node_in_parent(BSTree * map,
162                BSTreeNode * node,
163                BSTreeNode * new_value)
164    {
165        if (node->parent) {
166            if (node == node->parent->left) {
167                node->parent->left = new_value;
168            } else {
169                node->parent->right = new_value;
170            }
171        } else {
172            // this is the root so gotta change it
173            map->root = new_value;
174        }
175
176        if (new_value) {
177            new_value->parent = node->parent;
178        }
179    }
180
181    static inline void BSTree_swap(BSTreeNode * a, BSTreeNode * b)
182    {
183        void *temp = NULL;
184        temp = b->key;
185        b->key = a->key;
186        a->key = temp;
187        temp = b->data;
188        b->data = a->data;
189        a->data = temp;
190    }
191
192    static inline BSTreeNode *BSTree_node_delete(BSTree * map,
193                BSTreeNode * node,
194                void *key)
195    {
196        int cmp = map->compare(node->key, key);
197
198        if (cmp < 0) {
199            if (node->left) {
200                return BSTree_node_delete(map, node->left, key);
201            } else {
202                // not found
203                return NULL;
204            }
```

```
205         } else if (cmp > 0) {
206             if (node->right) {
207                 return BSTree_node_delete(map, node->right, key);
208             } else {
209                 // not found
210                 return NULL;
211             }
212         } else {
213             if (node->left && node->right) {
214                 // swap this node for the smallest node that is bigger than us
215                 BSTreeNode *successor = BSTree_find_min(node->right);
216                 BSTree_swap(successor, node);
217
218                 // this leaves the old successor with possibly a right child
219                 // so replace it with that right child
220                 BSTree_replace_node_in_parent(map, successor,
221                         successor->right);
222
223                 // finally it's swapped, so return successor instead of node
224                 return successor;
225             } else if (node->left) {
226                 BSTree_replace_node_in_parent(map, node, node->left);
227             } else if (node->right) {
228                 BSTree_replace_node_in_parent(map, node, node->right);
229             } else {
230                 BSTree_replace_node_in_parent(map, node, NULL);
231             }
232
233             return node;
234         }
235 }
236
237 void *BSTree_delete(BSTree * map, void *key)
238 {
239     void *data = NULL;
240
241     if (map->root) {
242         BSTreeNode *node = BSTree_node_delete(map, map->root, key);
243
244         if (node) {
245             data = node->data;
246             free(node);
247         }
248     }
249
250     return data;
251 }
```

Before getting into how BSTree_delete works, I want to explain a pattern for doing recursive function calls in a sane way. You'll find that many tree-based data structures are easy to write if you use recursion, but formulate a single recursive function. Part of the problem is that you need to set up some initial data for the first operation, *then* recurse into the data structure, which is hard to do with one function.

The solution is to use two functions: One function sets up the data structure and initial recursion conditions so that a second function can do the real work. Take a look at BSTree_get first to see what I mean.

- I have an initial condition: If map->root is NULL, then return NULL and don't recurse.

- I then set up a call to the real recursion, which is in BSTree_getnode. I create the initial condition of the root node to start with the key and then the map.

- In the BSTree_getnode, I then do the actual recursive logic. I compare the keys with map->compare(node->key, key) and go left, right, or equal to depending on the results.

- Since this function is self-similar and doesn't have to handle any initial conditions (because BSTree_get did), then I can structure it very simply. When it's done, it returns to the caller, and that return then comes back to BSTree_get for the result.

- At the end, the BSTree_get handles getting the node.data element but only if the result isn't NULL.

This way of structuring a recursive algorithm matches the way I structure my recursive data structures. I have an initial base function that handles initial conditions and some edge cases, and then it calls a clean recursive function that does the work. Compare that with how I have a base structure in BStree combined with recursive BSTreeNode structures, which all reference each other in a tree. Using this pattern makes it easy to deal with recursion and keep it straight.

Next, go look at BSTree_set and BSTree_setnode to see the exact same pattern. I use BSTree_set to configure the initial conditions and edge cases. A common edge case is that there's no root node, so I have to make one to get things started.

This pattern will work with nearly any recursive algorithm you have to figure out. The way I do it is by following this pattern:

- Figure out the initial variables, how they change, and what the stopping conditions are for each recursive step.

- Write a recursive function that calls itself, and has arguments for each stopping condition and initial variable.

- Write a setup function to set initial starting conditions for the algorithm and handle edge cases, then have it call the recursive function.

- Finally, the setup function returns the final result, and possibly alters it if the recursive function can't handle final edge cases.

This finally leads me to BSTree_delete and BSTree_node_delete. First, you can just look at BSTree_delete and see that it's the setup function. What it's doing is grabbing the resulting node data and freeing the node that's found. Things get more complex in BSTree_node_delete, because to delete a node at any point in the tree, I have to *rotate* that node's children up to the parent. Here's a breakdown of this function and the functions it uses:

bstree.c:190 I run the compare function to figure out which direction I'm going.

bstree.c:192-198 This is the usual less-than branch to use when I want to go left. I'm handling the case that left doesn't exist here, and returning NULL to say "not found." This covers deleting something that isn't in the BSTree.

bstree.c:199-205 This is the same thing, but for the right branch of the tree. Just keep recursing down into the tree just like in the other functions, and return NULL if it doesn't exist.

bstree.c:206 This is where I have found the node, since the key is equal (compare return 0).

bstree.c:207 This node has both a left and right branch, so it's deeply embedded in the tree.

bstree.c:209 To remove this node, I first need to find the smallest node that's greater than this node, which means I call BSTree_find_min on the right child.

bstree.c:210 Once I have this node, I'll swap its key and data with the current node's values. This will effectively take this node that was down at the bottom of the tree and put its contents here, so that I don't have to try and shuffle the node out by its pointers.

bstree.c:214 The successor is now this dead branch that has the current node's values. It could just be removed, but there's a chance that it has a right node value. This means I need to do a single rotate so that the successor's right node gets moved up to completely detach it.

bstree.c:217 At this point, the successor is removed from the tree, its values are replaced the current node's values, and any children it had are moved up into the parent. I can return the successor as if it were the node.

bstree.c:218 At this branch, I know that the node has a left but no right, so I want to replace this node with its left child.

bstree.c:219 I again use BSTree_replace_node_in_parent to do the replace, rotating the left child up.

bstree.c:220 This branch of the if-statement means I have a right child but no left child, so I want to rotate the right child up.

bstree.c:221 Again, I use the function to do the rotate, but this time, rotate the right node.

bstree.c:222   Finally, the only thing that's left is the condition where I've found the node, and it has no children (no left or right). In this case, I simply replace this node with NULL by using the same function I did with all of the others.

bstree.c:210   After all that, I have the current node rotated out of the tree and replaced with some child element that will fit in the tree. I just return this to the caller so it can be freed and managed.

This operation is very complex, and to be honest, I just don't bother doing deletes in some tree data structures, and I treat them like constant data in my software. If I need to do heavy inserting and deleting, I use a Hashmap instead.

Finally, you can look at the unit test to see how I'm testing it:

bstree_tests.c

```
1    #include "minunit.h"
2    #include <lcthw/bstree.h>
3    #include <assert.h>
4    #include <lcthw/bstrlib.h>
5    #include <stdlib.h>
6    #include <time.h>
7
8    BSTree *map = NULL;
9    static int traverse_called = 0;
10   struct tagbstring test1 = bsStatic("test data 1");
11   struct tagbstring test2 = bsStatic("test data 2");
12   struct tagbstring test3 = bsStatic("xest data 3");
13   struct tagbstring expect1 = bsStatic("THE VALUE 1");
14   struct tagbstring expect2 = bsStatic("THE VALUE 2");
15   struct tagbstring expect3 = bsStatic("THE VALUE 3");
16
17   static int traverse_good_cb(BSTreeNode * node)
18   {
19       debug("KEY: %s", bdata((bstring) node->key));
20       traverse_called++;
21       return 0;
22   }
23
24   static int traverse_fail_cb(BSTreeNode * node)
25   {
26       debug("KEY: %s", bdata((bstring) node->key));
27       traverse_called++;
28
29       if (traverse_called == 2) {
30           return 1;
31       } else {
32           return 0;
33       }
34   }
```

```
35
36    char *test_create()
37    {
38        map = BSTree_create(NULL);
39        mu_assert(map != NULL, "Failed to create map.");
40
41        return NULL;
42    }
43
44    char *test_destroy()
45    {
46        BSTree_destroy(map);
47
48        return NULL;
49    }
50
51    char *test_get_set()
52    {
53        int rc = BSTree_set(map, &test1, &expect1);
54        mu_assert(rc == 0, "Failed to set &test1");
55        bstring result = BSTree_get(map, &test1);
56        mu_assert(result == &expect1, "Wrong value for test1.");
57
58        rc = BSTree_set(map, &test2, &expect2);
59        mu_assert(rc == 0, "Failed to set test2");
60        result = BSTree_get(map, &test2);
61        mu_assert(result == &expect2, "Wrong value for test2.");
62
63        rc = BSTree_set(map, &test3, &expect3);
64        mu_assert(rc == 0, "Failed to set test3");
65        result = BSTree_get(map, &test3);
66        mu_assert(result == &expect3, "Wrong value for test3.");
67
68        return NULL;
69    }
70
71    char *test_traverse()
72    {
73        int rc = BSTree_traverse(map, traverse_good_cb);
74        mu_assert(rc == 0, "Failed to traverse.");
75        mu_assert(traverse_called == 3, "Wrong count traverse.");
76
77        traverse_called = 0;
78        rc = BSTree_traverse(map, traverse_fail_cb);
79        mu_assert(rc == 1, "Failed to traverse.");
80        mu_assert(traverse_called == 2, "Wrong count traverse for fail.");
81
82        return NULL;
83    }
84
```

```
85    char *test_delete()
86    {
87        bstring deleted = (bstring) BSTree_delete(map, &test1);
88        mu_assert(deleted != NULL, "Got NULL on delete.");
89        mu_assert(deleted == &expect1, "Should get test1");
90        bstring result = BSTree_get(map, &test1);
91        mu_assert(result == NULL, "Should delete.");
92
93        deleted = (bstring) BSTree_delete(map, &test1);
94        mu_assert(deleted == NULL, "Should get NULL on delete");
95
96        deleted = (bstring) BSTree_delete(map, &test2);
97        mu_assert(deleted != NULL, "Got NULL on delete.");
98        mu_assert(deleted == &expect2, "Should get test2");
99        result = BSTree_get(map, &test2);
100       mu_assert(result == NULL, "Should delete.");
101
102       deleted = (bstring) BSTree_delete(map, &test3);
103       mu_assert(deleted != NULL, "Got NULL on delete.");
104       mu_assert(deleted == &expect3, "Should get test3");
105       result = BSTree_get(map, &test3);
106       mu_assert(result == NULL, "Should delete.");
107
108       // test deleting non-existent stuff
109       deleted = (bstring) BSTree_delete(map, &test3);
110       mu_assert(deleted == NULL, "Should get NULL");
111
112       return NULL;
113   }
114
115   char *test_fuzzing()
116   {
117       BSTree *store = BSTree_create(NULL);
118       int i = 0;
119       int j = 0;
120       bstring numbers[100] = { NULL };
121       bstring data[100] = { NULL };
122       srand((unsigned int)time(NULL));
123
124       for (i = 0; i < 100; i++) {
125           int num = rand();
126           numbers[i] = bformat("%d", num);
127           data[i] = bformat("data %d", num);
128           BSTree_set(store, numbers[i], data[i]);
129       }
130
131       for (i = 0; i < 100; i++) {
132           bstring value = BSTree_delete(store, numbers[i]);
133           mu_assert(value == data[i],
134                   "Failed to delete the right number.");
```

```
135
136                     mu_assert(BSTree_delete(store, numbers[i]) == NULL,
137                         "Should get nothing.");
138
139                     for (j = i + 1; j < 99 - i; j++) {
140                         bstring value = BSTree_get(store, numbers[j]);
141                         mu_assert(value == data[j],
142                             "Failed to get the right number.");
143                     }
144
145                     bdestroy(value);
146                     bdestroy(numbers[i]);
147                 }
148
149             BSTree_destroy(store);
150
151             return NULL;
152         }
153
154         char *all_tests()
155         {
156             mu_suite_start();
157
158             mu_run_test(test_create);
159             mu_run_test(test_get_set);
160             mu_run_test(test_traverse);
161             mu_run_test(test_delete);
162             mu_run_test(test_destroy);
163             mu_run_test(test_fuzzing);
164
165             return NULL;
166         }
167
168         RUN_TESTS(all_tests);
```

I'll point you to the test_fuzzing function, which is an interesting technique for testing complex data structures. It is difficult to create a set of keys that cover all of the branches in BSTree_node_delete, and chances are, I would miss some edge case. A better way is to create a fuzz function that does all of the operations, but does them in a horrible and random way. In this case, I'm inserting a set of random string keys, and then I'm deleting them and trying to get the rest after each delete.

Doing this prevents you from testing only what you know to work, and then miss things you don't know. By throwing random junk at your data structures, you'll hit things you didn't expect and be able to work out any bugs you have.

How to Improve It

Do *not* do any of these yet. In the next exercise I'll be using this unit test to teach you some more performance-tuning tricks, and you'll come back and do these after you complete Exercise 41.

- As usual, you should go through all of the defensive programming checks and add assert``s for conditions that shouldn't happen. For example, you shouldn't be getting ``NULL values for the recursion functions, so assert that.

- The traverse function walks through the tree in order by traversing left, then right, and then the current node. You can create traverse functions for the reverse order, as well.

- It does a full string compare on every node, but I could use the Hashmap hashing functions to speed this up. I could hash the keys, and then keep the hash in the BSTreeNode. Then, in each of the setup functions, I can hash the key ahead of time and pass it down to the recursive function. Using this hash, I can then compare each node much quicker in a way that's similar to what I do in Hashmap.

Extra Credit

- There's an alternative way to do this data structure without using recursion. The Wikipedia page shows alternatives that don't use recursion but do the same thing. Why would this be better or worse?

- Read up on all of the different but similar trees you can find. There are AVL trees (named after Georgy Adelson-Velsky and E.M. Landis), red-black trees, and some non-tree structures like skip lists.

Project devpkg

You are now ready to tackle a new project called devpkg. In this project you're going to recreate a piece of software that I wrote specifically for this book called devpkg. You'll then extend it in a few key ways and improve the code, most importantly by writing some unit tests for it.

This exercise has a companion video to it, and also a project on GitHub (https://github.com) that you can reference if you get stuck. You should attempt to do this exercise using the description below, since that's how you'll need to learn to code from books in the future. Most computer science textbooks don't include videos for their exercises, so this project is more about trying to figure it out from this description.

If you get stuck, and you can't figure it out, *then* go watch the video and look at the GitHub project to see how your code differs from mine.

What Is devpkg?

Devpkg is a simple C program that installs other software. I made it specifically for this book as a way to teach you how a real software project is structured, and also how to reuse other people's libraries. It uses a portability library called the Apache Portable Runtime (APR), which has many handy C functions that work on tons of platforms, including Windows. Other than that, it just grabs code from the Internet (or local files) and does the usual ./configure, make, and make install that every program does.

Your goal in this exercise is to build devpkg from the source, finish each *challenge* I give, and use the source to understand what devpkg does and why.

What We Want to Make

We want a tool that has these commands:

devpkg -S Sets up a new installation on a computer.

devpkg -I Installs a piece of software from a URL.

devpkg -L Lists all of the software that's been installed.

devpkg -F Fetches some source code for manual building.

devpkg -B Builds the source code and installs it, even if it's already installed.

We want devpkg to be able to take almost any URL, figure out what kind of project it is, download it, install it, and register that it downloaded that software. We'd also like it to process a simple dependency list so that it can install all of the software that a project might need, as well.

The Design

To accomplish this goal, devpkg will have a very simple design:

Use External Commands   You'll do most of the work through external commands like curl, git, and tar. This reduces the amount of code devpkg needs to get things done.

Simple File Database   You could easily make it more complex, but you'll start by making just make a single simple file database at /usr/local/.devpkg/db to keep track of what's installed.

/usr/local Always   Again, you could make this more advanced, but for now just assume it's always /usr/local, which is a standard install path for most software on UNIX.

configure, make, make install   It's assumed that most software can be installed with just a configure, make, and make install—and maybe configure is optional. If the software at a minimum can't do that, there are some options to modify the commands, but otherwise, devpkg won't bother.

The User Can Be Root   We'll assume that the user can become root using sudo, but doesn't want to become root until the end.

This will keep our program small at first and work well enough for us to get it going, at which point you'll be able to modify it further for this exercise.

The Apache Portable Runtime

One more thing you'll do is leverage the APR Libraries to get a good set of portable routines for doing this kind of work. APR isn't necessary, and you could probably write this program without it, but it'd take more code than necessary. I'm also forcing you to use APR now so you get used to linking and using other libraries. Finally, APR also works on *Windows*, so your skills with it are transferable to many other platforms.

You should go get both the apr-1.5.2 and the apr-util-1.5.4 libraries, as well as browse through the documentation available at the main APR site at http://apr.apache.org.

Here's a shell script that will install all the stuff you need. You should write this into a file by hand, and then run it until it can install APR without any errors.

```
set -e

# go somewhere safe
cd /tmp

# get the source to base APR 1.5.2
curl -L -O http://archive.apache.org/dist/apr/apr-1.5.2.tar.gz

# extract it and go into the source
tar -xzvf apr-1.5.2.tar.gz
cd apr-1.5.2

# configure, make, make install
./configure
make
sudo make install

# reset and cleanup
cd /tmp
rm -rf apr-1.5.2 apr-1.5.2.tar.gz

# do the same with apr-util
curl -L -O http://archive.apache.org/dist/apr/apr-util-1.5.4.tar.gz

# extract
tar -xzvf apr-util-1.5.4.tar.gz
cd apr-util-1.5.4

# configure, make, make install
./configure --with-apr=/usr/local/apr
# you need that extra parameter to configure because
# apr-util can't really find it because...who knows.

make
sudo make install

#cleanup
cd /tmp
rm -rf apr-util-1.5.4* apr-1.5.2*
```

I'm having you write this script out because it's basically what we want devpkg to do, but with extra options and checks. In fact, you could just do it all in shell with less code, but then that wouldn't be a very good program for a C book would it?

Simply run this script and fix it until it works, then you'll have the libraries you need to complete the rest of this project.

Project Layout

You need to set up some simple project files to get started. Here's how I usually craft a new project:

```
mkdir devpkg
cd devpkg
touch README Makefile
```

Other Dependencies

You should have already installed apr-1.5.2 and apr-util-1.5.4, so now you need a few more files to use as basic dependencies:

- dbg.h from Exercise 20.
- bstrlib.h and bstrlib.c from http://bstring.sourceforge.net/. Download the .zip file, extract it, and copy just those two files.
- Type make bstrlib.o, and if it doesn't work, read the instructions for fixing bstring below.

WARNING! In some platforms, the bstring.c file will have an error like this:

```
bstrlib.c:2762: error: expected declaration\
specifiers or '...' before numeric constant
```

This is from a bad define that the authors added, which doesn't always work. You just need to change line 2759 that reads #ifdef __GNUC__ to read:

```
#if defined(__GNUC__) && !defined(__APPLE__)
```

and then it should work on OS X.

When that's all done, you should have a Makefile, README, dbg.h, bstrlib.h, and bstrlib.c ready to go.

The Makefile

A good place to start is the Makefile since this lays out how things are built and what source files you'll be creating.

```
PREFIX?=/usr/local
CFLAGS=-g -Wall -I${PREFIX}/apr/include/apr-1
CFLAGS+=-I${PREFIX}/apr/include/apr-util-1
LDFLAGS=-L${PREFIX}/apr/lib -lapr-1 -pthread -laprutil-1

all: devpkg

devpkg: bstrlib.o db.o shell.o commands.o

install: all
    install -d $(DESTDIR)/$(PREFIX)/bin/
    install devpkg $(DESTDIR)/$(PREFIX)/bin/

clean:
    rm -f *.o
    rm -f devpkg
    rm -rf *.dSYM
```

There's nothing in this that you haven't seen before, except maybe the strange ?= syntax, which says "set PREFIX equal to this unless PREFIX is already set."

WARNING! If you're on more recent versions of Ubuntu, and you get errors about apr_off_t or off64_t, then add –D_LARGEFILE64_SOURCE=1 to CFLAGS.
Another thing is that you need to add /usr/local/apr/lib to a file in /etc/ld.conf.so.d/ and then run ldconfig so that it correctly picks up the libraries.

The Source Files

From the Makefile, we see that there are five dependencies for devpkg:

bstrlib.o   This comes from bstrlib.c and the header file bstlib.h, which you already have.

db.o   This comes from db.c and header file db.h, and it will contain code for our little database routines.

shell.o   This is from shell.c and header shell.h, as well as a couple of functions that make running other commands like curl easier.

commands.o   This is from command.c and header command.h, and contains all of the commands that devpkg needs to be useful.

devpkg It's not explicitly mentioned, but it's the target (on the left) in this part of the Makefile. It comes from devpkg.c, which contains the main function for the whole program.

Your job is to now create each of these files, type in their code, and get them correct.

WARNING! You may read this description and think, "Man! How is it that Zed is so smart that he just sat down and typed these files out like this!? I could never do that." I didn't magically craft devpkg in this form with my awesome coding powers. Instead, what I did is this:

- I wrote a quick little README to get an idea of how I wanted it to work.

- I created a simple bash script (like the one you did earlier) to figure out all of the pieces that were needed.

- I made one .c file and hacked on it for a few days working through the idea and figuring it out.

- I got it mostly working and debugged, *then* I started breaking up the one big file into these four files.

- After getting these files laid down, I renamed and refined the functions and data structures so that they'd be more logical and pretty.

- Finally, after I had it working the *exact same* but with the new structure, I added a few features like the -F and -B options.

You're reading this in the order I want to teach it to you, but don't think this is how I always build software. Sometimes I already know the subject and I use more planning. Sometimes I just hack up an idea and see how well it'd work. Sometimes I write one, then throw it away and plan out a better one. It all depends on what my experience tells me is best or where my inspiration takes me.

If you run into a supposed expert who tries to tell you that there's only one way to solve a programming problem, they're lying to you. Either they actually use multiple tactics, or they're not very good.

The DB Functions

There must be a way to record URLs that have been installed, list these URLs, and check whether something has already been installed so we can skip it. I'll use a simple flat file database and the bstrlib.h library to do it.

First, create the db.h header file so you know what you'll be implementing.

db.h

```
#ifndef _db_h
#define _db_h

#define DB_FILE "/usr/local/.devpkg/db"
#define DB_DIR "/usr/local/.devpkg"

int DB_init();
int DB_list();
int DB_update(const char *url);
int DB_find(const char *url);

#endif
```

Then, implement those functions in db.c, and as you build this, use make to get it to compile cleanly.

db.c

```
1    #include <unistd.h>
2    #include <apr_errno.h>
3    #include <apr_file_io.h>
4
5    #include "db.h"
6    #include "bstrlib.h"
7    #include "dbg.h"
8
9    static FILE *DB_open(const char *path, const char *mode)
10   {
11       return fopen(path, mode);
12   }
13
14   static void DB_close(FILE * db)
15   {
16       fclose(db);
17   }
18
19   static bstring DB_load()
20   {
21       FILE *db = NULL;
22       bstring data = NULL;
23
24       db = DB_open(DB_FILE, "r");
25       check(db, "Failed to open database: %s", DB_FILE);
26
27       data = bread((bNread) fread, db);
28       check(data, "Failed to read from db file: %s", DB_FILE);
29
30       DB_close(db);
31       return data;
```

```
32
33    error:
34        if (db)
35            DB_close(db);
36        if (data)
37            bdestroy(data);
38        return NULL;
39    }
40
41    int DB_update(const char *url)
42    {
43        if (DB_find(url)) {
44            log_info("Already recorded as installed: %s", url);
45        }
46
47        FILE *db = DB_open(DB_FILE, "a+");
48        check(db, "Failed to open DB file: %s", DB_FILE);
49
50        bstring line = bfromcstr(url);
51        bconchar(line, '\n');
52        int rc = fwrite(line->data, blength(line), 1, db);
53        check(rc == 1, "Failed to append to the db.");
54
55        return 0;
56    error:
57        if (db)
58            DB_close(db);
59        return -1;
60    }
61
62    int DB_find(const char *url)
63    {
64        bstring data = NULL;
65        bstring line = bfromcstr(url);
66        int res = -1;
67
68        data = DB_load();
69        check(data, "Failed to load: %s", DB_FILE);
70
71        if (binstr(data, 0, line) == BSTR_ERR) {
72            res = 0;
73        } else {
74            res = 1;
75        }
76
77    error:                      // fallthrough
78        if (data)
79            bdestroy(data);
80        if (line)
81            bdestroy(line);
```

```
82
83          return res;
84      }
85
86      int DB_init()
87      {
88          apr_pool_t *p = NULL;
89          apr_pool_initialize();
90          apr_pool_create(&p, NULL);
91
92          if (access(DB_DIR, W_OK | X_OK) == -1) {
93              apr_status_t rc = apr_dir_make_recursive(DB_DIR,
94                      APR_UREAD | APR_UWRITE
95                      | APR_UEXECUTE |
96                      APR_GREAD | APR_GWRITE
97                      | APR_GEXECUTE, p);
98              check(rc == APR_SUCCESS, "Failed to make database dir: %s",
99                      DB_DIR);
100         }
101
102         if (access(DB_FILE, W_OK) == -1) {
103             FILE *db = DB_open(DB_FILE, "w");
104             check(db, "Cannot open database: %s", DB_FILE);
105             DB_close(db);
106         }
107
108         apr_pool_destroy(p);
109         return 0;
110
111     error:
112         apr_pool_destroy(p);
113         return -1;
114     }
115
116     int DB_list()
117     {
118         bstring data = DB_load();
119         check(data, "Failed to read load: %s", DB_FILE);
120
121         printf("%s", bdata(data));
122         bdestroy(data);
123         return 0;
124
125     error:
126         return -1;
127     }
```

Challenge 1: Code Review

Before continuing, read every line of these files carefully and confirm that you have them entered in *exactly* as they appear here. Read them backward line by line to practice that. Also, trace each function call and make sure you're using check to validate the return codes. Finally, look up *every* function that you don't recognize—either in the APR Web site documentation or in the bstrlib.h and bstrlib.c source.

The Shell Functions

A key design decision for devpkg is to have external tools like curl, tar, and git do most of the work. We could find libraries to do all of this internally, but it's pointless if we just need the base features of these programs. There is no shame in running another command in UNIX.

To do this, I'm going to use the apr_thread_proc.h functions to run programs, but I also want to make a simple kind of template system. I'll use a struct Shell that holds all of the information needed to run a program, but has holes in the arguments list that I can replace with values.

Look at the shell.h file to see the structure and the commands that I'll use. You can see that I'm using extern to indicate how other .c files can access variables that I'm defining in shell.c.

shell.h

```
#ifndef _shell_h
#define _shell_h

#define MAX_COMMAND_ARGS 100

#include <apr_thread_proc.h>

typedef struct Shell {
    const char *dir;
    const char *exe;

    apr_procattr_t *attr;
    apr_proc_t proc;
    apr_exit_why_e exit_why;
    int exit_code;

    const char *args[MAX_COMMAND_ARGS];
} Shell;

int Shell_run(apr_pool_t * p, Shell * cmd);
int Shell_exec(Shell cmd, ...);

extern Shell CLEANUP_SH;
extern Shell GIT_SH;
```

```
extern Shell TAR_SH;
extern Shell CURL_SH;
extern Shell CONFIGURE_SH;
extern Shell MAKE_SH;
extern Shell INSTALL_SH;

#endif
```

Make sure you've created shell.h exactly as it appears here, and that you've got the same names and number of extern Shell variables. Those are used by the Shell_run and Shell_exec functions to run commands. I define these two functions, and create the real variables in shell.c.

shell.c

```c
1    #include "shell.h"
2    #include "dbg.h"
3    #include <stdarg.h>
4
5    int Shell_exec(Shell template, ...)
6    {
7        apr_pool_t *p = NULL;
8        int rc = -1;
9        apr_status_t rv = APR_SUCCESS;
10       va_list argp;
11       const char *key = NULL;
12       const char *arg = NULL;
13       int i = 0;
14
15       rv = apr_pool_create(&p, NULL);
16       check(rv == APR_SUCCESS, "Failed to create pool.");
17
18       va_start(argp, template);
19
20       for (key = va_arg(argp, const char *);
21               key != NULL; key = va_arg(argp, const char *)) {
22           arg = va_arg(argp, const char *);
23
24           for (i = 0; template.args[i] != NULL; i++) {
25               if (strcmp(template.args[i], key) == 0) {
26                   template.args[i] = arg;
27                   break;                    // found it
28               }
29           }
30       }
31
32       rc = Shell_run(p, &template);
33       apr_pool_destroy(p);
34       va_end(argp);
35       return rc;
36
```

```
37    error:
38        if (p) {
39            apr_pool_destroy(p);
40        }
41        return rc;
42    }
43
44    int Shell_run(apr_pool_t * p, Shell * cmd)
45    {
46        apr_procattr_t *attr;
47        apr_status_t rv;
48        apr_proc_t newproc;
49
50        rv = apr_procattr_create(&attr, p);
51        check(rv == APR_SUCCESS, "Failed to create proc attr.");
52
53        rv = apr_procattr_io_set(attr, APR_NO_PIPE, APR_NO_PIPE,
54                APR_NO_PIPE);
55        check(rv == APR_SUCCESS, "Failed to set IO of command.");
56
57        rv = apr_procattr_dir_set(attr, cmd->dir);
58        check(rv == APR_SUCCESS, "Failed to set root to %s", cmd->dir);
59
60        rv = apr_procattr_cmdtype_set(attr, APR_PROGRAM_PATH);
61        check(rv == APR_SUCCESS, "Failed to set cmd type.");
62
63        rv = apr_proc_create(&newproc, cmd->exe, cmd->args, NULL, attr, p);
64        check(rv == APR_SUCCESS, "Failed to run command.");
65
66        rv = apr_proc_wait(&newproc, &cmd->exit_code, &cmd->exit_why,
67                APR_WAIT);
68        check(rv == APR_CHILD_DONE, "Failed to wait.");
69
70        check(cmd->exit_code == 0, "%s exited badly.", cmd->exe);
71        check(cmd->exit_why == APR_PROC_EXIT, "%s was killed or crashed",
72                cmd->exe);
73
74        return 0;
75
76    error:
77        return -1;
78    }
79
80    Shell CLEANUP_SH = {
81        .exe = "rm",
82        .dir = "/tmp",
83        .args = {"rm", "-rf", "/tmp/pkg-build", "/tmp/pkg-src.tar.gz",
84            "/tmp/pkg-src.tar.bz2", "/tmp/DEPENDS", NULL}
85    };
86
```

```
87    Shell GIT_SH = {
88        .dir = "/tmp",
89        .exe = "git",
90        .args = {"git", "clone", "URL", "pkg-build", NULL}
91    };
92
93    Shell TAR_SH = {
94        .dir = "/tmp/pkg-build",
95        .exe = "tar",
96        .args = {"tar", "-xzf", "FILE", "--strip-components", "1", NULL}
97    };
98
99    Shell CURL_SH = {
100       .dir = "/tmp",
101       .exe = "curl",
102       .args = {"curl", "-L", "-o", "TARGET", "URL", NULL}
103   };
104
105   Shell CONFIGURE_SH = {
106       .exe = "./configure",
107       .dir = "/tmp/pkg-build",
108       .args = {"configure", "OPTS", NULL}
109       ,
110   };
111
112   Shell MAKE_SH = {
113       .exe = "make",
114       .dir = "/tmp/pkg-build",
115       .args = {"make", "OPTS", NULL}
116   };
117
118   Shell INSTALL_SH = {
119       .exe = "sudo",
120       .dir = "/tmp/pkg-build",
121       .args = {"sudo", "make", "TARGET", NULL}
122   };
```

Read the shell.c from the bottom to the top (which is a common C source layout) and you see how I've created the actual Shell variables that you indicated were extern in shell.h. They live here, but are available to the rest of the program. This is how you make global variables that live in one .o file but are used everywhere. You shouldn't make many of these, but they are handy for things like this.

Continuing up the file we get to the Shell_run function, which is a base function that just runs a command according to what's in a Shell struct. It uses many of the functions defined in apr_thread_proc.h, so go look up each one to see how the base function works. This seems like a lot of work compared to just using the system function call, but it also gives you more control over the other program's execution. For example, in our Shell struct, we have a .dir attribute that forces the program to be in a specific directory before running.

Finally, I have the Shell_exec function, which is a variable argument function. You've seen this before, but make sure you grasp the stdarg.h functions. In the challenge for this section, you're going to analyze this function.

Challenge 2: Analyze Shell_exec

The challenge for these files (in addition to a full code review like you did in Challenge 1) is to fully analyze Shell_exec and break down exactly how it works. You should be able to understand each line, how the two for-loops work, and how arguments are being replaced.

Once you have it analyzed, add a field to struct Shell that gives you the number of variable args that must be replaced. Update all of the commands to have the right count of args, and have an error check to confirm that these args have been replaced, and then error exit.

The Command Functions

Now you get to make the actual commands that do the work. These commands will use functions from APR, db.h, and shell.h to do the real work of downloading and building the software that you want it to build. This is the most complex set of files, so do them carefully. As before, you start by making the commands.h file, then implementing its functions in the commands.c file.

commands.h

```
#ifndef _commands_h
#define _commands_h

#include <apr_pools.h>

#define DEPENDS_PATH "/tmp/DEPENDS"
#define TAR_GZ_SRC "/tmp/pkg-src.tar.gz"
#define TAR_BZ2_SRC "/tmp/pkg-src.tar.bz2"
#define BUILD_DIR "/tmp/pkg-build"
#define GIT_PAT "*.git"
#define DEPEND_PAT "*DEPENDS"
#define TAR_GZ_PAT "*.tar.gz"
#define TAR_BZ2_PAT "*.tar.bz2"
#define CONFIG_SCRIPT "/tmp/pkg-build/configure"

enum CommandType {
    COMMAND_NONE, COMMAND_INSTALL, COMMAND_LIST, COMMAND_FETCH,
    COMMAND_INIT, COMMAND_BUILD
};

int Command_fetch(apr_pool_t * p, const char *url, int fetch_only);
```

```
int Command_install(apr_pool_t * p, const char *url,
        const char *configure_opts, const char *make_opts,
        const char *install_opts);

int Command_depends(apr_pool_t * p, const char *path);

int Command_build(apr_pool_t * p, const char *url,
        const char *configure_opts, const char *make_opts,
        const char *install_opts);

#endif
```

There's not much in commands.h that you haven't seen already. You should see that there are some defines for strings that are used everywhere. The really interesting code is in commands.c.

commands.c

```
1    #include <apr_uri.h>
2    #include <apr_fnmatch.h>
3    #include <unistd.h>
4
5    #include "commands.h"
6    #include "dbg.h"
7    #include "bstrlib.h"
8    #include "db.h"
9    #include "shell.h"
10
11   int Command_depends(apr_pool_t * p, const char *path)
12   {
13       FILE *in = NULL;
14       bstring line = NULL;
15
16       in = fopen(path, "r");
17       check(in != NULL, "Failed to open downloaded depends: %s", path);
18
19       for (line = bgets((bNgetc) fgetc, in, '\n');
20               line != NULL;
21               line = bgets((bNgetc) fgetc, in, '\n'))
22       {
23           btrimws(line);
24           log_info("Processing depends: %s", bdata(line));
25           int rc = Command_install(p, bdata(line), NULL, NULL, NULL);
26           check(rc == 0, "Failed to install: %s", bdata(line));
27           bdestroy(line);
28       }
29
30       fclose(in);
31       return 0;
32
33   error:
34       if (line) bdestroy(line);
```

```
35          if (in) fclose(in);
36          return -1;
37      }
38
39      int Command_fetch(apr_pool_t * p, const char *url, int fetch_only)
40      {
41          apr_uri_t info = {.port = 0 };
42          int rc = 0;
43          const char *depends_file = NULL;
44          apr_status_t rv = apr_uri_parse(p, url, &info);
45
46          check(rv == APR_SUCCESS, "Failed to parse URL: %s", url);
47
48          if (apr_fnmatch(GIT_PAT, info.path, 0) == APR_SUCCESS) {
49              rc = Shell_exec(GIT_SH, "URL", url, NULL);
50              check(rc == 0, "git failed.");
51          } else if (apr_fnmatch(DEPEND_PAT, info.path, 0) == APR_SUCCESS) {
52              check(!fetch_only, "No point in fetching a DEPENDS file.");
53
54              if (info.scheme) {
55                  depends_file = DEPENDS_PATH;
56                  rc = Shell_exec(CURL_SH, "URL", url, "TARGET", depends_file,
57                          NULL);
58                  check(rc == 0, "Curl failed.");
59              } else {
60                  depends_file = info.path;
61              }
62
63              // recursively process the devpkg list
64              log_info("Building according to DEPENDS: %s", url);
65              rv = Command_depends(p, depends_file);
66              check(rv == 0, "Failed to process the DEPENDS: %s", url);
67
68              // this indicates that nothing needs to be done
69              return 0;
70
71          } else if (apr_fnmatch(TAR_GZ_PAT, info.path, 0) == APR_SUCCESS) {
72              if (info.scheme) {
73                  rc = Shell_exec(CURL_SH,
74                          "URL", url, "TARGET", TAR_GZ_SRC, NULL);
75                  check(rc == 0, "Failed to curl source: %s", url);
76              }
77
78              rv = apr_dir_make_recursive(BUILD_DIR,
79                      APR_UREAD | APR_UWRITE |
80                      APR_UEXECUTE, p);
81              check(rv == APR_SUCCESS, "Failed to make directory %s",
82                      BUILD_DIR);
83
84              rc = Shell_exec(TAR_SH, "FILE", TAR_GZ_SRC, NULL);
```

```
85              check(rc == 0, "Failed to untar %s", TAR_GZ_SRC);
86          } else if (apr_fnmatch(TAR_BZ2_PAT, info.path, 0) == APR_SUCCESS) {
87              if (info.scheme) {
88                  rc = Shell_exec(CURL_SH, "URL", url, "TARGET", TAR_BZ2_SRC,
89                          NULL);
90                  check(rc == 0, "Curl failed.");
91              }
92
93              apr_status_t rc = apr_dir_make_recursive(BUILD_DIR,
94                      APR_UREAD | APR_UWRITE
95                      | APR_UEXECUTE, p);
96
97              check(rc == 0, "Failed to make directory %s", BUILD_DIR);
98              rc = Shell_exec(TAR_SH, "FILE", TAR_BZ2_SRC, NULL);
99              check(rc == 0, "Failed to untar %s", TAR_BZ2_SRC);
100         } else {
101             sentinel("Don't now how to handle %s", url);
102         }
103
104         // indicates that an install needs to actually run
105         return 1;
106     error:
107         return -1;
108     }
109
110     int Command_build(apr_pool_t * p, const char *url,
111             const char *configure_opts, const char *make_opts,
112             const char *install_opts)
113     {
114         int rc = 0;
115
116         check(access(BUILD_DIR, X_OK | R_OK | W_OK) == 0,
117                 "Build directory doesn't exist: %s", BUILD_DIR);
118
119         // actually do an install
120         if (access(CONFIG_SCRIPT, X_OK) == 0) {
121             log_info("Has a configure script, running it.");
122             rc = Shell_exec(CONFIGURE_SH, "OPTS", configure_opts, NULL);
123             check(rc == 0, "Failed to configure.");
124         }
125
126         rc = Shell_exec(MAKE_SH, "OPTS", make_opts, NULL);
127         check(rc == 0, "Failed to build.");
128
129         rc = Shell_exec(INSTALL_SH,
130                 "TARGET", install_opts ? install_opts : "install",
131                 NULL);
132         check(rc == 0, "Failed to install.");
133
134         rc = Shell_exec(CLEANUP_SH, NULL);
```

```
135        check(rc == 0, "Failed to cleanup after build.");
136
137        rc = DB_update(url);
138        check(rc == 0, "Failed to add this package to the database.");
139
140        return 0;
141
142    error:
143        return -1;
144    }
145
146    int Command_install(apr_pool_t * p, const char *url,
147            const char *configure_opts, const char *make_opts,
148            const char *install_opts)
149    {
150        int rc = 0;
151        check(Shell_exec(CLEANUP_SH, NULL) == 0,
152                "Failed to cleanup before building.");
153
154        rc = DB_find(url);
155        check(rc != -1, "Error checking the install database.");
156
157        if (rc == 1) {
158            log_info("Package %s already installed.", url);
159            return 0;
160        }
161
162        rc = Command_fetch(p, url, 0);
163
164        if (rc == 1) {
165            rc = Command_build(p, url, configure_opts, make_opts,
166                    install_opts);
167            check(rc == 0, "Failed to build: %s", url);
168        } else if (rc == 0) {
169            // no install needed
170            log_info("Depends successfully installed: %s", url);
171        } else {
172            // had an error
173            sentinel("Install failed: %s", url);
174        }
175
176        Shell_exec(CLEANUP_SH, NULL);
177        return 0;
178
179    error:
180        Shell_exec(CLEANUP_SH, NULL);
181        return -1;
182    }
```

After you have this entered in and compiling, you can analyze it. If you've done the challenges thus far, you should see how the shell.c functions are being used to run shells, and how the arguments are being replaced. If not, then go back and make sure you *truly* understand how Shell_exec actually works.

Challenge 3: Critique My Design

As before, do a complete review of this code and make sure it's exactly the same. Then go through each function and make sure you know how they work and what they're doing. You should also trace how each function calls the other functions you've written in this file and other files. Finally, confirm that you understand all of the functions that you're calling from APR here.

Once you have the file correct and analyzed, go back through and assume that I'm an idiot. Then, criticize the design I have to see how you can improve it if you can. Don't *actually* change the code, just create a little notes.txt file and write down some thoughts about what you might change.

The devpkg Main Function

The last and most important file, but probably the simplest, is devpkg.c, which is where the main function lives. There's no .h file for this, since it includes all of the others. Instead, this just creates the executable devpkg when combined with the other .o files from our Makefile. Enter in the code for this file, and make sure it's correct.

devpkg.c

```
1    #include <stdio.h>
2    #include <apr_general.h>
3    #include <apr_getopt.h>
4    #include <apr_strings.h>
5    #include <apr_lib.h>
6
7    #include "dbg.h"
8    #include "db.h"
9    #include "commands.h"
10
11   int main(int argc, const char const *argv[])
12   {
13       apr_pool_t *p = NULL;
14       apr_pool_initialize();
15       apr_pool_create(&p, NULL);
16
17       apr_getopt_t *opt;
18       apr_status_t rv;
19
20       char ch = '\0';
21       const char *optarg = NULL;
```

```
22        const char *config_opts = NULL;
23        const char *install_opts = NULL;
24        const char *make_opts = NULL;
25        const char *url = NULL;
26        enum CommandType request = COMMAND_NONE;
27
28        rv = apr_getopt_init(&opt, p, argc, argv);
29
30        while (apr_getopt(opt, "I:Lc:m:i:d:SF:B:", &ch, &optarg) ==
31                APR_SUCCESS) {
32            switch (ch) {
33                case 'I':
34                    request = COMMAND_INSTALL;
35                    url = optarg;
36                    break;
37
38                case 'L':
39                    request = COMMAND_LIST;
40                    break;
41
42                case 'c':
43                    config_opts = optarg;
44                    break;
45
46                case 'm':
47                    make_opts = optarg;
48                    break;
49
50                case 'i':
51                    install_opts = optarg;
52                    break;
53
54                case 'S':
55                    request = COMMAND_INIT;
56                    break;
57
58                case 'F':
59                    request = COMMAND_FETCH;
60                    url = optarg;
61                    break;
62
63                case 'B':
64                    request = COMMAND_BUILD;
65                    url = optarg;
66                    break;
67            }
68        }
69
70        switch (request) {
71            case COMMAND_INSTALL:
```

```
72              check(url, "You must at least give a URL.");
73              Command_install(p, url, config_opts, make_opts, install_opts);
74              break;
75
76          case COMMAND_LIST:
77              DB_list();
78              break;
79
80          case COMMAND_FETCH:
81              check(url != NULL, "You must give a URL.");
82              Command_fetch(p, url, 1);
83              log_info("Downloaded to %s and in /tmp/", BUILD_DIR);
84              break;
85
86          case COMMAND_BUILD:
87              check(url, "You must at least give a URL.");
88              Command_build(p, url, config_opts, make_opts, install_opts);
89              break;
90
91          case COMMAND_INIT:
92              rv = DB_init();
93              check(rv == 0, "Failed to make the database.");
94              break;
95
96          default:
97              sentinel("Invalid command given.");
98      }
99
100         return 0;
101
102     error:
103         return 1;
104     }
```

Challenge 4: The README and Test Files

The challenge for this file is to understand how the arguments are being processed, what the arguments are, and then create the README file with instructions on how to use them. As you write the README, also write a simple test.sh that runs ./devpkg to check that each command is actually working against real, live code. Use the set -e at the top of your script so that it aborts on the first error.

Finally, run the program under your debugger and make sure it's working before moving on to the final challenge.

The Final Challenge

Your final challenge is a mini exam and it involves three things:

- Compare your code to my code that's available online. Starting at 100%, subtract 1% for each line you got wrong.

- Take the notes.txt file that you previously created and implement your improvements to the the code and functionality of devpkg.

- Write an alternative version of devpkg using your other favorite language or the one you think can do this the best. Compare the two, then improve your C version of devpkg based on what you've learned.

To compare your code with mine, do the following:

```
cd ..  # get one directory above your current one
git clone git://gitorious.org/devpkg/devpkg.git devpkgzed
diff -r devpkg devpkgzed
```

This will clone my version of devpkg into a directory called devpkgzed so you can then use the tool diff to compare what you've done to what I did. The files you're working with in this book come directly from this project, so if you get different lines, that's an error.

Keep in mind that there's no real pass or fail on this exercise. It's just a way for you to challenge yourself to be as exact and meticulous as possible.

Stacks and Queues

At this point in the book, you should know most of the data structures that are used to build all of the other data structures. If you have some kind of List, DArray, Hashmap, and Tree, then you can build almost anything else out there. Everything else you run into either uses these or some variant of these. If it doesn't, then it's most likely an exotic data structure that you probably won't need.

Stacks and Queues are very simple data structures that are really variants of the List data structure. All they do is use a List with a discipline or convention that says you always place elements on one end of the List. For a Stack, you always push and pop. For a Queue, you always shift to the front, but pop from the end.

I can implement both data structures using nothing but the CPP and two header files. My header files are 21 lines long and do all of the Stack and Queue operations without any fancy defines.

To see if you've been paying attention, I'm going to show you the unit tests, and then have *you* implement the header files needed to make them work. To pass this exercise, you can't create any stack.c or queue.c implementation files. Use only the stack.h and queue.h files to make the tests run.

stack_tests.c

```
1   #include "minunit.h"
2   #include <lcthw/stack.h>
3   #include <assert.h>
4
5   static Stack *stack = NULL;
6   char *tests[] = { "test1 data", "test2 data", "test3 data" };
7
8   #define NUM_TESTS 3
9
10  char *test_create()
11  {
12      stack = Stack_create();
13      mu_assert(stack != NULL, "Failed to create stack.");
14
15      return NULL;
16  }
17
18  char *test_destroy()
19  {
20      mu_assert(stack != NULL, "Failed to make stack #2");
21      Stack_destroy(stack);
22
```

```
23            return NULL;
24        }
25
26        char *test_push_pop()
27        {
28            int i = 0;
29            for (i = 0; i < NUM_TESTS; i++) {
30                Stack_push(stack, tests[i]);
31                mu_assert(Stack_peek(stack) == tests[i], "Wrong next value.");
32            }
33
34            mu_assert(Stack_count(stack) == NUM_TESTS, "Wrong count on push.");
35
36            STACK_FOREACH(stack, cur) {
37                debug("VAL: %s", (char *)cur->value);
38            }
39
40            for (i = NUM_TESTS - 1; i >= 0; i--) {
41                char *val = Stack_pop(stack);
42                mu_assert(val == tests[i], "Wrong value on pop.");
43            }
44
45            mu_assert(Stack_count(stack) == 0, "Wrong count after pop.");
46
47            return NULL;
48        }
49
50        char *all_tests()
51        {
52            mu_suite_start();
53
54            mu_run_test(test_create);
55            mu_run_test(test_push_pop);
56            mu_run_test(test_destroy);
57
58            return NULL;
59        }
60
61        RUN_TESTS(all_tests);
```

Then, the queue_tests.c is almost the same, only using Queue:

queue_tests.c

```
1    #include "minunit.h"
2    #include <lcthw/queue.h>
3    #include <assert.h>
4
5    static Queue *queue = NULL;
6    char *tests[] = { "test1 data", "test2 data", "test3 data" };
7
```

```
 8    #define NUM_TESTS 3
 9
10    char *test_create()
11    {
12        queue = Queue_create();
13        mu_assert(queue != NULL, "Failed to create queue.");
14
15        return NULL;
16    }
17
18    char *test_destroy()
19    {
20        mu_assert(queue != NULL, "Failed to make queue #2");
21        Queue_destroy(queue);
22
23        return NULL;
24    }
25
26    char *test_send_recv()
27    {
28        int i = 0;
29        for (i = 0; i < NUM_TESTS; i++) {
30            Queue_send(queue, tests[i]);
31            mu_assert(Queue_peek(queue) == tests[0], "Wrong next value.");
32        }
33
34        mu_assert(Queue_count(queue) == NUM_TESTS, "Wrong count on send.");
35
36        QUEUE_FOREACH(queue, cur) {
37            debug("VAL: %s", (char *)cur->value);
38        }
39
40        for (i = 0; i < NUM_TESTS; i++) {
41            char *val = Queue_recv(queue);
42            mu_assert(val == tests[i], "Wrong value on recv.");
43        }
44
45        mu_assert(Queue_count(queue) == 0, "Wrong count after recv.");
46
47        return NULL;
48    }
49
50    char *all_tests()
51    {
52        mu_suite_start();
53
54        mu_run_test(test_create);
55        mu_run_test(test_send_recv);
56        mu_run_test(test_destroy);
57
```

```
58        return NULL;
59    }
60
61    RUN_TESTS(all_tests);
```

What You Should See

Your unit test should run without your having to change the tests, and it should pass the debugger with no memory errors. Here's what it looks like if I run `stack_tests` directly:

Exercise 42.1 Session

```
$ ./tests/stack_tests
DEBUG tests/stack_tests.c:60: ----- RUNNING: ./tests/stack_tests
----
RUNNING: ./tests/stack_tests
DEBUG tests/stack_tests.c:53:
----- test_create
DEBUG tests/stack_tests.c:54:
----- test_push_pop
DEBUG tests/stack_tests.c:37: VAL: test3 data
DEBUG tests/stack_tests.c:37: VAL: test2 data
DEBUG tests/stack_tests.c:37: VAL: test1 data
DEBUG tests/stack_tests.c:55:
----- test_destroy
ALL TESTS PASSED
Tests run: 3
$
```

The `queue_test` is basically the same kind of output, so I shouldn't have to show it to you at this stage.

How to Improve It

The only real improvement you could make to this is switching from a `List` to a `DArray`. The Queue data structure is more difficult to do with a `DArray` because it works at both ends of the list of nodes.

One disadvantage of doing this entirely in a header file is that you can't easily performance tune it. Mostly, what you're doing with this technique is establishing a protocol for how to use a `List` in a certain style. When performance tuning, if you make `List` fast, then these two should improve as well.

Extra Credit

- Implement `Stack` using `DArray` instead of `List`, but without changing the unit test. That means you'll have to create your own STACK_FOREACH.

A Simple Statistics Engine

This is a simple algorithm that I use for collecting summary statistics online, or without storing all of the samples. I use this in any software that needs to keep some statistics, such as mean, standard deviation, and sum, but can't store all the samples needed. Instead, I can just store the rolling results of the calculations, which is only five numbers.

Rolling Standard Deviation and Mean

The first thing you need is a sequence of samples. This can be anything from the time it takes to complete a task to the number of times someone accesses something to star ratings on a Web site. It doesn't really matter what it is, just so long as you have a stream of numbers and you want to know the following summary statistics about them:

sum   This is the total of all the numbers added together.

sum squared (sumsq)   This is the sum of the square of each number.

count (n)   This is the number samples that you've taken.

min   This is the smallest sample you've seen.

max   This is the largest sample you've seen.

mean   This is the most likely middle number. It's not actually the middle, since that's the median, but it's an accepted approximation for it.

stddev   This is calculated using $sqrt(sumsq - (sum \times mean)) / (n - 1)))$ where sqrt is the square root function in the math.h header.

I will confirm this calculation works using R, since I know R gets these right:

Exercise 43.1 Session

```
> s <- runif(n=10, max=10)
> s
 [1] 6.1061334 9.6783204 1.2747090 8.2395131 0.3333483 6.9755066 1.0626275
 [8] 7.6587523 4.9382973 9.5788115
> summary(s)
   Min. 1st Qu.  Median    Mean 3rd Qu.    Max.
 0.3333  2.1910  6.5410  5.5850  8.0940  9.6780
> sd(s)
[1] 3.547868
> sum(s)
[1] 55.84602
```

```
> sum(s * s)
[1] 425.1641
> sum(s) * mean(s)
[1] 311.8778
> sum(s * s) - sum(s) * mean(s)
[1] 113.2863
> (sum(s * s) - sum(s) * mean(s)) / (length(s) - 1)
[1] 12.58737
> sqrt((sum(s * s) - sum(s) * mean(s)) / (length(s) - 1))
[1] 3.547868
>
```

You don't need to know R. Just follow along while I explain how I'm breaking this down to check my math:

Lines 1-4   I use the function `runif` to get a random uniform distribution of numbers, then print them out. I'll use these in the unit test later.

Lines 5-7   Here's the summary, so you can see the values that R calculates for these.

Lines 8-9   This is the `stddev` using the `sd` function.

Lines 10-11   Now I begin to build this calculation manually, first by getting the `sum`.

Lines 12-13   The next piece of the `stdev` formula is the `sumsq`, which I can get with `sum(s * s)` that tells R to multiply the whole s list by itself, and then `sum` those. The power of R is being able to do math on entire data structures like this.

Lines 14-15   Looking at the formula, I then need the `sum` multiplied by `mean`, so I do `sum(s) * mean(s)`.

Lines 16-17   I then combine the `sumsq` with this to get `sum(s * s) - sum(s) * mean(s)`.

Lines 18-19   That needs to be divided by $n-1$, so I do `(sum(s * s) - sum(s) * mean(s)) / (length(s) - 1)`.

Lines 20-21   Finally, I `sqrt` that and I get 3.547868, which matches the number R gave me for `sd` above.

Implementation

That's how you calculate the `stddev`, so now I can make some simple code to implement this calculation.

stats.h

```
#ifndef lcthw_stats_h
#define lcthw_stats_h

typedef struct Stats {
```

```
        double sum;
        double sumsq;
        unsigned long n;
        double min;
        double max;
    } Stats;

    Stats *Stats_recreate(double sum, double sumsq, unsigned long n,
            double min, double max);

    Stats *Stats_create();

    double Stats_mean(Stats * st);

    double Stats_stddev(Stats * st);

    void Stats_sample(Stats * st, double s);

    void Stats_dump(Stats * st);

    #endif
```

Here you can see that I've put the calculations I need to store in a `struct`, and then I have functions for sampling and getting the numbers. Implementing this is then just an exercise in converting the math:

stats.c

```
1    #include <math.h>
2    #include <lcthw/stats.h>
3    #include <stdlib.h>
4    #include <lcthw/dbg.h>
5
6    Stats *Stats_recreate(double sum, double sumsq, unsigned long n,
7            double min, double max)
8    {
9        Stats *st = malloc(sizeof(Stats));
10       check_mem(st);
11
12       st->sum = sum;
13       st->sumsq = sumsq;
14       st->n = n;
15       st->min = min;
16       st->max = max;
17
18       return st;
19
20   error:
```

```
21          return NULL;
22      }
23
24      Stats *Stats_create()
25      {
26          return Stats_recreate(0.0, 0.0, 0L, 0.0, 0.0);
27      }
28
29      double Stats_mean(Stats * st)
30      {
31          return st->sum / st->n;
32      }
33
34      double Stats_stddev(Stats * st)
35      {
36          return sqrt((st->sumsq - (st->sum * st->sum / st->n)) /
37                  (st->n - 1));
38      }
39
40      void Stats_sample(Stats * st, double s)
41      {
42          st->sum += s;
43          st->sumsq += s * s;
44
45          if (st->n == 0) {
46              st->min = s;
47              st->max = s;
48          } else {
49              if (st->min > s)
50                  st->min = s;
51              if (st->max < s)
52                  st->max = s;
53          }
54
55          st->n += 1;
56      }
57
58      void Stats_dump(Stats * st)
59      {
60          fprintf(stderr,
61                  "sum: %f, sumsq: %f, n: %ld, "
62                  "min: %f, max: %f, mean: %f, stddev: %f",
63                  st->sum, st->sumsq, st->n, st->min, st->max, Stats_mean(st),
64                  Stats_stddev(st));
65      }
```

Here's a breakdown of each function in `stats.c`:

Stats_recreate   I'll want to load these numbers from some kind of database, and this function let's me recreate a `Stats` struct.

Stats_create   This simply called `Stats_recreate` with all 0 (zero) values.

Stats_mean   Using the sum and n, it gives the mean.

Stats_stddev   This implements the formula I worked out; the only difference is that I calculate the mean with `st->sum / st->n` in this formula instead of calling `Stats_mean`.

Stats_sample   This does the work of maintaining the numbers in the `Stats` struct. When you give it the first value, it sees that n is 0 and sets `min` and `max` accordingly. Every call after that keeps increasing `sum`, `sumsq`, and n. It then figures out if this new sample is a new `min` or `max`.

Stats_dump   This is a simple debug function that dumps the statistics so you can view them.

The last thing I need to do is confirm that this math is correct. I'm going to use numbers and calculations from my R session to create a unit test that confirms that I'm getting the right results.

stats_tests.c

```
1    #include "minunit.h"
2    #include <lcthw/stats.h>
3    #include <math.h>
4
5    const int NUM_SAMPLES = 10;
6    double samples[] = {
7        6.1061334, 9.6783204, 1.2747090, 8.2395131, 0.3333483,
8        6.9755066, 1.0626275, 7.6587523, 4.9382973, 9.5788115
9    };
10
11   Stats expect = {
12       .sumsq = 425.1641,
13       .sum = 55.84602,
14       .min = 0.333,
15       .max = 9.678,
16       .n = 10,
17   };
18
19   double expect_mean = 5.584602;
20   double expect_stddev = 3.547868;
21
22   #define EQ(X,Y,N) (round((X) * pow(10, N)) == round((Y) * pow(10, N)))
23
24   char *test_operations()
25   {
26       int i = 0;
27       Stats *st = Stats_create();
```

```
28          mu_assert(st != NULL, "Failed to create stats.");
29
30          for (i = 0; i < NUM_SAMPLES; i++) {
31              Stats_sample(st, samples[i]);
32          }
33
34          Stats_dump(st);
35
36          mu_assert(EQ(st->sumsq, expect.sumsq, 3), "sumsq not valid");
37          mu_assert(EQ(st->sum, expect.sum, 3), "sum not valid");
38          mu_assert(EQ(st->min, expect.min, 3), "min not valid");
39          mu_assert(EQ(st->max, expect.max, 3), "max not valid");
40          mu_assert(EQ(st->n, expect.n, 3), "max not valid");
41          mu_assert(EQ(expect_mean, Stats_mean(st), 3), "mean not valid");
42          mu_assert(EQ(expect_stddev, Stats_stddev(st), 3),
43                  "stddev not valid");
44
45          return NULL;
46      }
47
48      char *test_recreate()
49      {
50          Stats *st = Stats_recreate(
51                  expect.sum, expect.sumsq, expect.n, expect.min, expect.max);
52
53          mu_assert(st->sum == expect.sum, "sum not equal");
54          mu_assert(st->sumsq == expect.sumsq, "sumsq not equal");
55          mu_assert(st->n == expect.n, "n not equal");
56          mu_assert(st->min == expect.min, "min not equal");
57          mu_assert(st->max == expect.max, "max not equal");
58          mu_assert(EQ(expect_mean, Stats_mean(st), 3), "mean not valid");
59          mu_assert(EQ(expect_stddev, Stats_stddev(st), 3),
60                  "stddev not valid");
61
62          return NULL;
63      }
64
65      char *all_tests()
66      {
67          mu_suite_start();
68
69          mu_run_test(test_operations);
70          mu_run_test(test_recreate);
71
72          return NULL;
73      }
74
75      RUN_TESTS(all_tests);
```

There's nothing new in this unit test, except maybe the EQ macro. I felt lazy and didn't want to look up the standard way to tell if two `double` values are close, so I made this macro. The problem with `double` is that equality assumes totally equal results, but I'm using two different systems with slightly different rounding errors. The solution is to say that I want the numbers to be "equal to X decimal places."

I do this with EQ by raising the number to a power of 10, then using the round function to get an integer. This is a simple way to round to N decimal places and compare the results as an integer. I'm sure there are a billion other ways to do the same thing, but this works for now.

The expected results are then in a `Stats struct` and I simply make sure that the number I get is close to the number R gave me.

How to Use It

You can use the standard deviation and mean to determine if a new sample is interesting, or you can use this to collect statistics on statistics. The first one is easy for people to understand, so I'll explain that quickly using an example for login times.

Imagine you're tracking how long users spend on a server, and you're using statistics to analyze it. Every time someone logs in, you keep track of how long they are there, then you call `Stats_sample`. I'm looking for people who are on too long and also people who seem to be on too quickly.

Instead of setting specific levels, what I'd do is compare how long someone is on with the mean `(plus or minus) 2 * stddev` range. I get the mean and `2 * stddev`, and consider login times to be interesting if they are outside these two ranges. Since I'm keeping these statistics using a rolling algorithm, this is a very fast calculation, and I can then have the software flag the users who are outside of this range.

This doesn't necessarily point out people who are behaving badly, but instead it flags potential problems that you can review to see what's going on. It's also doing it based on the behavior of all of the users, which avoids the problem of picking some arbitrary number that's not based on what's really happening.

The general rule you can get from this is that the mean `(plus or minus) 2 * stddev` is an estimate of where 90% of the values are expected to fall, and anything outside that range is interesting.

The second way to use these statistics is to go meta and calculate them for other `Stats` calculations. You basically do your `Stats_sample` like normal, but then you run `Stats_sample` on the `min`, `max`, `n`, `mean`, and `stddev` on that sample. This gives a two-level measurement, and lets you compare samples of samples.

Confusing, right? I'll continue my example above, but let's say you have 100 servers that each hold a different application. You're already tracking users' login times for each application server, but you want to compare all 100 applications and flag any users that are logging in too much on all of them. The easiest way to do that is to calculate the new login stats each time someone logs in, and then add *that* Stats structs element to a second Stat.

What you end up with is a series of statistics that can be named like this:

mean of means   This is a full Stats struct that gives you mean and stddev of the means of all the servers. Any server or user who is outside of this is worth looking at on a global level.

mean of stddevs   Another Stats struct that produces statistics on how *all* of the servers range. You can then analyze each server and see if any of them have unusually wide-ranging numbers by comparing their stddev to this mean of stddevs statistic.

You could do them all, but these are the most useful. If you then wanted to monitor servers for erratic login times, you'd do this:

- User John logs in to and out of server A. Grab server A's statistics and update them.

- Grab the mean of means statistics, and then take A's mean and add it as a sample. I'll call this m_of_m.

- Grab the mean of stddevs statistics, and add A's stddev to it as a sample. I'll call this m_of_s.

- If A's mean is outside of m_of_m.mean + 2 * m_of_m.stddev, then flag it as possibly having a problem.

- If A's stddev is outside of m_of_s.mean + 2 * m_of_s.stddev, then flag it as possibly behaving too erratically.

- Finally, if John's login time is outside of A's range, or A's m_of_m range, then flag it as interesting.

Using this mean of means and mean of stddevs calculation, you can efficiently track many metrics with a minimal amount of processing and storage.

Extra Credit

- Convert the Stats_stddev and Stats_mean to static inline functions in the stats.h file instead of in the stats.c file.

- Use this code to write a performance test of the string_algos_test.c. Make it optional, and have it run the base test as a series of samples, and then report the results.

- Write a version of this in another programming language you know. Confirm that this version is correct based on what I have here.

- Write a little program that can take a file full of numbers and spit these statistics out for them.

- Make the program accept a table of data that has headers on one line, then all of the other numbers on lines after it are separated by any number of spaces. Your program should then print out these statistics for each column by the header name.

Ring Buffer

Ring buffers are incredibly useful when processing asynchronous I/O. They allow one side to receive data in random intervals of random sizes, but feed cohesive chunks to another side in set sizes or intervals. They are a variant on the Queue data structure but focus on blocks of bytes instead of a list of pointers. In this exercise, I'm going to show you the RingBuffer code, and then have you make a full unit test for it.

ringbuffer.h

```
1    #ifndef _lcthw_RingBuffer_h
2    #define _lcthw_RingBuffer_h
3
4    #include <lcthw/bstrlib.h>
5
6    typedef struct {
7        char *buffer;
8        int length;
9        int start;
10       int end;
11   } RingBuffer;
12
13   RingBuffer *RingBuffer_create(int length);
14
15   void RingBuffer_destroy(RingBuffer * buffer);
16
17   int RingBuffer_read(RingBuffer * buffer, char *target, int amount);
18
19   int RingBuffer_write(RingBuffer * buffer, char *data, int length);
20
21   int RingBuffer_empty(RingBuffer * buffer);
22
23   int RingBuffer_full(RingBuffer * buffer);
24
25   int RingBuffer_available_data(RingBuffer * buffer);
26
27   int RingBuffer_available_space(RingBuffer * buffer);
28
29   bstring RingBuffer_gets(RingBuffer * buffer, int amount);
30
31   #define RingBuffer_available_data(B) (\
32           ((B)->end + 1) % (B)->length - (B)->start - 1)
33
34   #define RingBuffer_available_space(B) (\
35           (B)->length - (B)->end - 1)
36
37   #define RingBuffer_full(B) (RingBuffer_available_data((B))\
38           - (B)->length == 0)
```

```
39
40    #define RingBuffer_empty(B) (\
41            RingBuffer_available_data((B)) == 0)
42
43    #define RingBuffer_puts(B, D) RingBuffer_write(\
44            (B), bdata((D)), blength((D)))
45
46    #define RingBuffer_get_all(B) RingBuffer_gets(\
47            (B), RingBuffer_available_data((B)))
48
49    #define RingBuffer_starts_at(B) (\
50            (B)->buffer + (B)->start)
51
52    #define RingBuffer_ends_at(B) (\
53            (B)->buffer + (B)->end)
54
55    #define RingBuffer_commit_read(B, A) (\
56            (B)->start = ((B)->start + (A)) % (B)->length)
57
58    #define RingBuffer_commit_write(B, A) (\
59            (B)->end = ((B)->end + (A)) % (B)->length)
60
61    #endif
```

Looking at the data structure, you see I have a buffer, start, and end. A RingBuffer does nothing more than move the start and end around the buffer so that it loops whenever it reaches the buffer's end. Doing this gives the illusion of an infinite read device in a small space. I then have a bunch of macros that do various calculations based on this.

Here's the implementation, which is a much better explanation of how this works.

ringbuffer.c

```
1     #undef NDEBUG
2     #include <assert.h>
3     #include <stdio.h>
4     #include <stdlib.h>
5     #include <string.h>
6     #include <lcthw/dbg.h>
7     #include <lcthw/ringbuffer.h>
8
9     RingBuffer *RingBuffer_create(int length)
10    {
11        RingBuffer *buffer = calloc(1, sizeof(RingBuffer));
12        buffer->length = length + 1;
13        buffer->start = 0;
14        buffer->end = 0;
15        buffer->buffer = calloc(buffer->length, 1);
16
17        return buffer;
18    }
```

```
19
20    void RingBuffer_destroy(RingBuffer * buffer)
21    {
22        if (buffer) {
23            free(buffer->buffer);
24            free(buffer);
25        }
26    }
27
28    int RingBuffer_write(RingBuffer * buffer, char *data, int length)
29    {
30        if (RingBuffer_available_data(buffer) == 0) {
31            buffer->start = buffer->end = 0;
32        }
33
34        check(length <= RingBuffer_available_space(buffer),
35                "Not enough space: %d request, %d available",
36                RingBuffer_available_data(buffer), length);
37
38        void *result = memcpy(RingBuffer_ends_at(buffer), data, length);
39        check(result != NULL, "Failed to write data into buffer.");
40
41        RingBuffer_commit_write(buffer, length);
42
43        return length;
44    error:
45        return -1;
46    }
47
48    int RingBuffer_read(RingBuffer * buffer, char *target, int amount)
49    {
50        check_debug(amount <= RingBuffer_available_data(buffer),
51                "Not enough in the buffer: has %d, needs %d",
52                RingBuffer_available_data(buffer), amount);
53
54        void *result = memcpy(target, RingBuffer_starts_at(buffer), amount);
55        check(result != NULL, "Failed to write buffer into data.");
56
57        RingBuffer_commit_read(buffer, amount);
58
59        if (buffer->end == buffer->start) {
60            buffer->start = buffer->end = 0;
61        }
62
63        return amount;
64    error:
65        return -1;
66    }
67
68    bstring RingBuffer_gets(RingBuffer * buffer, int amount)
```

```
69    {
70        check(amount > 0, "Need more than 0 for gets, you gave: %d ",
71                amount);
72        check_debug(amount <= RingBuffer_available_data(buffer),
73                "Not enough in the buffer.");
74
75        bstring result = blk2bstr(RingBuffer_starts_at(buffer), amount);
76        check(result != NULL, "Failed to create gets result.");
77        check(blength(result) == amount, "Wrong result length.");
78
79        RingBuffer_commit_read(buffer, amount);
80        assert(RingBuffer_available_data(buffer) >= 0
81                && "Error in read commit.");
82
83        return result;
84    error:
85        return NULL;
86    }
```

This is all there is to a basic `RingBuffer` implementation. You can read and write blocks of data to it. You can ask how much is in it and how much space it has. There are some fancier ring buffers that use tricks on the OS to create an imaginary infinite store, but those aren't portable.

Since my `RingBuffer` deals with reading and writing blocks of memory, I'm making sure that any time end `==` start, I reset them to 0 (zero) so that they go to the beginning of the buffer. In the Wikipedia version it isn't writing blocks of data, so it only has to move end and `start` around in a circle. To better handle blocks, you have to drop to the beginning of the internal buffer whenever the data is empty.

The Unit Test

For your unit test, you'll want to test as many possible conditions as you can. The easiest way to do that is to preconstruct different `RingBuffer` structs, and then manually check that the functions and math work right. For example, you could make one where end is right at the end of the buffer and `start` is right before the buffer, and then see how it fails.

What You Should See

Here's my `ringbuffer_tests` run:

Exercise 44.1 Session

```
$ ./tests/ringbuffer_tests
DEBUG tests/ringbuffer_tests.c:60: ----- RUNNING: ./tests/ringbuffer_tests
----
RUNNING: ./tests/ringbuffer_tests
```

```
DEBUG tests/ringbuffer_tests.c:53:
----- test_create
DEBUG tests/ringbuffer_tests.c:54:
----- test_read_write
DEBUG tests/ringbuffer_tests.c:55:
----- test_destroy
ALL TESTS PASSED
Tests run: 3
$
```

You should have at least three tests that confirm all of the basic operations, and then see how much more you can test beyond what I've done.

How to Improve It

As usual, you should go back and add defensive programming checks to this exercise. Hopefully you've been doing this, because the base code in most of `liblcthw` doesn't have the common defensive programming checks that I'm teaching you. I leave this to you so that you can get used to improving code with these extra checks.

For example, in this ring buffer, there's not a lot of checking that an access will actually be inside the buffer.

If you read the "Circular buffer" page on Wikipedia, you'll see the "Optimized POSIX implementation" that uses Portable Operating System Interface (POSIX)-specific calls to create an infinite space. Study that and I'll have you try it in the Extra Credit section.

Extra Credit

- Create an alternative implementation of `RingBuffer` that uses the POSIX trick and then create a unit test for it.

- Add a performance comparison test to this unit test that compares the two versions by fuzzing them with random data and random read/write operations. Make sure that you set up this fuzzing so that the same operations are done to each version, and you can compare them between runs.

A Simple TCP/IP Client

I'm going to use the RingBuffer to create a very simplistic network testing tool that I call netclient. To do this, I have to add some stuff to the Makefile to handle little programs in the bin/ directory.

Augment the Makefile

First, add a variable for the programs just like the unit test's TESTS and TEST_SRC variables:

```
PROGRAMS_SRC=$(wildcard bin/*.c)
PROGRAMS=$(patsubst %.c,%,$(PROGRAMS_SRC))
```

Then, you want to add the PROGRAMS to the all target:

```
all: $(TARGET) $(SO_TARGET) tests $(PROGRAMS)
```

Then, add PROGRAMS to the rm line in the clean target:

```
rm -rf build $(OBJECTS) $(TESTS) $(PROGRAMS)
```

Finally, you just need a target at the end to build them all:

```
$(PROGRAMS): CFLAGS += $(TARGET)
```

With these changes, you can drop simple .c files into bin, and make will build them and link them to the library just like unit tests do.

The netclient Code

The code for the little netclient looks like this:

netclient.c

```
1    #undef NDEBUG
2    #include <stdlib.h>
3    #include <sys/select.h>
4    #include <stdio.h>
5    #include <lcthw/ringbuffer.h>
6    #include <lcthw/dbg.h>
7    #include <sys/socket.h>
```

```
 8    #include <sys/types.h>
 9    #include <sys/uio.h>
10    #include <arpa/inet.h>
11    #include <netdb.h>
12    #include <unistd.h>
13    #include <fcntl.h>
14
15    struct tagbstring NL = bsStatic("\n");
16    struct tagbstring CRLF = bsStatic("\r\n");
17
18    int nonblock(int fd)
19    {
20        int flags = fcntl(fd, F_GETFL, 0);
21        check(flags >= 0, "Invalid flags on nonblock.");
22
23        int rc = fcntl(fd, F_SETFL, flags | O_NONBLOCK);
24        check(rc == 0, "Can't set nonblocking.");
25
26        return 0;
27    error:
28        return -1;
29    }
30
31    int client_connect(char *host, char *port)
32    {
33        int rc = 0;
34        struct addrinfo *addr = NULL;
35
36        rc = getaddrinfo(host, port, NULL, &addr);
37        check(rc == 0, "Failed to lookup %s:%s", host, port);
38
39        int sock = socket(AF_INET, SOCK_STREAM, 0);
40        check(sock >= 0, "Cannot create a socket.");
41
42        rc = connect(sock, addr->ai_addr, addr->ai_addrlen);
43        check(rc == 0, "Connect failed.");
44
45        rc = nonblock(sock);
46        check(rc == 0, "Can't set nonblocking.");
47
48        freeaddrinfo(addr);
49        return sock;
50
51    error:
52        freeaddrinfo(addr);
53        return -1;
54    }
55
56    int read_some(RingBuffer * buffer, int fd, int is_socket)
57    {
```

```
58          int rc = 0;
59
60          if (RingBuffer_available_data(buffer) == 0) {
61              buffer->start = buffer->end = 0;
62          }
63
64          if (is_socket) {
65              rc = recv(fd, RingBuffer_starts_at(buffer),
66                      RingBuffer_available_space(buffer), 0);
67          } else {
68              rc = read(fd, RingBuffer_starts_at(buffer),
69                      RingBuffer_available_space(buffer));
70          }
71
72          check(rc >= 0, "Failed to read from fd: %d", fd);
73
74          RingBuffer_commit_write(buffer, rc);
75
76          return rc;
77
78      error:
79          return -1;
80      }
81
82      int write_some(RingBuffer * buffer, int fd, int is_socket)
83      {
84          int rc = 0;
85          bstring data = RingBuffer_get_all(buffer);
86
87          check(data != NULL, "Failed to get from the buffer.");
88          check(bfindreplace(data, &NL, &CRLF, 0) == BSTR_OK,
89                  "Failed to replace NL.");
90
91          if (is_socket) {
92              rc = send(fd, bdata(data), blength(data), 0);
93          } else {
94              rc = write(fd, bdata(data), blength(data));
95          }
96
97          check(rc == blength(data), "Failed to write everything to fd: %d.",
98                  fd);
99          bdestroy(data);
100
101          return rc;
102
103     error:
104          return -1;
105     }
106
107     int main(int argc, char *argv[])
```

```
108    {
109        fd_set allreads;
110        fd_set readmask;
111
112        int socket = 0;
113        int rc = 0;
114        RingBuffer *in_rb = RingBuffer_create(1024 * 10);
115        RingBuffer *sock_rb = RingBuffer_create(1024 * 10);
116
117        check(argc == 3, "USAGE: netclient host port");
118
119        socket = client_connect(argv[1], argv[2]);
120        check(socket >= 0, "connect to %s:%s failed.", argv[1], argv[2]);
121
122        FD_ZERO(&allreads);
123        FD_SET(socket, &allreads);
124        FD_SET(0, &allreads);
125
126        while (1) {
127            readmask = allreads;
128            rc = select(socket + 1, &readmask, NULL, NULL, NULL);
129            check(rc >= 0, "select failed.");
130
131            if (FD_ISSET(0, &readmask)) {
132                rc = read_some(in_rb, 0, 0);
133                check_debug(rc != -1, "Failed to read from stdin.");
134            }
135
136            if (FD_ISSET(socket, &readmask)) {
137                rc = read_some(sock_rb, socket, 0);
138                check_debug(rc != -1, "Failed to read from socket.");
139            }
140
141            while (!RingBuffer_empty(sock_rb)) {
142                rc = write_some(sock_rb, 1, 0);
143                check_debug(rc != -1, "Failed to write to stdout.");
144            }
145
146            while (!RingBuffer_empty(in_rb)) {
147                rc = write_some(in_rb, socket, 1);
148                check_debug(rc != -1, "Failed to write to socket.");
149            }
150        }
151
152        return 0;
153
154    error:
155        return -1;
156    }
```

This code uses select to handle events from both stdin (file descriptor 0) and socket, which it uses to talk to a server. The code uses RingBuffers to store the data and copy it around. You can consider the functions read_some and write_some early prototypes for similar functions in the RingBuffer library.

This little bit of code contains quite a few networking functions that you may not know. As you come across a function that you don't know, look it up in the man pages and make sure you understand it. This one little file might inspire you to then research all of the APIs required to write a little server in C.

What You Should See

If you have everything building, then the quickest way to test the code is see if you can get a special file off of http://learncodethehardway.org.

Exercise 45.1 Session

```
$
$ ./bin/netclient learncodethehardway.org 80
GET /ex45.txt HTTP/1.1
Host: learncodethehardway.org

HTTP/1.1 200 OK
Date: Fri, 27 Apr 2012 00:41:25 GMT
Content-Type: text/plain
Content-Length: 41
Last-Modified: Fri, 27 Apr 2012 00:42:11 GMT
ETag: 4f99eb63-29
Server: Mongrel2/1.7.5

Learn C The Hard Way, Exercise 45 works.
^C
$
```

What I do here is type in the syntax needed to make the HTTP request for the file /ex45.txt, then the Host: header line, and then I press ENTER to get an empty line. I then get the response, with headers and the content. After that, I just hit CTRL-C to exit.

How to Break It

This code could definitely have bugs, and currently in the draft of this book, I'm going to have to keep working on it. In the meantime, try analyzing the code I have here and thrashing it against other servers. There's a tool called netcat that's great for setting up these kinds of servers. Another thing to do is use a language like Python or Ruby to create a simple junk server that spews out junk and bad data, randomly closes connections, and does other nasty things.

If you find bugs, report them in the comments, and I'll fix them up.

Extra Credit

- As I mentioned, there are quite a few functions you may not know, so look them up. In fact, look them all up even if you think you know them.

- Run this under the debugger and look for errors.

- Go back through and add various defensive programming checks to the functions to improve them.

- Use the getopt function to allow the user the option *not* to translate \n to \r\n. This is only needed on protocols that require it for line endings, like HTTP. Sometimes you don't want the translation, so give the user the option.

Ternary Search Tree

The final data structure that I'll show you is called the *TSTree*, which is similar to the BSTree, except it has three branches: `low`, `equal`, and `high`. It's primarily used just like BSTree and Hashmap to store key/value data, but it works off of the individual characters in the keys. This gives the TSTree some abilities that neither BSTree nor Hashmap has.

In a TSTree, every key is a string, and it's inserted by walking through and building a tree based on the equality of the characters in the string. It starts at the root, looks at the character for that node, and if it's lower, equal to, or higher than that, then it goes in that direction. You can see this in the header file:

tstree.h

```
#ifndef _lcthw_TSTree_h
#define _lcthw_TSTree_h

#include <stdlib.h>
#include <lcthw/darray.h>

typedef struct TSTree {
    char splitchar;
    struct TSTree *low;
    struct TSTree *equal;
    struct TSTree *high;
    void *value;
} TSTree;

void *TSTree_search(TSTree * root, const char *key, size_t len);

void *TSTree_search_prefix(TSTree * root, const char *key, size_t len);

typedef void (*TSTree_traverse_cb) (void *value, void *data);

TSTree *TSTree_insert(TSTree * node, const char *key, size_t len,
        void *value);

void TSTree_traverse(TSTree * node, TSTree_traverse_cb cb, void *data);

void TSTree_destroy(TSTree * root);

#endif
```

The TSTree has the following elements:

splitchar   The character at this point in the tree.

low   The branch that's lower than `splitchar`.

equal The branch that's equal to splitchar.

high The branch that's higher than splitchar.

value The value set for a string at that point with splitchar.

You can see that this implementation has the following operations:

search A typical operation to find a value for this key.

search_prefix This operation finds the first value that has this as a prefix of its key. This is the an operation that you can't easily do in a BSTree or Hashmap.

insert This breaks the key down by each character and inserts them into the tree.

traverse This walks through the tree, allowing you to collect or analyze all the keys and values it contains.

The only thing missing is a TSTree_delete, and that's because it's a horribly expensive operation, even more expensive than BSTree_delete. When I use TSTree structures, I treat them as constant data that I plan on traversing many times, and not removing anything from them. They are very fast for this, but aren't good if you need to insert and delete things quickly. For that, I use Hashmap, since it beats both BSTree and TSTree.

The implementation for the TSTree is actually simple, but it might be hard to follow at first. I'll break it down after you enter it in:

tstree.c

```
 1     #include <stdlib.h>
 2     #include <stdio.h>
 3     #include <assert.h>
 4     #include <lcthw/dbg.h>
 5     #include <lcthw/tstree.h>
 6
 7     static inline TSTree *TSTree_insert_base(TSTree * root, TSTree * node,
 8             const char *key, size_t len,
 9             void *value)
10     {
11         if (node == NULL) {
12             node = (TSTree *) calloc(1, sizeof(TSTree));
13
14             if (root == NULL) {
15                 root = node;
16             }
17
18             node->splitchar = *key;
19         }
20
```

```
21          if (*key < node->splitchar) {
22              node->low = TSTree_insert_base(
23                      root, node->low, key, len, value);
24          } else if (*key == node->splitchar) {
25              if (len > 1) {
26                  node->equal = TSTree_insert_base(
27                          root, node->equal, key + 1, len - 1, value);
28              } else {
29                  assert(node->value == NULL && "Duplicate insert into tst.");
30                  node->value = value;
31              }
32          } else {
33              node->high = TSTree_insert_base(
34                      root, node->high, key, len, value);
35          }
36
37      return node;
38  }
39
40  TSTree *TSTree_insert(TSTree * node, const char *key, size_t len,
41          void *value)
42  {
43      return TSTree_insert_base(node, node, key, len, value);
44  }
45
46  void *TSTree_search(TSTree * root, const char *key, size_t len)
47  {
48      TSTree *node = root;
49      size_t i = 0;
50
51      while (i < len && node) {
52          if (key[i] < node->splitchar) {
53              node = node->low;
54          } else if (key[i] == node->splitchar) {
55              i++;
56              if (i < len)
57                  node = node->equal;
58          } else {
59              node = node->high;
60          }
61      }
62
63      if (node) {
64          return node->value;
65      } else {
66          return NULL;
67      }
68  }
69
70  void *TSTree_search_prefix(TSTree * root, const char *key, size_t len)
```

```
71    {
72        if (len == 0)
73            return NULL;
74
75        TSTree *node = root;
76        TSTree *last = NULL;
77        size_t i = 0;
78
79        while (i < len && node) {
80            if (key[i] < node->splitchar) {
81                node = node->low;
82            } else if (key[i] == node->splitchar) {
83                i++;
84                if (i < len) {
85                    if (node->value)
86                        last = node;
87                    node = node->equal;
88                }
89            } else {
90                node = node->high;
91            }
92        }
93
94        node = node ? node : last;
95
96        // traverse until we find the first value in the equal chain
97        // this is then the first node with this prefix
98        while (node && !node->value) {
99            node = node->equal;
100        }
101
102        return node ? node->value : NULL;
103    }
104
105    void TSTree_traverse(TSTree * node, TSTree_traverse_cb cb, void *data)
106    {
107        if (!node)
108            return;
109
110        if (node->low)
111            TSTree_traverse(node->low, cb, data);
112
113        if (node->equal) {
114            TSTree_traverse(node->equal, cb, data);
115        }
116
117        if (node->high)
118            TSTree_traverse(node->high, cb, data);
119
120        if (node->value)
```

```
121                    cb(node->value, data);
122        }
123
124        void TSTree_destroy(TSTree * node)
125        {
126            if (node == NULL)
127                return;
128
129            if (node->low)
130                TSTree_destroy(node->low);
131
132            if (node->equal) {
133                TSTree_destroy(node->equal);
134            }
135
136            if (node->high)
137                TSTree_destroy(node->high);
138
139            free(node);
140        }
```

For TSTree_insert, I'm using the same pattern for recursive structures where I have a small function that calls the real recursive function. I'm not doing any additional checks here, but you should add the usual defensive programming checks to it. One thing to keep in mind is that it's using a slightly different design that doesn't have a separate TSTree_create function. However, if you pass it a NULL for the node, then it will create it and return the final value.

That means I need to break down TSTree_insert_base so that you understand the insert operation:

tstree.c:10-18 As I mentioned, if given a NULL, then I need to make this node and assign the *key (current character) to it. This is used to build the tree as we insert keys.

tstree.c:20-21 If the *key is less than this, then recurse, but go to the low branch.

tstree.c:22 This splitchar is equal, so I want to go and deal with equality. This will happen if we just create this node, so we'll be building the tree at this point.

tstree.c:23-24 There are still characters to handle, so recurse down the equal branch, but go to the next *key character.

tstree.c:26-27 This is the last character, so I set the value and that's it. I have an assert here in case of a duplicate.

tstree.c:29-30 The last condition is that this *key is greater than splitchar, so I need to recurse down the high branch.

The key to this data structure is the fact that I'm only incrementing the character when a splitchar is equal. For the other two conditions, I just walk through the tree until I hit an equal character to recurse into next. What this does is make it very fast *not* to find a key. I can get a bad key, and simply walk through a few high and low nodes until I hit a dead end before I know that this key doesn't exist. I don't need to process every character of the key or every node of the tree.

Once you understand that, then move on to analyzing how TSTree_search works.

tstree.c:46   I don't need to process the tree recursively in the TSTree. I can just use a while-loop and a node for where I currently am.

tstree.c:47-48   If the current character is less than the node splitchar, then go low.

tstree.c:49-51   If it's equal, then increment i and go equal as long as it's not the last character. That's why the if(i < len) is there, so that I don't go too far past the final value.

tstree.c:52-53   Otherwise, I go high, since the character is greater.

tstree.c:57-61   If I have a node after the loop, then return its value, otherwise return NULL.

This isn't too difficult to understand, and you can see that it's almost exactly the same algorithm for the TSTree_search_prefix function. The only difference is that I'm not trying to find an exact match, but find the longest prefix I can. To do that, I keep track of the last node that was equal, and then after the search loop, walk through that node until I find a value.

Looking at TSTree_search_prefix, you can start to see the second advantage a TSTree has over the BSTree and Hashmap for finding strings. Given any key of X length, you can find any key in X moves. You can also find the first prefix in X moves, plus N more depending on how big the matching key is. If the biggest key in the tree is ten characters long, then you can find any prefix in that key in ten moves. More importantly, you can do all of this by comparing each character of the key *once*.

In comparison, to do the same with a BSTree, you would have to check the prefixes of each character in every possible matching node in the BSTree against the characters in the prefix. It's the same for finding keys or seeing if a key doesn't exist. You have to compare each character against most of the characters in the BSTree to find or not find a match.

A Hashmap is even worse for finding prefixes, because you can't hash just the prefix. Basically, you can't do this efficiently in a Hashmap unless the data is something you can parse, like a URL. Even then, that usually requires whole trees of Hashmaps.

The last two functions should be easy for you to analyze since they're the typical traversing and destroying operations that you've already seen in other data structures.

Finally, I have a simple unit test for the whole thing to make sure it works right:

tstree_tests.c

```
1    #include "minunit.h"
2    #include <lcthw/tstree.h>
3    #include <string.h>
4    #include <assert.h>
5    #include <lcthw/bstrlib.h>
6
7    TSTree *node = NULL;
8    char *valueA = "VALUEA";
9    char *valueB = "VALUEB";
10   char *value2 = "VALUE2";
11   char *value4 = "VALUE4";
12   char *reverse = "VALUER";
13   int traverse_count = 0;
14
15   struct tagbstring test1 = bsStatic("TEST");
16   struct tagbstring test2 = bsStatic("TEST2");
17   struct tagbstring test3 = bsStatic("TSET");
18   struct tagbstring test4 = bsStatic("T");
19
20   char *test_insert()
21   {
22       node = TSTree_insert(node, bdata(&test1), blength(&test1), valueA);
23       mu_assert(node != NULL, "Failed to insert into tst.");
24
25       node = TSTree_insert(node, bdata(&test2), blength(&test2), value2);
26       mu_assert(node != NULL,
27               "Failed to insert into tst with second name.");
28
29       node = TSTree_insert(node, bdata(&test3), blength(&test3), reverse);
30       mu_assert(node != NULL,
31               "Failed to insert into tst with reverse name.");
32
33       node = TSTree_insert(node, bdata(&test4), blength(&test4), value4);
34       mu_assert(node != NULL,
35               "Failed to insert into tst with second name.");
36
37       return NULL;
38   }
39
40   char *test_search_exact()
41   {
42       // tst returns the last one inserted
43       void *res = TSTree_search(node, bdata(&test1), blength(&test1));
44       mu_assert(res == valueA,
45               "Got the wrong value back, should get A not B.");
46
47       // tst does not find if not exact
```

```
48          res = TSTree_search(node, "TESTNO", strlen("TESTNO"));
49          mu_assert(res == NULL, "Should not find anything.");
50
51          return NULL;
52      }
53
54      char *test_search_prefix()
55      {
56          void *res = TSTree_search_prefix(
57                  node, bdata(&test1), blength(&test1));
58          debug("result: %p, expected: %p", res, valueA);
59          mu_assert(res == valueA, "Got wrong valueA by prefix.");
60
61          res = TSTree_search_prefix(node, bdata(&test1), 1);
62          debug("result: %p, expected: %p", res, valueA);
63          mu_assert(res == value4, "Got wrong value4 for prefix of 1.");
64
65          res = TSTree_search_prefix(node, "TE", strlen("TE"));
66          mu_assert(res != NULL, "Should find for short prefix.");
67
68          res = TSTree_search_prefix(node, "TE--", strlen("TE--"));
69          mu_assert(res != NULL, "Should find for partial prefix.");
70
71          return NULL;
72      }
73
74      void TSTree_traverse_test_cb(void *value, void *data)
75      {
76          assert(value != NULL && "Should not get NULL value.");
77          assert(data == valueA && "Expecting valueA as the data.");
78          traverse_count++;
79      }
80
81      char *test_traverse()
82      {
83          traverse_count = 0;
84          TSTree_traverse(node, TSTree_traverse_test_cb, valueA);
85          debug("traverse count is: %d", traverse_count);
86          mu_assert(traverse_count == 4, "Didn't find 4 keys.");
87
88          return NULL;
89      }
90
91      char *test_destroy()
92      {
93          TSTree_destroy(node);
94
95          return NULL;
96      }
97
```

```
 98    char *all_tests()
 99    {
100        mu_suite_start();
101
102        mu_run_test(test_insert);
103        mu_run_test(test_search_exact);
104        mu_run_test(test_search_prefix);
105        mu_run_test(test_traverse);
106        mu_run_test(test_destroy);
107
108        return NULL;
109    }
110
111    RUN_TESTS(all_tests);
```

Advantages and Disadvantages

There are other interesting, practical things you can do with a TSTree:

- In addition to finding prefixes, you can reverse all of the keys you insert, and then find things by *suffix*. I use this to look up host names, since I want to find *.learncodethe hardway.com. If I go backward, I can match them quickly.

- You can do approximate matching, by gathering all of the nodes that have most of the same characters as the key, or using other algorithms to find a close match.

- You can find all of the keys that have a part in the middle.

I've already talked about some of the things TSTrees can do, but they aren't the best data structure all the time. Here are the disadvantages of the TSTree:

- As I mentioned, deleting from them is murder. They are better used for data that needs to be looked up fast and rarely removed. If you need to delete, then simply disable the value and then periodically rebuild the tree when it gets too big.

- It uses a ton of memory compared to BSTree and Hashmaps for the same key space. Think about it. It's using a full node for each character in every key. It might work better for smaller keys, but if you put a lot in a TSTree, it will get huge.

- They also don't work well with large keys, but large is subjective. As usual, test it first. If you're trying to store 10,000-character keys, then use a Hashmap.

How to Improve It

As usual, go through and improve this by adding the defensive programming preconditions, asserts, and checks to each function. There are some other possible improvements, but you don't necessarily have to implement all of these:

- You could allow duplicates by using a DArray instead of the value.

- As I mentioned earlier, deleting is hard, but you could simulate it by setting the values to NULL so that they are effectively gone.

- There are no ways to collect all of the possible matching values. I'll have you implement that in an Extra Credit exercise.

- There are other algorithms that are more complex but have slightly better properties. Take a look at suffix array, suffix tree, and radix tree structures.

Extra Credit

- Implement a TSTree_collect that returns a DArray containing all of the keys that match the given prefix.

- Implement TSTree_search_suffix and a TSTree_insert_suffix so you can do suffix searches and inserts.

- Use the debugger to see how this structure stores data compared to the BSTree and Hashmap.

A Fast URL Router

I m now going to show you how I use the TSTree to do fast URL routing in Web servers that I've written. This works for simple URL routing that you might use at the edge of an application, but it doesn't really work for the more complex (and sometimes unnecessary) routing found in many Web application frameworks.

To play with routing, I'm going to make a little command line tool that I'm calling urlor, which reads a simple file of routes, and then prompts the user to enter in URLs.

urlor.c

```c
1    #include <lcthw/tstree.h>
2    #include <lcthw/bstrlib.h>
3
4    TSTree *add_route_data(TSTree * routes, bstring line)
5    {
6        struct bstrList *data = bsplit(line, ' ');
7        check(data->qty == 2, "Line '%s' does not have 2 columns",
8                bdata(line));
9
10       routes = TSTree_insert(routes,
11               bdata(data->entry[0]),
12               blength(data->entry[0]),
13               bstrcpy(data->entry[1]));
14
15       bstrListDestroy(data);
16
17       return routes;
18
19   error:
20       return NULL;
21   }
22
23   TSTree *load_routes(const char *file)
24   {
25       TSTree *routes = NULL;
26       bstring line = NULL;
27       FILE *routes_map = NULL;
28
29       routes_map = fopen(file, "r");
30       check(routes_map != NULL, "Failed to open routes: %s", file);
31
32       while ((line = bgets((bNgetc) fgetc, routes_map, '\n')) != NULL) {
33           check(btrimws(line) == BSTR_OK, "Failed to trim line.");
34           routes = add_route_data(routes, line);
```

```
35              check(routes != NULL, "Failed to add route.");
36              bdestroy(line);
37          }
38
39          fclose(routes_map);
40          return routes;
41
42      error:
43          if (routes_map) fclose(routes_map);
44          if (line) bdestroy(line);
45
46          return NULL;
47      }
48
49      bstring match_url(TSTree * routes, bstring url)
50      {
51          bstring route = TSTree_search(routes, bdata(url), blength(url));
52
53          if (route == NULL) {
54              printf("No exact match found, trying prefix.\n");
55              route = TSTree_search_prefix(routes, bdata(url), blength(url));
56          }
57
58          return route;
59      }
60
61      bstring read_line(const char *prompt)
62      {
63          printf("%s", prompt);
64
65          bstring result = bgets((bNgetc) fgetc, stdin, '\n');
66          check_debug(result != NULL, "stdin closed.");
67
68          check(btrimws(result) == BSTR_OK, "Failed to trim.");
69
70          return result;
71
72      error:
73          return NULL;
74      }
75
76      void bdestroy_cb(void *value, void *ignored)
77      {
78          (void)ignored;
79          bdestroy((bstring) value);
80      }
81
82      void destroy_routes(TSTree * routes)
83      {
84          TSTree_traverse(routes, bdestroy_cb, NULL);
```

```
85          TSTree_destroy(routes);
86      }
87
88      int main(int argc, char *argv[])
89      {
90          bstring url = NULL;
91          bstring route = NULL;
92          TSTree *routes = NULL;
93
94          check(argc == 2, "USAGE: urlor <urlfile>");
95
96          routes = load_routes(argv[1]);
97          check(routes != NULL, "Your route file has an error.");
98
99          while (1) {
100             url = read_line("URL> ");
101             check_debug(url != NULL, "goodbye.");
102
103             route = match_url(routes, url);
104
105             if (route) {
106                 printf("MATCH: %s == %s\n", bdata(url), bdata(route));
107             } else {
108                 printf("FAIL: %s\n", bdata(url));
109             }
110
111             bdestroy(url);
112         }
113
114         destroy_routes(routes);
115         return 0;
116
117     error:
118         destroy_routes(routes);
119         return 1;
120     }
```

I'll then make a simple file with some fake routes to play with:

```
/ MainApp

/hello Hello

/hello/ Hello

/signup Signup

/logout Logout

/album/ Album
```

What You Should See

Once you have `urlor` working, and a routes file, you can try it out here:

```
$ ./bin/urlor urls.txt
URL> /
MATCH: / == MainApp
URL> /hello
MATCH: /hello == Hello
URL> /hello/zed
No exact match found, trying prefix.
MATCH: /hello/zed == Hello
URL> /album
No exact match found, trying prefix.
MATCH: /album == Album
URL> /album/12345
No exact match found, trying prefix.
MATCH: /album/12345 == Album
URL> asdfasfdasfd
No exact match found, trying prefix.
FAIL: asdfasfdasfd
URL> /asdfasdfasf
No exact match found, trying prefix.
MATCH: /asdfasdfasf == MainApp
URL>
$
```

You can see that the routing system first tries an exact match, and if it can't find one, it will give a prefix match. This is mostly done to try out the difference between the two. Depending on the semantics of your URLs, you may want to always match exactly, always to prefixes, or do both and pick the best one.

How to Improve It

URLs are weird because people want them to magically handle all of the insane things their Web applications do, even if that's not very logical. In this simple demonstration of how to use the TSTree to do routing, there are some flaws that people wouldn't be able to articulate. For example, the TSTree will match /al to Album, which generally isn't what they want. They want /album/* to match Album, and /al to be a 404 error.

This isn't difficult to implement, though, since you could change the prefix algorithm to match any way you want. If you change the matching algorithm to find *all* matching prefixes, and then pick the best one, you'll be able to do it easily. In this case, /al could match MainApp or Album. Take those results, and then do a little logic to determine which is better.

Another thing you can do in a real routing system is use the TSTree to find all possible matches, but these matches are a small set of patterns to check. In many Web applications, there's a list of regular expressions (regex) that has to be matched against URLs on each request. Running all of the regex can be time consuming, so you can use a TSTree to find all of the possible matches by their prefixes. That way you narrow down the patterns to try to a few very quickly.

Using this method, your URLs will match exactly since you're actually running real regex patterns, and they'll match much faster since you're finding them by possible prefixes.

This kind of algorithm also works for anything else that needs to have flexible user-visible routing mechanisms: domain names, IP addresses, registries and directories, files, or URLs.

Extra Credit

- Instead of just storing the string for the handler, create an actual engine that uses a Handler struct to store the application. The structure would store the URL to which it's attached, the name, and anything else you'd need to make an actual routing system.

- Instead of mapping URLs to arbitrary names, map them to .so files and use the dlopen system to load handlers on the fly and call callbacks they contain. Put these callbacks in your Handler struct, and then you have yourself a fully dynamic callback handler system in C.

A Simple Network Server

W e now start the part of the book where you do a long-running, more involved project in a series of exercises. The last five exercises will present the problem of creating a simple network server in a similar fashion as you did with the logfind project. I'll describe each phase of the project, you'll attempt it, and then you'll compare your implementation to mine before continuing.

These descriptions are purposefully vague so that you have the freedom to attempt to solve the problems on your own, but I'm still going to help you. Included with each of these exercises are *two* videos. The first video shows you how the project for the exercise should work, so you can see it in action and try to emulate it. The second video shows you how *I* solved the problem, so you can compare your attempt to mine. Finally, you'll have access to all of the code in the GitHub project, so you can see real code by me.

You should attempt the problem first, then after you get it working (or if you get totally stuck), go watch the second video and take a look at my code. When you're done, you can either keep using your code, or just use mine for the next exercise.

The Specification

In this first small program you'll lay the first foundation for the remaining projects. You'll call this program statserve, even though this specification doesn't mention statistics or anything. That will come later.

The specification for this project is very simple:

1. Create a simple network server that accepts a connection on port 7899 from netclient or the nc command, and that echoes back anything you type.

2. You'll need to learn how to bind a port, listen on the socket, and answer it. Use your research skills to study how this is done and attempt to implement it yourself.

3. The more important part of this project is laying out the project directory from the c-skeleton, and making sure you can build everything and get it working.

4. Don't worry about things like daemons or anything else. Your server just has to run from the command line and keep running.

The important challenge for this project is figuring out how to create a socket server, but everything you've learned so far makes this possible. Watch the first lecture video where I teach you about this if you find that it's too hard to figure out on your own.

A Statistics Server

The next phase of your project is to implement the very first feature of the statserve server. Your program from Exercise 48 should be working and not crashing. Remember to think defensively and attempt to break and destroy your project as best you can before continuing. Watch both Exercise 48 videos to see how I do this.

The purpose of statserve is for clients to connect to it and submit commands for modifying statistics. If you remember, we learned a little bit about doing incremental basic statistics, and you know how to use data structures like hash maps, dynamic arrays, binary search trees, and ternary search trees. These are going to be used in statserve to implement this next feature.

Specification

You have to implement a protocol that your network client can use to store statistics. If you remember from Exercise 43, you have three simple operations you can do to in the stats.h API:

create   Create a new statistic.

mean   Get the current mean of a statistic.

sample   Add a new sample to a statistic.

dump   Get all of the elements of a statistic (sum, sumsq, n, min, and max).

This will make the beginning of your protocol, but you'll need to do some more things:

1.   You'll need to allow people to name these statistics, which means using one of the map style data structures to map names to Stats structs.

2.   You'll need to add the CRUD standard operations for each name. CRUD stands for create read update delete. Currently, the list of commands above has create, mean, and dump for reading; and sample for updating. You need a delete command now.

3.   You may also need to have a list command for listing out all of the available statistics in the server.

Given that your statserve should handle a protocol that allows the above operations, let's create statistics, update their sample, delete them, dump them, get the mean, and finally, list them.

Do your best to design a simple (and I mean *simple*) protocol for this using plain text, and see what you come up with. Do this on paper first, then watch the lecture video for this exercise to find out how to design a protocol and get more information about the exercise.

I also recommend using unit tests to test that the protocol is parsing separately from the server. Create separate .c and .h files for just processing strings with protocol in them, and then test those until you get them right. This will make things much easier when you add this feature to your server.

Routing the Statistics

O nce you've solved the problem of the protocol and putting statistics into a data structure, you'll want to make this much richer. This exercise may require that you redesign and refactor some of your code. That's on purpose, as this is an absolute requirement when writing software. You must frequently throw out old code to make room for new code. Never get too attached to something you've written.

In this exercise, you're going to use the URL routing from Exercise 47 to augment your protocol, allowing statistics to be stored at arbitrary URL paths.

This is all the help you get. It's a simple requirement that you have to attempt on your own, modifying your protocol, updating your data structures, and changing your code to make it work.

Watch the lecture video to see what I want, and then try your best before watching the second video to see how I implemented it.

Storing the Statistics

The next problem to solve is how to store the statistics. There is an advantage to having the statistics in memory, because it's much faster than storing them. In fact, there are large data storage systems that do this very thing, but in our case, we want a smaller server that can store some of the data to a hard drive.

The Specification

For this exercise, you'll add two commands for storing to and loading statistics from a hard drive:

store   If there's a URL, store it to a hard drive.

load   If there are two URLs, load the statistic from the hard drive based on the first URL, and then put it into the second URL that's in memory.

This may seem simple, but you'll have a few battles when implementing this feature:

1.   If URLs have / characters in them, then that conflicts with the filesystem's use of slashes. How will you solve this?

2.   If URLs have / characters in them, then someone can use your server to overwrite files on a hard drive by giving paths to them. How will you solve this?

3.   If you choose to use deeply nested directories, then traversing directories to find files will be very slow. What will you do here?

4.   If you choose to use one directory and hash URLs (oops, I gave a hint), then directories with too many files in them are slow. How will you solve this?

5.   What happens when someone loads a statistic from a hard drive into a URL that already exists?

6.   How will someone running statserve know where the storage should be?

An alternative to using a filesystem to store the data is using something like SQLite and SQL. Another option is to use a system like GNU dbm (GDBM) to store them in a simpler database.

Research all of your options and watch the lecture video, and then pick the simplest option and try it. Take your time figuring out this feature because the next exercise will involve figuring out how to destroy your server.

Hacking and Improving Your Server

The final exercise consists of three videos. The first video is a lecture on how to hack your server and attempt to destroy it. In the video, I show you a great many tools and tricks for breaking protocols, using my *own* implementation to demonstrate flaws in the design. This video is fun, and if you've been following along with your own code, you can compete with me to see who made the more robust server.

The second video then demonstrates how I'd add improvements to the server. You should attempt your own improvements first, before watching this video, and then see if your improvements are similar to mine.

The third and final video teaches you how to make further improvements and design decisions in the project. It covers everything I'd think about to complete the project and refine it. Typically, to complete a project, I'd do the following:

1. Get it online and accessible to people.

2. Document it and improve the usability to make sure that the documents are easy to read.

3. Do as much test coverage as possible.

4. Improve any corner cases and add defenses against any attacks that I can find.

The second video demonstrates each of these and explains how you can do them yourself.

Next Steps

This book is most likely a monumental undertaking for a beginner programmer, or even a programmer with no experience with many of the topics covered inside. You have successfully learned an introductory amount of knowledge of C, testing, secure coding, algorithms, data structures, unit testing, and general applied problem solving. Congratulations. You should be a much better programmer now.

I recommend that you now go read other books on the C programming language. You can't go wrong with *The C Programming Language* (Prentice Hall 1988) by Brian W. Kernighan and Dennis M. Ritchie, the creators of the C language. My book teaches you an initial, practical version of C that gets the job done, mostly as a means of teaching you other topics. Their book will teach you deeper C as defined by the creators and the C standard.

If you want to continue improving as a programmer, I recommend that you learn at least four programming languages. If you already knew one language, and now you know C, then I recommend you try learning any of these programming languages as your next ones:

- Python, with my book *Learn Python The Hard Way, Third Edition* (Addison-Wesley, 2014)
- Ruby, with my book *Learn Ruby The Hard Way, Third Edition* (Addison-Wesley, 2015)
- Go, with its list of documentation at http://http://golang.org/doc, another language by the authors of the C language, and frankly, a much better one
- Lua, which is a very fun language that has a decent API for C that you might enjoy now
- JavaScript, although I'm not sure which book is best for this language

There are many programming languages available, so choose whichever language interests you and learn it. I recommend this because the easiest way to become adept at programming and build confidence is to strengthen your ability to learn multiple languages. Four languages seems to be the breaking point where a beginner transitions to being a capable programmer. It's also just a lot of fun.

Index

DVD-ROM Warranty

Addison-Wesley warrants the enclosed DVD-ROM to be free of defects in materials and faulty workmanship under normal use for a period of ninety days after purchase (when purchased new). If a defect is discovered in the DVD-ROM during this warranty period, a replacement DVD-ROM can be obtained at no charge by sending the defective DVD-ROM, postage prepaid, with proof of purchase to:

> Disc Exchange
> Addison-Wesley
> Pearson Technology Group
> 800 East 96th Street
> Indianapolis, IN 46240
>
> Email: disc.exchange@pearson.com

Addison-Wesley makes no warranty or representation, either expressed or implied, with respect to this software, its quality, performance, merchantability, or fitness for a particular purpose. In no event will Addison-Wesley, its distributors, or dealers be liable for direct, indirect, special, incidental, or consequential damages arising out of the use or inability to use the software. The exclusion of implied warranties is not permitted in some states. Therefore, the above exclusion may not apply to you. This warranty provides you with specific legal rights. There may be other rights that you may have that vary from state to state. The contents of this DVD-ROM are intended for personal use only.

More information and updates are available at:

> informit.com/aw